ALL ABOUT
LOW VOLATILITY
INVESTING

OTHER TITLES IN THE "ALL ABOUT" FINANCE SERIES

ALL ABOUT
LOW VOLATILITY
INVESTING

Peter Sander

New York   Chicago   San Francisco   Athens   London
Madrid   Mexico City   Milan   New Delhi
Singapore   Sydney   Toronto

1 2 3 4 5 6 7 8 9 0   QFR/QFR   1 9 8 7 6 5 4 3

ISBN   978-0-07-181984-8
MHID   0-07-181984-3

e-ISBN   978-0-07-181985-5
e-MHID   0-07-181985-1

This publication is designed to provide accurate and authoritative information in regard to the subject matter covered. It is sold with the understanding that neither the author nor the publisher is engaged in rendering legal, accounting, securities trading, or other professional services. If legal advice or other expert assistance is required, the services of a competent professional person should be sought.

—*From a Declaration of Principles Jointly Adopted by a Committee of the American Bar Association and a Committee of Publishers and Associations*

Library of Congress Cataloging-in-Publication Data

Sander, Peter J.
    All about low volatility investing / by Peter Sander.
        pages cm
    ISBN 978-0-07-181984-8 (alk. paper) — ISBN 0-07-181984-3 (alk. paper)
1. Investments.   2. Financial risk.   3. Portfolio management.   I. Title.
    HG4521.S33168 2014
    332.6—dc23   2013027447

McGraw-Hill Education books are available at special quantity discounts to use as premiums and sales promotions or for use in corporate training programs. To contact a representative, please visit the Contact Us pages at www.mhprofessional.com.

I dedicate this book to all of you active investors who have the sense of purpose and independence of thought to make your own investing decisions, or at least to ask the right questions. You're wise enough to realize that sleeping at night and productive investing are not mutually exclusive and prudent enough to seek wisdom on how to pull it off.

CONTENTS

ACKNOWLEDGMENTS

I would like to thank my editor Zach Gajewski and his colleagues at McGraw-Hill for bringing this idea my way and helping to make it a reality. Then there's my exercise buddies, for no book happens without the added value of exercise to keep a body in shape and a mind clear. Finally, I recognize my life partner Marjorie and my boys Julian and Jonathan as guarantors of a low volatility lifestyle as well as ongoing inspiration to do this sort of work.

Return with Peace of Mind

"A ship is safe in port. But that's not what a ship is for."

You may have heard this quote before. It is attributed to, of all people, computer programming pioneer Grace Murray Hopper, inventor of the COBOL computing language.

I will admit that, throughout my life, this quote has been dusted off as a theme from time to time. I left the relative stability and security of life in the Midwest in 1980, moving west to a job in California, a state I had just set foot in for the job interview. Twenty-one years later I left the relative stability and security of that job to enter the life of a freelance researcher and writer.

My ship was safe in port, but this was not what ships were for.

So, you might rightly ask as you hold this book (or e-reader) in your hands, what does this quote have to do with investing?

Recently, it dawned on me that this quote has *everything* to do with investing. Probably more to do with it than anything else in my life—or yours, for that matter.

I've been investing since I was 12 years old. That's a long time. My exact age is unimportant, but suffice it to say I've lived through the storms of the 1970s' OPEC oil embargo, stagflation, the early 1980s' recession, the Gulf wars, the dot-com bust, and, most recently and vividly in the minds of investors of all stripes, the Great Recession of 2008–2011.

I have seen many investors over the years seek those safe ports to bear with these crises—and all the other crises that *didn't* happen. They save in banks, CDs, bond funds, and other "plain vanilla" investment forms, often purchased at high prices through financial advisors and the funds they purvey. The reason, of course, is for safety and security; they choose to avoid the choppy waters of the global economy and, in the typical case, want some-one else to skipper their boat.

They want to sleep at night. I get that, and I've been there, too.

But the world is changing, and it continues to change. First, we're all more responsible for our own financial destinies. I can't speculate on the future of Social Security, but what I do know is that for most of us, Social Security won't pay all the bills when we retire, at least beyond a bare minimum lifestyle. The other thing I know for sure is that the traditional "defined benefit" pension—in which the employer takes all the risks while you get safe, secure income for life—has also become an endangered species. Instead, you're required to save and invest, to create a "nest egg" through a 401(k) or some similar plan.

That's the key. You must invest. You must produce a return. You can't just leave that ship in port, or else you might never really reach that nest egg, that "number" you have in mind. Now, instead of losing sleep about investing and volatility in the markets, you lose sleep about *not having enough* someday.

And that's not all. There's another unfortunate and now all-too-familiar trend—really a context—that's emerged in today's world of slow growth (which I attribute to the absence of true value add in the economy, but that's another topic). Our gov-ernment—and governments around the world, for that matter—have come to take extreme defensive stances against economic malaise. There are a lot of reasons for that, which, again, are beyond the scope of this book. They defend against this mal-aise by pumping money into the economic system, which at the end of the day produces extremely low interest rates—rates of return—on money. Money is everywhere, so the price to borrow it or use it declines.

This all comes back to us in the form of extremely low interest rates and rates offered for fixed income, or fixed return investments. Absurdly low, near zero in some economies. In Germany, there are even negative interest rates: you have to *pay* the government to keep certain short-term cash for you safe for a rainy day.

So what does that mean? Our investment ships in port earn less and less. Not enough to achieve our number or anything close. Sure, they're still safe. But they're not performing. They may not even be all that safe if the winds of inflation start to blow harder. To achieve our goals, we must set sail to achieve *something* with our investments. Now we're not day traders, and we're not trying to double our money or hit "ten-baggers" in with our investments in hopes of becoming the center of attention at the next cocktail party. We're just trying to achieve decent returns.

Returns with peace of mind.

I ASSUME YOU'VE DONE THIS BEFORE

You're not a novice or first-time investor. You've done this before. You've probably done this for years.

In fact, you've been burned before. You jumped on the bandwagon, perhaps in 1999 or 2007, and bought in. You may have bought individual stocks, or you may have moved some of your chips into a small-cap stock fund, a tech fund, perhaps an international or emerging markets fund. Then the tide washed out and you got left "swimming naked," as Warren Buffett would say.

You may have endured a few years of reluctance. That's natural and normal. Should I do this again? Or should I just keep my ship in port, so I never have to endure the jitters, the awful feeling in my stomach, when the squalls of the investing world start to blow?

How do I venture out from port again, but with the confidence that I won't have to stay up all night watching the Asian markets and Dow futures, fearing the worst? How can I plot a safer route, and sail a safer ship, on the high seas of investing?

Indeed, you, I, and many others, seek something that has only recently been put into words and into the investment vernacular, so much so that it has even led to the creation of new investment products.

We have entered the era of *low volatility* investing. And yes, there are now low volatility funds recently created to address the needs of the low volatility investor.

INTO CALMER WATERS

Low volatility investing? Sounds pretty technical. Volatility? I can now tell you from 250-plus pages of experience that it's even a hard work to *type*, let alone set it into precise mathematical stone for everyone to grasp.

Have no fear. While the financial engineers of the Wall Street geek world have had a heyday measuring and managing volatility through sophisticated algorithms and databases, we won't go there, at least not all the way.

All About Low Volatility Investing may be a misnomer. It may not be *all* about low volatility investing. Instead, I proudly present it to you as everything you, as an *individual investor*, should know about it.

And just exactly what is low volatility investing? I guess I should define it here, which I'll embellish as we move forward. It is really about managing—*reducing*—volatility, and the elephant that sits in the room behind volatility: *downside risk*. Now, we could all do that by stuffing money under our mattresses—literally or figuratively— right? Keeping our ship in port by buying the safe stuff, the CDs and Treasury securities and bond funds. But we'd earn what, 2 percent on our money at the most?

So that suggests the second dimension of low volatility investing: *return*. Low volatility investing sets our ship to sail in open waters—in smooth waters we can understand and chart for ourselves—to achieve a decent return. Twenty percent annual returns? No, not at all. Simply, returns maybe 1 or 2 percent ahead of the market averages, that's all. In Chapter 3, as I derive the true definition of low volatility investing, I'll explain why it's so important to sail that ship toward these safe return waters.

FROM A USER PERSPECTIVE

I used to teach a tax class. Now mind you, I'm not a CPA, and I don't do taxes for a living. But I've been an entrepreneur for a while, have done my own taxes for 40 years, and have come to understand the system.

I taught that tax class to professional writers: writers like me. I gave tips on how to keep track of income and expenses and, importantly, what items could be written off in the business. Research materials, reasonable travel, coffee for the home office coffeepot.

Most writers aren't too savvy with taxes and live on modest incomes, so they appreciated the advice. One time I gave my little talk, and the head of the writers' group decided to schedule a real CPA to give a similar talk after me. I thought, *that's interesting* and attended the talk. He probably thought the same and attended mine.

I gave my talk. After my talk, he walked up to the podium, smiled, and opened, quite earnestly: "That was interesting—to see this all from a user perspective!" The audience chuckled. He gave his talk and, indeed, with one minor exception, we were on the same page.

What's my point? Very simple. There are a million ways to measure volatility, and the measurement of volatility across hundreds—*thousands*—of portfolio choices can become mind-bogglingly complex. It can be done, but it's a very scientific and technical exercise requiring computing power and know-how well beyond what we individual investors can grasp, or would even carry out if we could grasp it. People *major* in financial engineering, and in doing so, turn investing into a mathematical exercise that may—*may*—eke out a few fractions of incremental return.

I say there's a user's perspective—a commonsense approach—that will get you most of the way to where you need to go. It will get you there, just as writers can do their taxes without the help of a CPA and certainly without understanding the 44,000 some-odd pages of the U.S. tax code.

That commonsense user perspective is the core idea of this book.

CHARTING THE COURSE

All About Low Volatility Investing is divided into two parts. *Part One: What You Need to Know About Volatility* is designed to bring you up to speed on volatility itself—what it is, what we've experienced through history, how it's measured and applied mathematically, and most of all, how it becomes part of your investing thought process. *Part Two: Becoming a Low Volatility Investor* takes the thought process from Part One and applies it to your investing habits and practice. The contents outlines the two parts to our book.

So, stow your gear, chart your course, motor to clear water, haul up your main, unfurl your jib, and sail forth into the rewarding waters of investing success. You'll enjoy the destination, and maybe for the first time as an investor—okay, it's an overused cliché—you'll enjoy the journey. Or at least you won't dread or regret it.

Anchors aweigh!

PART ONE

What You Need to Know About Volatility

A Short History of Investment Risk

If you drive across the United States, coast to coast, you'll experience a unique profile of hills, plains, mountains, and elevation changes, some gradual and some not so gradual. If you start from the east, you'll run through some ups and downs—steep and sharp but not very long or high—as you travel through, say, central Pennsylvania. By the time you reach Ohio, things flatten out considerably: "stand on a nickel, you'll see twice as far" country. Things stay flat and the going is easy. Maybe a few rolling hills, maybe a few episodes of wind and rain, but otherwise a smooth trip.

Then you cross the Missouri River, and things stay flat for a while. Almost without notice, you begin to rise. You start rising through the Great Plains, say, in Nebraska and eastern Wyoming or Colorado, depending on the route you choose. You don't even notice that you're climbing. Pretty smooth, still, but slowly and gradually, you climb. By the time you reach the Front Range of the Rocky Mountains, you've climbed a full mile and are higher than all but a few peaks across the 2,000 miles to the east. As you move still farther west, the profile changes drastically. It's up and down, up and down, almost the rest of the way to the Pacific.

I'll bet you're wondering: Did the publisher make a mistake? Did they bind the first page of a travel book into the book you *thought* you bought: *All About Low Volatility Investing*?

No. You are reading the right book, and this is the correct page.

The profile of ups and downs would describe your long multiday trek to the Left Coast. But it also would more or less describe your trip through the investment world, from the 1920s to the present. It is a trip that started with a surprising amount of volatility with the events of 1929 and the Great Depression and went into a period of relative quiet and prosperity (although not without some volatility) through the remainder of the twentieth century. At the turn of the millennium, markets for most assets—not only stocks but also gold, real estate, and most commodities—entered another age of more recognizable volatility, one that we're still in today and probably will be for the indeterminate future. In this chapter we'll share the story of volatility: what it is, where it comes from, and its journey through time.

VOLATILITY ENTERS THE INVESTING STAGE

It started rough. A major financial and industrial boom capped off the end of the Roaring Twenties. It became a debt-fueled boom of speculative greed, which, like most do, went sour. Because there were few banking and financial protections and controls at the time, there were no safety nets; what was gone was gone.

Although the world economy had experienced bubbles and down market cycles many times before the 1930s—in 1907, 1893, and, well, back to the 1600s, in the case of tulip bulbs—the magnitude and influence of the stock market crash and Great Depression showed us not just bad economic times but also served to etch the effects and principles of volatility onto our minds forever. It's no wonder many people learned to fear the markets during the Depression.

As we'll see, and as the following charts and tables will show, things went pretty smoothly for a number of years—our crossing of the Midwest and Great Plains—only to get pretty jumpy again as we came to the past fifteen years and the present.

Figure 1.1 clearly shows the topography of the S&P 500 journey since 1929. The S&P 500 Index is the most representative

FIGURE 1.1

S&P 500 Year-End Close, 1929–2012

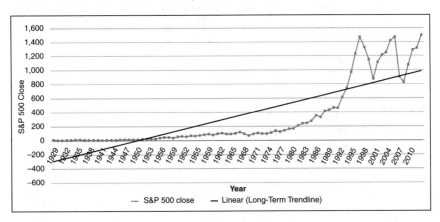

of the multitudes of stock market indexes we will look at. You can clearly see the Rockies and the mountains farther west as jagged ups and downs starting in the 1990s after a long, relatively steady period of some 60 years. The initial Appalachian-style volatility of the eastern portion of the journey doesn't show so well, but we'll see shortly that, especially on a percentage basis, it was there. The ups and downs were sharp and scary, although not gaining or losing so much nominal altitude.

As we'll see, it isn't just stocks that have enjoyed such an uptrend or such volatility in more recent times.

The S&P 500 chart rather dramatically shows (1) the relatively recent and substantial rise in the markets and (2) the *size* of the peaks and valleys, as more and more investors get involved and commit more and more capital to the markets. Although compared to recent times the ups and downs of the twentieth-century portion of the graph seem fairly subdued, it will also become clear that even in these quiet times there was a fair amount of volatility on a percentage basis.

To be sure, volatility isn't the only thing that's happening here. A significant portion of the change we see in these charts is growth, and as we all know, economic growth doesn't always come in steady and equally divided increments. At this point we should set the stage a little more by examining the market growth over time, and then by overlaying an analysis of volatility on top of that long-term performance. You'll get an idea of how much the markets *should* grow over the long run and how much volatility you should expect along the way.

WHAT TO EXPECT WHEN YOU'RE INVESTING

So, the million-dollar question asked by most investors, whether they buy individual stocks or participate in the markets through funds, retirement accounts, and so forth is: What should *I* expect from my investments? What is *achievable*? What is *realistic*? If I'm going to take the risks and experience the volatility, what's my reward for doing so?

For years, 10 percent was the rule of thumb offered by the financial community for long-term stock market returns. From the 1920s through the end of the millennium, the facts supported this truth. Stock market returns, including dividend payouts, approached the 10 percent figure over an 80-year period.

Now, you might ask, how can a stock market, which really is a sum of the values of all corporations traded in that market, return 10 percent per year when the total economy, measured by Gross Domestic Product (GDP) is growing say, between 2 and 4 percent a year *at the most*? Does the 10 percent figure make sense? Can corporations, taken as a whole, grow faster than the economy as a whole? And, if so, is such a growth pattern sustainable?

These are great questions, and all investors should wrap themselves around the answers. In fact, stock market investing returns have outperformed the economy as a whole over the long haul, but not by as much as the numbers on the surface suggest. Furthermore, it appears that the rule-of-thumb 10 percent return has moderated somewhat to something closer to 7 to 8 percent, which is evident in the S&P 500 chart after the millennium: lots of ups and downs, but not a lot of true upward progress.

So where did the premillennium 10-percent figure come from? There were three primary components:

- GDP growth—real economic growth—averaging about 3 percent
- Inflation averaging perhaps 3 to 4 percent over the long haul
- Dividends and payouts: cash earned and paid out by companies and not retained as part of the company's value. The average long-term payout for S&P 500 stocks is a bit over 2 percent.

These figures suggest a total somewhere in the range of 8 or 9 percent. Where does the final 1 to 2 percent come from to get to 10 percent? That final percent or two is probably attributable to large publically traded companies doing an increased share of total business as they force smaller competitors and mom-and-pops aside. So the 10-percent figure, so long as this market share gain was intact and so long as the economy as a whole pulled forward in the 2- to 4- percent range, made sense.

Today, however, economic growth as measured by GDP has waned somewhat, and that market share growth has probably also waned. Many companies are seeing renewed competition from smaller, more nimble firms, especially as larger firms downsize and outsource more of their business. A rather dramatic case in point (pardon the pun) is offered by the beer industry, in which big is no longer best and market share enjoyed by the larger brewers is reverting back to small brewers, microbrewers, and so forth. On the flip side, many companies have boosted their payout by repurchasing shares, perhaps raising the dividends and payouts figure to something closer to 2.5 percent.

So, for a long-term stock market performance, what is reasonable to expect today?

When you measure long-term *compounded* stock market returns from 1920 through 2012, again using the S&P 500 Index as the barometer, the markets have gained an average of 5.1 percent per year over the 83-year long term. That is more or less the slope of the trend line depicted in Figure 1.1. This figure includes inflation, GDP growth, and market share gains over the period.

But as GDP growth has softened, and as market share gains have also probably largely disappeared, the more recent expectation for stock market performance has waned. The analysis would now look something like this:

- GDP growth—real economic growth—2 percent
- Inflation perhaps 2 to 3 percent
- Corporate market share growth zero
- Dividends and payouts 2.5 to 3 percent, including buybacks

Now, as you can see, expected stock market growth barely reaches 5 percent and, in terms of real (inflation adjusted) growth, is far less. Add the 2.5 percent in payouts, and you get a true expectation for annualized stock market returns somewhere in the 7.5 percent range. So while reasonable stock market returns have declined to the 7.5 percent range from the old rule of thumb 10 percent, they still compare favorably to today's paltry fixed income returns of 1 percent or less for most savings accounts, and even a historically minuscule 2 percent for 10-year government bonds. Who wouldn't want to be in stocks? Well, the answer is simple: that 7.5 percent comes with considerable variation or, as market pros call it, *volatility* from one year to the next. As we'll discuss in more detail—and as you probably already know well as an experienced investor—higher returns don't come without some risk.

VOLATILITY IN THE SPOTLIGHT

Figure 1.1 gives one view of the 83-year history of the S&P 500, a view that shows the absolute growth over time, and the movement away from a steady growth and toward a more up-and-down, volatile path after the turn of the millennium. It's a good picture, and one that every investor should know and internalize.

FIGURE 1.2

S&P 500 Percent Change by Year, 1929–2012

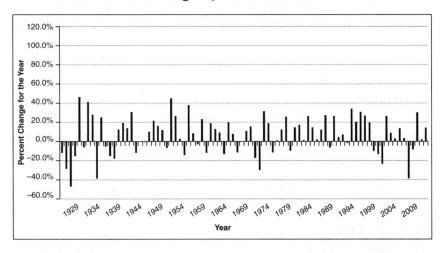

But to get a true understanding of volatility, one should look at the variation and change from year to year *expressed as a percentage*. Ten points up, 10 points down isn't much, unless we're talking about an index that is at 50 or 100 points. The ups and downs expressed as a percentage convey more meaning and help us understand how volatile the markets truly are. Figure 1.2 shows annual S&P 500 Index changes, expressed as a percentage, from year to year.

From this chart you can really start to see the roller-coaster ride we've been on. While the overall growth trajectory has been 5.1 percent per year, there is considerable variation around this figure. In fact, the annual change seldom comes in anywhere near the single-digit growth figure suggested by the long-term average.

You can also see the sharp ups and downs—the Rockies and westward—in this chart, occurring between 2000 and the present. With such a profound signature on the S&P 500 average chart (Figure 1.1), one might expect them to show more dramatically on this chart, too. Why don't they? Because this chart shows percentages, and the ups and downs, while significant, aren't as dramatic *as a percentage*. The real message here is that volatility, when thought of as a percentage change from a norm or expectation, has been relatively consistent through the years.

Perhaps the questions have already popped into your mind: Of the 83 years we're looking at, how many of them showed an annual performance within, say, zero and 10 percent positive, a relatively calm performance relative to the long-term average? How many of the 83 years showed this slow and steady growth?

Figure 1.3 answers that question rather dramatically.

In fact, in only 14 of the 83 years in question did the S&P 500 grow in single digits. That means that in 69 of the 83 years, the change was something larger or smaller. How could any investor sleep at night?

While this sounds pretty scary, there is some good news. First, some 55 of the 83 years are positive. Second, 46 of the 83 years are within a relatively benign 0 to 30 percent range. If you think of it as rolling dice, most of the outcomes are positive, and most are better than the 5.1 percent long-term average. Still, in the really bad years, in the 1930s and more recently 2008, things can get really bad, and

FIGURE 1.3

S&P 500 Annual Change Distribution

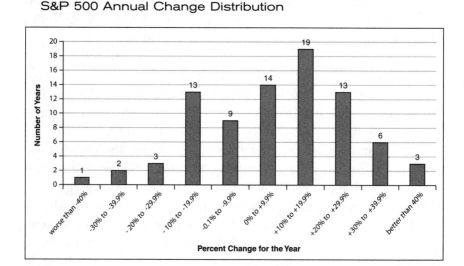

those assaults and corrections can really ding the long-term growth in the averages.

And, it should be noted, even this analysis doesn't convey the complete volatility story. The chart shows monthly figures, which mask the volatility experienced *during* the month: week to week, day to day, even within the day itself. There have been days, like the so-called flash crash of May 6, 2010, when the averages moved more than 10 percent from high to low *within the day*. The upshot: depending on how you look at it, volatility can be even greater—and more nerve wracking—than our simple analysis shows.

SHOULD INVESTORS EXPECT 20 PERCENT PER YEAR?

Particularly in the wake of the boom years of the late 1990s, and some of the better years that followed, many investors came to naively expect annual returns of 15 percent, 20 percent, or even more. If they owned the right stocks (or commodities or real estate, etc.) they would easily match these numbers, paving the way to a secure retirement, if nothing else. As you can see, while 20 percent did happen some of the time—like 22 of the 83 times depicted in Figures 1.2 and 1.3—it's pretty difficult to count on such sustained performance. And, knowing what we know about real economic growth, market share growth, payouts, and so forth, such gains are indeed unsustainable.

Rational, realistic investors are aware of these figures and should be quite happy with 5 percent growth with some current payout in the 2 percent range. It's reasonable to expect a little bit more, but 20 percent year after year simply does not make sense. If that's the expectation, volatility will most likely get in the way of reality. However, we as prudent investors can manage the volatility and perhaps turn some of it toward our favor, allowing us to earn maybe a little better than the market return of 5 percent.

That's what this book is all about.

VOLATILE FROM THE BEGINNING

Those of you who were investing actively back in 2008 certainly remember gut-wrenching volatility when the collapse of Lehman Brothers and the threat to the remainder of the financial industry took hold as the real estate bubble burst. In 2008 it felt like 200-point drops—and some gains—in the ever-popular Dow Jones Industrial Average were a daily occurrence.

Indeed, compared to other years, the numbers show that they *were* an almost daily occurrence. The following table shows the calms and the storms of the Dow Jones Industrial Average from 2000 through 2012.

Year	2000	2001	2002	2003	2004	2005	2006	2007	2008	2009	2010	2011	2012
# days 200-point change, Dow Jones Industrials	79	64	94	16	4	7	10	53	173	68	42	81	29

Source: *USA Today/Scanshift*

But to really get a handle on volatility, as suggested above, one should look not only at the big point gains and losses but also at the percentage represented by those movements. By that measure, the 2008–2012 period is significant, but we can see that tremendous damage was done during the Great Depression as well.

The following set of tables depict the largest *point* gains and losses, this time for the S&P 500 Index, and the *percentage* gains and losses.

S&P 500 Top 20 Largest *Point* Gains 1929–2011	
Time Period	**# of Gains**
1997–2001	6
2008–2012	14

S&P 500 Top 20 Largest *Point* Losses 1929–2011	
Time Period	**# of Losses**
1987	1
1997–2001	7
2008–2011	12

S&P 500 Top 20 Largest *Percent* Gains 1929–2011	
Time Period	**# of Gains**
1929–1939	16
1948	1
1987	1
2008	2

S&P 500 Top 20 Largest *Percent* Losses 1929–2011	
Time Period	**# of Losses**
1929–1939	13
1940	1
1987	2
2008	4

Source: *Wall Street Journal*

Yes, the year 2008 was a bad one, and hopefully, at least for most of us, it won't be repeated. But we may all be too young to remember the real heyday of gut-wrenching volatility back in the 1930s. Don't forget, no matter how calm the markets might seem at a given time, the next stretch of volatility may be just around the corner.

A SHORT TRIP THROUGH THE ASSET CLASSES

Up to this point, we've mainly addressed the volatility of stocks as an entire investment class, just to give us a primer on the nature of volatility and its timing through history. Obviously, stocks aren't the only thing you can invest in; it makes sense to understand the volatility of other assets: commodities, gold, real estate, bonds, and others.

As we look at other types of assets, it may surprise you that assets we consider to be safe and reliable can be fairly volatile as well. As more and more investors get into the markets, as business and boom-bust cycles get faster, and as information flow brings news and events more quickly than ever before, even such steady assets as gold, real estate, corn, and wheat have become more volatile.

Additionally, even within the asset class we all know as stocks—equities—there are different groupings of companies we can invest in: large cap, mid cap, small cap, value, growth, international. Each of these classes has a different volatility profile, but virtually all have been volatile. As we progress through this book, we'll see that it's not so important which class you choose to invest in but which assets *within* that class you choose.

First up is a closer look at what most people perceive to be the safest asset of all: gold.

Gold: Volatile Up and to the Right

A quick glance at the price of gold reveals anything but a flat or slowly rising, 5-percent-per-year trajectory. In fact, at first glance it looks more like the stock market, except that it doesn't have the steep peaks and valleys we found after the turn of the millennium.

Figure 1.4 shows the history of the price of gold from 1929 through 2012:

FIGURE 1.4

Gold Price, Year-End Close, 1929–2012

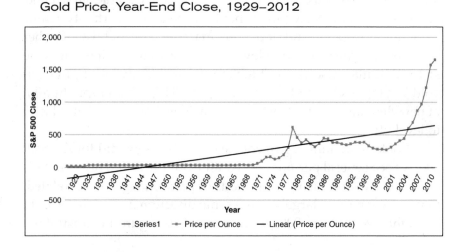

Now, to be fair, the price of gold was fixed by the U.S. government at $35 per ounce until 1971, so volatility was, well, illegal. (Now, wouldn't we all like to see that with some of our other investments?) So it makes more sense to look at the price of gold from 1971 on (Figure 1.5):

FIGURE 1.5

Gold Price, Year-End Close, 1971–2012

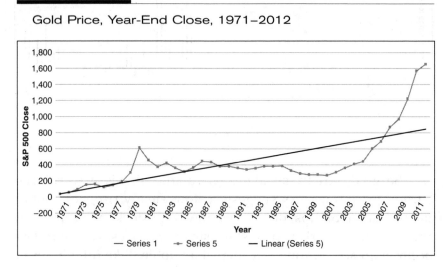

Now we can see a little more volatility corresponding to the inflation-driven peak in early 1980, followed by a gradual decline, before recent monetary policy, banking system uncertainty, China demand, European and Japanese malaise, and a host of other factors drove the price on a slow, steady rise to where it is now. One factor that may also account for the rise is the advent of physical-gold buying exchange-traded funds, or ETFs, which brought a lot of new demand into the gold market, a "new" demand that is likely to level off.

Looking at annual percentage changes, as we did for the S&P 500, we see several periods of volatility. But the difference—and it's a big one—is that the major periods of price change are correlated; that is, they moved largely in the same direction in the late 1970s to 1980, then again from 2003 to the present, as Figure 1.6 illustrates:

FIGURE 1.6

Gold, Percent Change by Year, 1971–2012

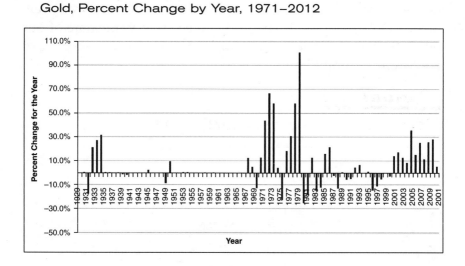

So gold, strictly speaking, is volatile. But is it risky? The current price trajectory suggests a slow, steady rise, not a lot of up-and-down bumps. But as we know from stocks and especially the real estate market, such slow, steady rises, especially if they occur at an accelerating rate, depict a bubble. Like tulip bulbs in

the 1600s and many assets since, when investors jump in "just because the price is going up," at some point there are no more investors to buy, and the price heads downhill, sometimes also at an accelerating rate as panic sets in.

If we were watching gold on a purely technical price behavior basis, we might be concerned. Of course, we must also consider the fundamentals of supply and demand, which may dictate a steady course even if the chart indicates danger. That's one of the tricks of low volatility investing: you can't just depend on the chart. It helps to know the volatility and the track record for the investment. But when you invest, you're investing in the future, which may not always be dictated by the past. Past behavior is an indicator but not a clear determinant of future behavior.

The bottom line: gold is a pretty solid investment but may be more volatile than you thought.

OBSERVATIONS: LOW, MEDIUM, AND HIGH VOLATILITY ASSET CLASSES

This chapter is designed as a primer on how to look at volatility and how different kinds of assets compare in their volatility characteristics. There are a lot of ways to display and examine this subject, and it's easy to get bogged down in endless charts and descriptions of how assets fluctuate over varying periods of time.

To give an overview, what probably works best is to move through each asset class and some subsets like growth, value, international, etc., for stocks, and give a few figures representing change as observed over a 20-year period. Why 20 years? Two reasons: first, that time frame takes us through two major business cycles, and second, observations farther back probably aren't that useful for most investors.

We will look at 12 asset classes and subclasses:

- Stocks
  - S&P 500 Growth
  - S&P 500 Value

- o Russell 2000 Growth
- o Russell 2000 Value
- o MSCI Emerging Markets
- o MSCI EAFE
- Bonds—Barclays Aggregate Bond Index
- Gold—spot price per Troy ounce
- Commodities—IMF Commodity Price Index
- Commodities—IMF Commodity Food Price Index
- Oil—IMF Crude Price Index
- Real Estate—Federal Housing Finance Agency All-Transactions U.S. Home Price Index

Pictures are worth a thousand words, but this chapter would expand beyond the limits of easy comprehension, especially for a first chapter, if we showed charts for all of these classes. Therefore, I'll show a few brief, low-tech statistics to characterize for each class here.

LOW VOLATILITY ASSET CLASSES

Particularly in the last 20 years, because of the rather dramatic business cycles we've experienced and the arrival of more investors and more funds to the market, it's not easy to identify an asset class that truly—and on its own accord—exhibits the characteristics of low volatility.

One could identify low volatility investments in a number of ways, and the true meaning of low volatility and low volatility investing will emerge in the next two chapters. For now, and for the sake of comparing asset classes, let's suppose that a true low volatility investment would produce a steady, predictable, and positive return over the 20-year period (better than a zero return, or else why invest?) and would generally not move more than 20 percent in either direction in a year. Sure, 20 percent up is nice, but it sets us up for pullbacks—or worse.

With that definition and some stretching and a few important caveats, we can define three of the 12 asset classes under review as having exhibited low volatility behavior over the past 20 years: bonds, housing, and food commodities.

Housing, you ask? Yes, it fits, with one very important caveat we'll get to in a minute.

Bonds

Over the past 20 years, at least as the statistics lead us, bonds have been the true safe and steady, with an average return of a healthy 6.3 percent, 18 years of positive returns, and no 20-percenters. Here we expose one caveat: this index includes all types of bonds and, naturally, within this asset class there are subclasses—such as high-yield, or so-called junk bonds—that have a different profile.

The second caveat is a big one: The recent accommodative policies of the Federal Reserve have driven bond prices upward in an attempt to drive interest rates downward and to bolster the economy. That's all well and good, but it has also most likely artificially increased returns (in the form of higher bond prices) and steadied the markets. Thus, the slow, steady returns of the bond market may not be real and in the view of many investors (myself included may) be exposed to a correction. It might not be a bubble, but it has inflated to the point where there's exposure to greater volatility going forward.

- Average annual percent change: 6.3 percent
- Number of years positive: 18
- Number of years negative: 2
- Number of years between 0 and 10 percent positive: 16
- Number of years more than 20 percent positive: 0
- Number of years more than 20 percent negative: 0

We'll cover bonds and other fixed income investments in Chapter 8.

Housing

Yes, housing. You wonder, perhaps from your own experience, *How could this be?* Indeed, the long-term chart for housing shows an asymptotic rise (that is, getting steeper as it goes) much like gold and the S&P 500 through 2006, then—wham!—the correction of the financial crisis and the housing bust.

But the statistics below show that housing on the whole is a relatively tame investment:

- Average annual percent change: 3.1 percent
- Number of years positive: 15
- Number of years negative: 5
- Number of years between 0 and 10 percent positive: 13
- Number of years more than 20 percent positive: 0
- Number of years more than 20 percent negative: 0

How could this be? What about the housing boom in 2004 to 2006, and the housing bust we all went through after that?

Again, there are two caveats. One is that the sheer price—the base, or denominator—in the calculation is very large: the price of a house. So a 5-percent move on a $200,000 asset is significant, and a 20-percent move is gigantic. That lesson carries forward as we look at other investment classes, too, as the price of gold, stocks, and so forth rise, an equal percentage gain or loss can have a much greater impact. Volatility as a percentage *should* naturally attenuate as the base of an index rises, although that isn't always the case; sometimes we've seen the opposite when bubbles go into correction.

The second caveat is huge, and is an important lesson for all of investing: leverage magnifies volatility. If you borrow money to invest, say, 50 percent of the amount of the investment, the volatility you will experience will, mathematically, double. Obviously that's an important consideration in housing, as the box shows:

A DOUBLE-EDGED SWORD CALLED LEVERAGE

Leverage—borrowing money to buy an asset or to fund a business—can be a great tool so long as everything works out right. But when it doesn't, look out below.

Consider the clear-cut example of housing. We just presented housing as an example of low volatility, with a tame and steady 3.1 percent annual gain with 15 positive years out of 20 and no 20 percent annual fluctuations. Nice, and you get to live in it, too.

Suppose you buy a $200,000 house. Suppose it goes up (or down) $10,000 in price in a year. No problem, right? A 5-percent fluctuation and we can all sleep at night. But now suppose that you, as most Americans do, borrowed 80 percent of the value. Your equity is $40,000. Now about that $10,000 price decrease— it's now a 25-percent change. That's the math: if your equity is only a fifth of the asset value, you must multiply the volatility figures by five. If you put 50 percent down, like some investors do for stocks, volatility doubles. Here again are the housing volatility figures, this time assuming an 80-percent mortgage:

- Average annual percent change: 15.5 percent
- Number of years positive: 15
- Number of years negative: 5
- Number of years between 0 and 10 percent positive: 2
- Number of years more than 20 percent positive: 10
- Number of years more than 20 percent negative: 2

Note especially the decline in the number of years between 0 and 10 percent positive: from 13 to 2. Looked at in this light, housing is a volatile investment indeed, at least for most people.

Remember the impact of leverage on volatility. It comes into play, too, when looking at companies to invest in. If they've borrowed a lot to finance the business, that, too, can lead to higher volatility.

VOLATILITY AND LEVERAGE: A VICIOUS CIRCLE?

If we get the binoculars out and look far downfield at the causes and consequences of volatility, we can see how it frequently can become a self-fulfilling prophecy, particularly where leverage is involved. Why? Because, as we just saw, a small loss is magnified into a big one when leverage is involved. That bigger loss creates considerable indigestion for the losers. They see what's happening and rush to *deleverage:* that is, to sell assets to reduce exposure to volatility. That rush to the exits creates—you guessed it—*more* volatility. The cycle continues. This deleveraging cycle goes a long way to explain the 2008 financial crisis: the volatility that created it and that it created.

Food Commodities—IMF Commodity Food Index

We all need to eat, and supply and demand in the food and food-stuffs markets tend to be fairly steady, although they've been a little more volatile in recent years as ethanol production and increased world standards of living have had their impact. On the flip side, increased globalization and additions of more world land to the mix have attenuated the effects of increased demands, as well as draughts and other natural hiccups. Compared to other assets, food prices, and prices of companies in the food business, for that matter, have been generally steady:

- Average annual percent change: 4.0 percent
- Number of years positive: 10
- Number of years negative: 10
- Number of years between 0 and 10 percent positive: 4
- Number of years more than 20 percent positive: 2
- Number of years more than 20 percent negative: 0

Food gives us a good example of how volatility is determined not just by technical or market characteristics, but fundamentals like long-term supply and demand. The markets may trade corn or sugar temporarily higher or lower, but in the long term, supply and demand aren't likely to change too much. Agriculture is subject to fewer technological upheavals, management missteps, competitive uncertainty, or other forms of change than many other things you can invest in.

MEDIUM VOLATILITY ASSET CLASSES

Here, we examine six asset classes best described as "medium" volatility:

Gold

We've already covered the long-term picture of gold, but here is how it stacks up in the 20-year comparison:

- Average annual percent change: 9.5 percent
- Number of years positive: 13
- Number of years negative: 7
- Number of years between 0 and 10 percent positive: 3
- Number of years more than 20 percent positive: 6
- Number of years more than 20 percent negative: 1

The trend has been positive to strongly positive; most of the volatility has been on the upside, with several years of up in a row. When we think about volatility, we think about the down volatility and random ups and downs, not a series of ups. Furthermore, it isn't as volatile as some of the popular measures might tell us, since it moves in a consistent direction—without random fluctuations—more than most assets. Here again, the technicals of persistent and accelerating upward price movement suggest a correction, but the fundamentals may not.

Large-Cap Growth Stocks: S&P 500 Growth Index

Now it's time to take a closer look at equities as an asset class, and to gain a better understanding of how different components of this asset class behave. Stocks, of course, come in all shapes and sizes. Most often stocks are grouped by *capitalization*, or the underlying size of the company, and by orientation: that is, whether the company is a growth or a value investment.

The precise definition of growth and value isn't important here; growth stocks typically have strong sales growth and high valuations compared to underlying assets values; value stocks are relatively more established with relatively moderate growth (although, strictly speaking, growth is *part* of value) and relatively low valuations compared to underlying assets.

In this first grouping, we examine the S&P Large-Cap Growth Index. As we'll see, most U.S. stocks are more similar than they are different, with a strong growth record over the 20 years and fairly sharp moves up and down.

- Average annual percent change: 10.1 percent
- Number of years positive: 16
- Number of years negative: 4
- Number of years between 0 and 10 percent positive: 6
- Number of years more than 20 percent positive: 7
- Number of years more than 20 percent negative: 3

Large-Cap Value Stocks: S&P 500 Value Index

The results are surprisingly similar to the S&P 500 Growth Index shown above:

- Average annual percent change: 9.9 percent
- Number of years positive: 15
- Number of years negative: 5
- Number of years between 0 and 10 percent positive: 3

- Number of years more than 20 percent positive: 6
- Number of years more than 20 percent negative: 2

In fact, the pattern is so similar that it deserves a picture (Figure 1.7):

FIGURE 1.7

Comparison of Annual Change Between S&P 500 Growth and S&P 500 Value Indexes

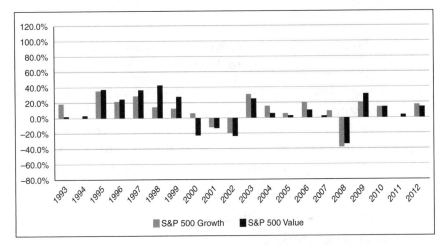

Large-cap stocks, whether growth or value, tend to run together and tend to be more volatile than one might think, as we saw when looking at the S&P 500 chart as a whole at the beginning of this chapter. The growth stocks actually have more years in the favorable 0 to 10-percent range, mostly because for several years the value stocks slightly exceed 10 percent.

Broad Market Growth: Russell 2000 Growth Index

Our look at stocks continues with the Russell 2000 indexes, which now include a broader array of companies in the mid- and small-cap tiers. Mid-cap usually refers to companies with capitalizations (number of shares outstanding times share price) between

$1 billion and $5 billion; small-cap companies are less than $1 billion.

- Average annual percent change: 8.7 percent
- Number of years positive: 14
- Number of years negative: 6
- Number of years between 0 and 10 percent positive: 3
- Number of years more than 20 percent positive: 5
- Number of years more than 20 percent negative: 3

Broad Market Value: Russell 2000 Value Index

Again, this is a similar analysis and result as compared to the large-cap S&P groupings. Notable is the higher overall annual percentage change with the value stocks, and the absence of drops greater than 20 percent, indicating that mid- and small-cap value stocks have done well over the years, with relatively less volatility.

- Average annual percent change: 14.0 percent
- Number of years positive: 14
- Number of years negative: 6
- Number of years between 0 and 10 percent positive: 1
- Number of years more than 20 percent positive: 11
- Number of years more than 20 percent negative: 0

General Commodities: IMF Commodity Price Index

Next, we arrive at a general commodity index that includes not only the food and food products covered above, under low volatility asset classes, but also energy, metals, and other mostly mined commodities, adding an element of volatility to the mix.

- Average annual percent change: 8.9 percent
- Number of years positive: 14

- Number of years negative: 6
- Number of years between 0 and 10 percent positive: 6
- Number of years more than 20 percent positive: 7
- Number of years more than 20 percent negative: 2

On the whole, the volatility of this class is not that much different than stocks, which might reflect their sensitivity and synchronization with the overall U.S. and global economy.

HIGH VOLATILITY ASSET CLASSES

There are no surprises in the three groups that tend to exhibit higher volatility: international stocks, emerging market stocks (a special subset of international stocks), and crude oil.

International Stocks: MSCI EAFE Index

MSCI is a company that provides "decision support tools," in this case indexes, and EAFE stands for Europe, Australasia, and Far East, and is the broadest indicator of company and stock performance for companies headquartered in so-called developed countries:

- Average annual percent change: 12.8 percent
- Number of years positive: 16
- Number of years negative: 4
- Number of years between 0 and 10 percent positive: 4
- Number of years more than 20 percent positive: 7
- Number of years more than 20 percent negative: 1

Emerging Market Stocks: MSCI Emerging Markets Index

Emerging markets are in countries with emerging economies at the frontiers of the larger regions. Currently the index includes 22 countries, including larger economies like China, India, Russia, and

Brazil (the BRICs) and smaller economies like Chile, Colombia, Mexico, Egypt, Poland, South Africa, Korea, Malaysia, and Indonesia:

- Average annual percent change: 11.5 percent
- Number of years positive: 11
- Number of years negative: 9
- Number of years between 0 and 10 percent positive: 1
- Number of years more than 20 percent positive: 7
- Number of years more than 20 percent negative: 3

One would expect a higher volatility with this group than with the more established EAFE economies, and there is somewhat more volatility. There is some overlap between these indexes, and the volatility difference isn't as large as one might expect—but if you look at some of the individual countries, that's where the volatility comes in. Again, when several assets are combined, the volatility for the combination is usually reduced. It's important to keep in mind the components of any asset class.

Crude Oil

We've all felt it at the gas pump: yes, crude oil is volatile.

- Average annual percent change: 9.5 percent
- Number of years positive: 12
- Number of years negative: 8
- Number of years between 0 and 10 percent positive: 2
- Number of years more than 20 percent positive: 8
- Number of years more than 20 percent negative: 4

The volatility is caused by tips in the balance in supply and demand—and, most likely, by the perception of future volatility, which causes a lot of big players, like airlines, to buy now to avoid future shocks. As with many commodities, demand frenzies are followed by supply frenzies (and, sometimes, recessions) tipping the balance back in the other direction. Again, understanding the volatility requires understanding the fundamentals.

WHERE TO NOW?

It's not just the asset class, it's the investments, timing, and time frame. As we'll see, it's very difficult to put a precise and actionable handle on volatility. There are many ways to measure it, but none is perfect, and at the end of the day almost anything can be volatile, depending on when you buy it and how closely you watch it. And, of course, any measure of volatility, including visual, commonsense glances at the historical patterns of an investment, is just that: history. There's no telling what's in store for the future, as investors in housing, BP, Eastman Kodak, Hewlett-Packard, BlackBerry, and many other companies over the years have found out. There are clearly other forces at work. Knowing the history helps, but it isn't the whole story.

KEY CONCEPTS

▶ Most assets—even gold—are more volatile than you think.

▶ In percentage terms, volatility has been high in the past 10 years, but was even higher during the Great Depression.

▶ The S&P 500 Index returned between zero and 9.9 percent only 14 times in its 82-year history.

▶ Investors should be content with annual returns in the 5 to 8 percent range, maybe a bit more.

▶ Bonds and housing have the lowest 20-year volatility among 12 asset classes. However, leverage from debt financing makes housing more volatile in practice.

▶ So far as volatility is concerned, there is less difference than you might expect between growth and value stocks as defined in the S&P 500 Index. Stocks are stocks.

CHAPTER 2

The Anatomy of Risk and Volatility

Chapter 1 gave us a mental picture of volatility in the various investment markets over time. Having that picture helps us to embrace what will happen if we invest, but only in very big-picture sense. We know that there is risk if we invest, and that risk presents itself to us in the form of volatility. Business is business, markets are markets, and nothing follows a smooth path up and to the right forever. So what do we do?

In this chapter, we'll further develop the big picture of volatility, centered on getting a clearer view of where it comes from and how it affects you as an investor. People tend to be afraid of what they don't understand and can't control. When they're afraid of something, they tend to avoid it. Our discussion of volatility is aimed to develop an understanding of what it is and how it works so that you can *deal* with it—so you can work with it and around it and thus achieve more with your investments. The main idea is that if you understand and then accept and embrace volatility rather than avoiding it, you'll achieve greater returns on your investments and ultimately achieve your investment goals. When you achieve investment goals, you'll sleep better at night than if you simply avoid volatility per se.

While this chapter explores the nature and sources of volatility with the idea of helping you understand and think clearly about it, Chapter 3—"What Is Low Volatility Investing?"—lays out an approach to managing volatility in your investments according to your perception and tolerance of risk and what is rational and makes sense as an investor. From these concepts we'll arrive at a definition of low volatility investing you can use and work with through the acquisition of individual investments and the creation of your own portfolio.

VOLATILITY: WHAT IT IS AND WHERE IT COMES FROM

Volatility? Certainly we all know what that is, if not in mind, certainly in body, when we experience the tightened chest, increased pulse, and gritted teeth of a 500-point Dow drop or several 200-point moves in a row. Volatility is one of the few experiences in investing that can actually produce a physiological response. For most of us, volatility creates fear. For some of us, it creates opportunity.

What do I mean by that? When most of us think of volatility, we think of the downside. We think of risk. Statisticians define *uncertainty* as the movement of data above *and* below a mean or trend line. Risk, on the other hand, concerns the movements—and possible movements—*below* the norm, below the trend line. Most of us are concerned about risk—the downside—the fear factor.

So, although most of us think of volatility and risk as being one and the same, there is actually an upside to consider, too. Volatility is directly related to the concept of uncertainty, and a little less directly related to risk. If one considers greed and fear to be the two major emotional forces in the market, volatility serves both of those masters.

Still, as a practical matter for most of us, volatility should be thought of as a fairly strong proxy for risk, an equivalent of risk, a correlated indicator of risk. If something is volatile, it's risky, and if it's risky, it should be considered carefully, if not avoided altogether.

This is true, so far as it goes. Think of your experiences with anything "scary"—your first date, or perhaps high school chemistry, or maybe even a snake. You approached it with considerable caution. You knew there were downside possibilities; the date might not work out, the chemistry might be too hard and you might flunk, and the snake might bite or lunge at you or do something unpredictable, disruptive, or discomforting. But the more you got used to dating, or the more small successes you rang up in chemistry, the better; you were able to accept some of those downsides, because, well, you were seeing some of the upside as well.

And as for the snake—well, some of us never really overcome that fear. But once we understand snakes better—what kind of snake we're dealing with, and whether a particular snake won't bite or poison us—does it get a little better? Even for the most averse-averse person, I say it probably does.

LIVING WITH THE TRUE NATURE OF VOLATILITY

To gain a better understanding of the volatility snake, it makes sense to diverge into where that snake comes from. We already know something about its nature from Chapter 1. Now, unlike a snake, we have the opportunity to apply logic and experience to understand its behavior and what drives it. If we could understand that about snakes, or any wild animal, wouldn't that help?

That said, perhaps it isn't so simple. We can get the courage to look at the snake, and even touch it, knowing we won't have to deal with it on an ongoing basis. The fact that it is always with us, and never goes away, may be what makes the volatility snake so fearsome for some people. Even with this long-term component, I maintain that we can get used to being with the snake on an ongoing basis.

While the snake analogy may be a bit drastic, the point really is that by understanding the snake—where it comes from and how it behaves—you'll still be wary that it might bite, but you'll learn to live with it anyway. If a snake could bite, but also provide financial and retirement security, wouldn't you try to, and learn to, live with it?

Learning where volatility comes from, and what causes it, is a good place to start.

THE PRIMORDIAL CAUSES OF VOLATILITY

To gain a better understanding of the volatility beast, we should discuss some of the most basic causes. From there, we can get into the real-world behaviors, what triggers them, and what can harm us.

At its roots, volatility arises from three main forces: business activity and change, knowns vs. unknowns, and perceptions vs. reality.

Business Activity and Change

Business involves the exchange of goods and services between willing parties, and the nature of that exchange can evolve and change considerably over time. Business can change dramatically in the short term, as in a new product being introduced or a contract not being renewed. Business also changes gradually over time, as the forces of "creative destruction" make old businesses, like film photography, obsolete in favor of new technologies like digital photography. The forces of change are always at work, and those forces will cause volatility.

Sometimes the change is factored in gradually over time; everyone knows about it and can embrace it. Sometimes it comes as a shock or a surprise—in either case, something changes and someone loses—but in the latter, the surprise creates more volatility. Eastman Kodak didn't flame out in a drastic crash; it faded away over time. But the BP Deepwater Horizon disaster came on suddenly and was clearly not part of anyone's plan, yet it changed offshore oil production drastically in the short term and, in some ways, forever. The event created a downside—and volatility—in the oil industry.

The point is, change creates volatility, and the more sudden or unexpected the change, or the *less understood* the change, the more volatility is created.

Knowns and Unknowns

Nobody can predict the future, and it is this very fact that creates volatility. All markets—stock and others—are simply a guess at what something will be worth in the future. Stock valuations are based on what a company has, but even more on how much it will earn and pay to investors down the road. Prices for commodities, real estate, and other investments are dictated not only by current value but also by future expectations. Current value can change fundamentally, but it's really the expectation of future value and the uncertainty of what that future value will be that cause much of the volatility in the markets.

As an example, oil markets in 2008 became volatile not so much because of the current supply and demand situation, which was impacted by China demand, but because of the lack of certainty about both future demand and supply, in part *because* of the new China demand. The future price became a guessing game, and the current price became more volatile as people in the markets tried to guess. That volatility made market players even more uncertain, leading to, yes, even more volatility.

Volatility, indeed, can be a self-fulfilling prophecy, especially as the unknowns in a market become *more* unknown. This is why bond markets are typically less volatile; the returns are far more known and understood. But if a major player goes bankrupt, the unknowns turn into fear, and that fear turns rather readily into volatility.

Perceptions and Reality

It would have been easy to throw in the towel on low oil prices in the summer of 2008, or even on the entire financial industry later that year in the wake of the debt-fueled real estate market and Lehman Brothers collapse. These events were real, and they did a lot of real damage to markets and to asset prices.

But often the perceptions exceed reality and sometimes go in the opposite direction. Perceptions cause markets to go too far negative or positive, often resulting in volatile reversals or corrections to the normal market pattern. Perceptions tend to amplify—or sometimes attenuate—real changes as what might arise from normal business or market activity. The volatility is real, but the causal factors may not be, or may be less significant than the market makes them out to be.

VOLATILITY vs. RISK: SHORT TERM vs. LONG TERM?

When one thinks of the term *volatility*, one thinks of relatively short-term ups and downs—a pulse, if you will—around a fairly steady long-term pattern of behavior. Gyrations around a steady average or trend, either downward or upward, usually aren't significant or even real when it comes to determining long-term investing performance. But what is the definition of short and *long term*? In the course of business history, even the existence of a company like Microsoft (MSFT)—30 years—could be considered a short-term event. Is Microsoft's meteoric rise and subsequent reversion to a more normal valuation, a short-term blip? Volatility? Most would say no. But the cycle of upward growth, followed by a correction and then years of relative price inactivity—with the ever-growing concern that MSFT's core products could someday become obsolete—could definitely be considered volitility in the context of long-term investing performance, say, long into retirement.

Many consider volatility short-term gyrations, mostly irrational or not explained by real events, around a more stable pattern, while risk is a more long-term, causal change in something. Perhaps it's easier to consider the Microsoft case as risk: risk of technology obsolescence, rising acceptance of competitive products, or something else entirely. Whether short or long term, one must decide whether gyrations or fluctuations in price are genuine and indicative of larger business change, or are a result of forces of perception, unknowns, and even the day-to-day operations of the markets. It isn't so much whether change is short term or long, it's whether it's real and here to stay. That said, whether real or perceived, both short- term and long-term volatility or risk can affect your investing performance.

It isn't so much about what we call it, it's how we deal with it that counts.

RISK—THE WAY THE PROS VIEW IT

Upside volatility is nice, but most investment professionals tend to focus on the downside part of the equation: risk. When considering the risk of a particular investment, many divide the risk into two categories: *systemic* and *unsystemic*:

- *Systemic* risk comes from sources not directly related to the investment itself: in other words, the markets or the economy at large. If a company's stock rises and falls in direct correlation to what's happening in the overall market in which it trades, the rises and falls are considered to by systemic, that is, from the system the investment is part of. Since—in theory, at least—one cannot change these events or avoid them by switching to another investment, one cannot diversify away from systemic risk.

- *Unsystemic* risk arises from the characteristics, performance, and/or supply vs. demand fundamentals of an investment separate from the overall market and economy. The fortunes of, say, Microsoft, are tied to the overall economy and market. But they are also tied to the individual decisions, products, marketing effectiveness, and financial performance of the company and its leaders and managers. You can diversify away from Microsoft's risks by buying another company (although with their market-dominant products in the computing market, it's more difficult than with most companies).

This construct is meaningful, especially in theory, but breaks down a bit because some risks are difficult to classify. The cost of manufacturing or labor inputs can be affected by the overall economy or news headlines far from a company's front door, but how a company *uses* those inputs is wholly an unsystemic issue. Still, it's important to understand that even if you buy an investment that correlates perfectly with the market, there is some risk, and by buying a company or some other investment, you're acquiring both the systemic and unsystemic risks inherent to that investment. By buying smart or by diversifying, it is easier to control unsystemic than systemic risks.

RISK–CONSIDERING THE SOURCE

I think there's a slightly more useful model, one that breaks down the risks a bit more descriptively aligned to where they come from. Somewhat coincident with the systemic-vs.-unsystemic risk model, investing risks break down into three categories: *external, internal,* and *personal.*

Recognizing that it's practically impossible to list all the different kinds of investing risks, what follows are some examples of each category of risk. It would be easy to be frightened away from investing altogether after reviewing these lists, but one should keep in mind three things: (1) the probability of major failure caused by any of these factors is relatively small; (2) these sources of uncertainty can sometimes cancel each other out; and (3) in most cases, commodities being the notable exception, investments can be managed (at least by competent managers) to avoid or reduce these risks.

These lists of risks may seem obvious and are not intended to be memorized or placed in some kind of checklist of risk factors to check before making any investment. Rather, they should become part of your thought process, part of the sensory experience of selecting or managing a given investment and your investment portfolio as a whole.

External Risks

Call it what you want—external, extrinsic, exogenous, macro, or something else—but a considerable amount of risk with any investment comes from forces and factors external to or outside the investment itself. Like all risk factors, there is a reality component—what is changing—and a component of unknowns, uncertainties, and perceptions surrounding the reality, which may cause more volatility than the reality itself. Your job as an investor is to assess both the reality and the unknowns around in and what they might do to your investments.

Examples of external risks include:

- *Economic risk*: The economy has its ups and downs, which can provide considerable headwinds or tailwinds to investments. What might be a headwind to one investment, such as housing, might be a tailwind to another, such as gold. Investors should always keep tabs on the economy, economic cycles, and signs of change in the economic cycle (like employment figures and such).

- *Headline risk*: Headlines can directly concern the economy or be about some other geopolitical event of importance that might cause substantial real change or bring new unknowns, uncertainties, or perceptions to the markets. The September 11, 2001, terrorist attacks are, of course, a classic example. Elections, important congressional actions or bills, or tax changes are also at the top of a long list of such risks.

- *Policy risk*: Policy risk is closely related to headline risk, except that not all changes in policy will make headlines. Changes in tax policy, monetary policy, health care, energy policy, deficit reduction, and others can all create or obliterate a favorable climate for a particular investment, or investments in general. We're not just talking about U.S. policy here; policy change in other countries can affect all kinds of investments, notably currency investments.

- *Input risks*: Now we get a little closer to the actual investment you intend to make, yet these factors are entirely out of your control or the control of a business manager if you're investing in stocks. Shortages and higher energy prices, food commodity prices, and other supply risks provide solid examples.

- *Interest rate risk*: Interest rate risk could really be lumped into policy risk, headline risk, or even input risk, as money is an input into any business, especially financial businesses, real estate, etc. Uncertainty about interest rates can cause considerable volatility in specific investments and the markets as a whole.

- *Inflation risk*: Inflation risk is often the result of policy or other headline events like shortages, labor cost pressures, and others. Inflation is a good example of where the unknowns and perceptions can cause more damage than the reality, as evidenced by gold prices in the past five years.

- *Channel risks*: Like input risks, channel risks can be one step removed from an investment. If you were investing in a company in the publishing industry, the demise of Borders Group, an event totally outside your control or a publisher's control, had a dramatic effect on the publishing industry. More globally, the advent of e-commerce has disrupted a lot of businesses and industries.

- *Financial market risks*: The financial markets and the system behind them are a complex and well-oiled machine that works well to provide fast and fair trading almost all of the time. But as we learned with the May 6, 2010, Flash Crash, things can go wrong. The risk of outright system failure is not the only thing to consider here; if a stock is illiquid or thinly traded—that is, if there aren't many buyers or sellers in the market at a given time—price swings can be more severe, especially if any disruptive event happens with the company or the investment. Liquidity and market robustness can be a marketwide issue, too, as found with foreign and especially emerging markets, which are typically more volatile than the United States and larger, more developed countries. Differences in accounting policies and other business practices can also create uncertainty and volatility in these different and smaller markets.

- *Technology risk*: Technology risk is not as likely as some of these other factors to cause immediate short-term volatility but can cause changes or disruptions in the long term. The long term sometimes isn't so long, especially when uncertainty and perception enter the picture. The primary risk is that a company—or even a commodity—becomes obsolete. The demise of film photography obviously affected Eastman Kodak and, a little less obviously, the silver industry. These events did not cause immediate volatility, but did Apple's 2010 introduction of the iPad signal a more volatile period for makers of PC-based products?

WHAT IS A BLACK SWAN?

It may seem that most external events are part of the normal course and twitter of the business day, and for the most part, that's right. But what about those huge game-changing events, like September 11, 2001, that nobody saw coming?

Such an event—or, more recently, an event like the BP Deepwater Horizon oil spill in 2010—is highly uncorrelated and unexpected, something that few could have foreseen, and obviously, it created a lot of volatility for both individual investments and the markets as a whole. Market observers refer to something like this as a *black swan event*.

Just as a black swan is unusual among a group of white swans, a black swan event is a surprise to the observer and has a major effect. But author Nassim Nicholas Taleb, in his 2007 classic *The Black Swan* (which was revised in 2010, following the financial crisis), adds more to the definition.

1. Black swan events are rare events that are beyond the realm of normal expectations in history, science, finance, or technology. They are hard to predict and so rare that they largely defy scientific or statistical prediction, but play a huge and disproportionate role when they happen.

2. Because they are so rare, people are blind to their possibility and tend to see only after the fact that they could have happened and rationalize accordingly: "I should have seen that, and managed my investments differently." The 2008 financial crisis is a clear example, but investors in BP or any other oil company should look at the Deepwater Horizon disaster as a possibility.

One of the key features of a black swan event is the psychological bias or predisposition to ignoring it until it happens and, naturally, when it does, people will become overly fearful for a period of time afterward. It's like when a tornado hits a small town; everyone fears it will happen again, but that fear naturally subsides. In the meantime, they head for the basement at the first rumble of thunder. The next black swan becomes a matter of perception for individuals and the collective masses.

Other cited examples of black swan events include World War I, Pearl Harbor, the financial meltdown and failure of Lehman Brothers, the 2011 Japan earthquake, and even the rise of the Internet (some are slower and more deliberate in nature than others). Some might consider the newfound U.S. energy independence from shale formation fracking a black swan event, as would a major breakthrough in alternative energy. Black swans aren't always negative, but they are disruptive.

Taleb doesn't advocate attempting to predict black swans; nobody can. The point is to know they can happen, to strengthen your fortress against the ones that might occur, and to be able to take advantage of the positive ones. When leverage is involved—as shown in the financial industry in 2008—black swans can be magnified. In the case of the financial industry, firms were both complacent about the black swan possibilities and way out on a limb, thus extremely vulnerable.

Taleb also contends that world and financial events aren't normally distributed; that is, they don't occur randomly. Normally distributed, random models for measuring and managing risk probably don't work (more on this in Chapters 4 and 5). Black swans increase volatility, and even the less extreme events don't happen randomly or independently. Think about oil shortages, inflation, and corresponding changes in interest rates, for example.

There are important lessons for investors, especially low volatility investors. They should know that black swans can happen and should provide some protection for their invest-ments. The key word is *some*; you can't guard against every-thing, and overprotection against these events can wipe out any chance of achieving investment returns—and you'll probably still get hurt by the swan anyway!

Knowing that black swans are out there is part of the thought process, but by definition can't be part of any investing formula. You just need to ask "what if" a little more often.

Internal Risks

Internal, or intrinsic or endogenous, risks are risks inherent to the investment. When talking about stocks or bonds, these are *company-specific* risks (or agency-specific, in the case of public sector bonds) that affect that company's business alone. When talking about a commodity, these are risks inherent to the commodity itself and affect production, distribution, or demand. While most external risks, like systemic risks, are hard to avoid, internal risks can usually be avoided—or diversified away from—simply by finding an alternative investment.

Like most external risks, volatility is affected both by the reality of the item and the unknowns and perceptions that may surround it. If a company becomes known for issuing negative earnings warnings prior to regular earnings announcements, that perception will continue, like the tornado experience in the small town, long after the most recent event, and will often increase volatility.

- *News and event risk*: For companies, this category broadly covers news about or affecting the performance of the business, including earnings announcements, preannouncements and warnings, recalls, layoffs, and a host of other events that might happen to the business. Most of us have seen a dramatic increase in volatility immediately prior to—and often immediately prior to—earnings announcements. This volatility is wholly caused by anticipation of the unknown rather than actual fact. For commodities, volatility-causing events might include draughts, releases of production statistics (which are comparable to earnings reports), or other production or market disruptions

The risks that follow pertain mainly to companies and thus to stocks and bonds of those companies:

- *Product risks*: All companies carry the risk of something bad happening to their product or service. Defects, recalls, errors, and the costs incurred to correct them can all create volatility. Sometimes the source of these problems may be external, like the Tylenol poisoning scare that hit Johnson &

Johnson back in the 1980s, but the risk and volatility that follows are specific to the company. *Technology risk* is a form of product risk; the introduction of the iPad and other mobile computing devices put many traditional PC and PC-related products at risk. Again, it's often the news and perception surrounding the event of a product failure or technical competitor that set off the volatility.

- *Market risks*: All companies that market products incur risks in doing so. Companies may stumble with their customers (usually related to a product failure) or fail to respond to competitive threats. Price changes or channel or distribution problems can also create risk and volatility, for example, if a key retailer decides to stop carrying a company's product.

- *Operational risks*: A production problem, a fire in a factory or a hurricane, a long or complex supply chain, or low-cost foreign competition can create risk and volatility for a company or, really, a commodity. High inventories that consume cash and increase the risk of obsolescence are a risk factor. One must also remember how dependent most businesses are on IT performance; a server glitch or even a virus can become a black swan event for any given company.

- *Financial risks*: Companies take on financial risk routinely by borrowing money or letting customers pay on credit (receivables) or with large inventories or high capital spending requirements. Just as in your own personal finances, a lot of debt or financial commitments make you more vulnerable to the unexpected, and companies that incur these risks are likely to be more volatile.

- *Management risks*: Companies are complex, and as we've seen, there are a lot of risks to be managed or avoided. Managers must lead, set the right objectives and strategies, hire the right employees, and make the right decisions. A solid, proven management team helps, but as we've often seen in the corporate world, not all management teams are up to the task. When managers make mistakes; come and go in revolving-door fashion; or, even worse, lie, cheat, and steal, perceived risk, actual risk, and, ultimately, volatility, can increase dramatically. Volatile management teams—or even stable management teams that deliver volatile performance—can lead to volatile investment performance in a hurry.

WHY DO SOME INVESTORS PREFER COMMODITIES?

Commodities have unique supply-and-demand characteristics, and many investors will say they invest in commodities because, especially with the emergence of China, more people with an increasing standard of living are in the market buying the same amount of produced oil, wheat, corn, gold, silver—you name it.

This is true. But many investors prefer commodities because they are pure investments; there is no management team to depend on to make the right decisions, be honest and upfront with shareholders, keep the finances straight, or just plain do a good job. While managers *should* work to reduce the risks outlined above—and better yet, create a positive upside gain from the resources they have—it doesn't always work out that way.

While commodities still have some market and production risk factors, like draught or overproduction, inherent to their existence, by and large they have fewer internal risks.

Personal Risks

Finally, we get to the third category of risk, one not so well identified or documented in today's investment literature. It is what I call personal risk: the additional risk contributed by personal characteristics, behaviors, and knowledge (or lack thereof) that might affect your investing decisions and that can become another source of volatility for your investments.

Emotions, greed, fear, hope, lack of knowledge or understanding, and lack of time can all lead to investment decisions (or indecisions) that will make your investing life *seem* more volatile and probably *be* measurably more volatile. How many of us have hung on to a stock too long because we failed to recognize the signs of failure, only to experience more volatility as that failure came to be? How many times have we chosen an investment that turned out to be more volatile than we expected simply because we overlooked something in our analysis?

We've all done it.

And these personal or behavioral risks don't just apply to us as individual investors; they apply to the entire investing community. Markets are really just collections of individuals; more precisely, they are collections of individual *decisions*. They are collections of individual hopes, fears, ideas, impulses, and, indeed, sometimes greed. When investors as a group let emotion carry the day, things happen to these markets, or prices of individual securities, that might not otherwise have happened in a purely rational, formula-driven environment. People overreact, perception overrides reality, perception *becomes* reality, and the markets overreact as a whole.

Wise investors are aware that volatility and volatile investment performance can arise from a number of human factors, some of which may be seen in the bathroom mirror every morning:

- *Insufficient knowledge*: Warren Buffett said it best: "Risk comes from not knowing what you're doing." Most of us don't have the time or the ability to research an investment well enough to fully understand the dynamics, causes of change, and long-term factors of success and failure. The Buffett school of value investing teaches us to invest "as though we were buying the whole business," a treatise to the level of knowledge and understanding we should have. But even if we were able to see into every corner of a business or investment, most of us wouldn't have the time to pursue it. The lack of knowledge about what's really going on with investments breeds risk, and that risk can turn into unforeseen and unwanted volatility. Naturally, this turns into a core theme later in this book; you can reduce volatility—at least unexpected volatility—by knowing what you're doing.

- *Insufficient time*: Closely related to insufficient knowledge is the fact of life for most of us that, unless we are professional investors, there isn't enough time in the day to fully research every investment and to track what's going on with it. Lack of time leads to lack of knowledge and a diminished ability to make the most rational, timely investment decisions, so we reluctantly accept additional risk and volatility as a consequence.

- *Emotional override*: Now we arrive at one of the most fascinating—and pervasive—sources of volatility, both for us as individual investors and for investors as a collective group, that is, for markets. It's what I call emotional override: the tendency to let emotions carry the day. These emotions trump otherwise rational decisions and behaviors with greed, fear, and other quirks of personality, usually leading to overreaction—or even underreaction—to the facts of the day. Both individually and collectively, these factors lead to volatility.

  o *Greed and fear*. It's been said that markets are fueled by greed and fear. While this may be a bit of an overstatement, we all get greedy and we all get fearful. When entire markets get greedy or fearful, we know what happens to volatility.

  o *Failing to accept failure*. More often attributed to the male gender—and studies have shown, as a result, that females have been known to deliver better investing performance—is the good, old-fashioned ego. "I know I'm right; the market is wrong" is the oft-repeated slogan of this group. People "marry" their investments and can't let go, especially at a loss. As a corollary, knowing when to sell is a big, and often much overlooked, part of investing, and when we don't know when to sell, we can become more vulnerable to volatility.

o *Not knowing when (or how) to sell.* Obviously related to the first two bullet points above, buying is easy. But if we can't make a *sell* decision on certain investments when needed or prudent, we hang on to some investments too long. That doesn't increase volatility, but it does increase our exposure to volatility.

Can you see the pattern? Volatility is a function of the markets and the external and internal characteristics of our investments. But we can't just look in the direction of the markets and the companies or commodities or currencies we invest in; volatility can often arise from our own habits and investing behaviors. As we'll see, a rational, disciplined investment approach should help reduce the volatility we experience and is a critical component of low volatility investing.

When Personal Risk Isn't So Personal

What we learned of as personal risk can become so pervasive that it becomes more like an external risk—when entire populations exhibit aspects of personal risk: greed, fear, doubt, lack of knowledge—we arrive at a collective market behavior we can't control and can diversify only away from with difficulty. What happens? We get a statistically measurable increase in volatility, particularly volatility far away from what would be expected in the normal course of business and market behavior.

Consider the work of the economist Eugene Fama, a student of stock prices and stock price behavior, who once pointed out that if prices followed a normal distribution you'd expect a really big jump—what he specified as a movement five standard deviations from the mean—once every 7,000 years. What he found, in fact, was that jumps of that magnitude happen in the stock market every three or four years, because investors don't behave in a statistically orderly fashion.

What do investors do? They do stupid things, they get greedy, they get fearful, they panic, they change their minds, and they follow each other. It becomes a herd mentality, a stampede. Fama overlaid this on the normal distribution of stock price behavior, as depicted by the statistically normal distribution in Figure 2.1, to add a "fat tail." The fat tail signals many more outlying events than statisticians would normally find in a normal world with normal behavior.

FIGURE 2.1

Fat Tail Distribution

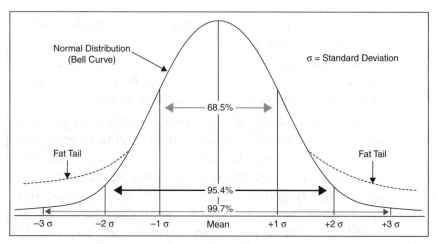

Source: Stockcharts.com

What does this mean? Normal volatility is volatile enough. But when these personal and collective behavior factors enter the picture, behavior ceases to be normal and volatility can exceed what is normally predictable. As investors, we must know about these black swans and also know that our own behaviors—and market behaviors—as rational as we want them to be, often fail. We also see once again that collective behavior often isn't normal and thus isn't always measurable or predicable.

Once again, we can't control this kind of volatility precisely, but it becomes an important part of our thought process.

MANAGING RISK: THE INSURANCE
INDUSTRY APPROACH

As a final look at the nature of risk, and as the beginning of a necessary transition to what to do about it, the next stop is a look at risk the way the insurance industry looks at it. For years, insurers, mostly of the property or casualty stripe, have broken down risk into four categories defined by the best ways to manage that risk. As you approach any risk, you have one of four choices:

- *Avoid the risk.* If you can, simply choose something else. This would pertain to large risks you can't—or choose not to—do anything about. Don't want to get killed skydiving? Don't go skydiving. Don't want to experience the volatility of Facebook stock? Don't buy Facebook stock.

- *Retain the risk.* Some risks are small enough that you can simply afford to take—to *absorb* them—without engaging in any further steps, behavior modifications, or buying insurance. These are frequent and noncatastrophic risks, like the risk of getting a flat tire on the way to work. You don't want it to happen, but if it does, it's not the end of the world. You won't avoid driving to work, and you probably won't insure against the event. In some cases, doing anything other than absorbing the risk simply doesn't make sense. In investing, you're absorbing some risk and volatility just by buying the investment.

- *Reduce the risk.* In many cases, there is risk, and the consequence can be catastrophic. So what do you do? Put on a seat belt. Driving to work is important, so you don't want to avoid the risk. An accident is catastrophic, so you don't want to absorb it. You can't avoid having steps up to the front of your house, but you can make them safer. You want to invest and you need to invest to achieve goals. The trick is to figure out ways to do it that reduce the risk.

> • *Transfer the risk.* You can't avoid it, you can't absorb it, and you can't really reduce it, at least not as much as you'd like. You need to drive, and anything might happen. So how do you protect yourself? You transfer the risk to someone else. Easy, huh? Except the privilege of doing that costs money. That's where insurance comes in: you pay an insurance company a premium to absorb your risk for you, *transferring* your risk to them. Can you do this in investing? Yes, you can, and we'll get to that.

Avoid, absorb, reduce, transfer; understand these four choices and you'll be a long way toward understanding low volatility investing.

JUST AROUND THE CORNER: LOW VOLATILITY INVESTING

In the first two chapters we laid out the concepts of volatility, how they affect various investments over time, and how volatility affects you as an investor. From that, we will proceed to explore how to achieve success in the form of decent investment returns while managing these risks as we define low volatility investing in the next chapter. In Chapters 4 and 5 we'll finally come to wrestling with how volatility is measured. Wrestle? Do we normally wrestle with things in books? In this case, yes, because as you'll see, the measures aren't perfect, and volatility as most investors should approach it is more conceptual; there is no perfect measure of volatility and, as a consequence, there is no mathematically precise method to incorporate volatility into your investments. Thus—and you knew this—you cannot delegate your investing to a precise mathematical formula.

KEY CONCEPTS

▶ Volatility comes from external, internal, and personal sources. This expands the idea of systemic and unsystemic risks often presented in the investment media to include personal behaviors that cause volatility.

▶ Volatility arises from events that actually do occur but, importantly, also unknowns and perceptions around those realities

▶ Personal perceptions and behaviors can cause considerable overreaction and underreaction to actual events, especially when investors are taken as a whole as markets. Rational, predictable, normal behavior doesn't happen as often as we would like. We cannot create a formula to deal with volatility; it must be dealt with in our thought processes.

▶ When dealing with risk (or volatility), you can avoid, retain, reduce, or transfer that risk.

CHAPTER 3

What Is Low Volatility Investing?

Up to this point, we've talked a lot about risk and volatility. What it is, where it comes from, how much. But we haven't really finished that discussion, because we haven't delved into the lengthy topic of historical and future volatility for the individual investments you might want to make.

As an investor, you've no doubt heard it before: *Where there's risk, there's reward.* And the reason you invest is to make money, right? The reward is the important part. Sure, you can avoid most risk by simply not seeking the reward, but that's not why you're here, right? You want to invest to achieve a reward, only you want to achieve the most reward possible without taking too much risk—or without losing too much sleep.

So we need to explore the risk/reward trade-off. What amount of risk are you willing to take to achieve a given reward? Oh, if only it were that simple. You tell me how much risk you're willing to take, express it as a number, and I'll tell you the reward you should expect. There's got to be formula for this somewhere, with all the quantitative tools and analysis available for today's investors. Right?

That's where the bad news comes in. There is no formula. There is no magic mathematical equation or spreadsheet that allows you to say "I want to take this much risk" and thus "here's the reward I'm entitled to for taking that risk." Formulas can help measure risk (and we'll explore a lot of them in Chapter 5), but they can't nail down the risk you might be about to take.

"Why?" you might rightly ask. Because markets don't behave predictably, or even randomly. What happened in the past may give you *an idea* of the future, but it doesn't predict the future with any degree of precision. You can't drive forward by looking in the rearview mirror. The world is too complex, and there are too many moving parts for that, external and internal moving parts, with a dose of personal and collective personal moving parts thrown in. We can make pretty good numbers-based guesses, but we can't predict the future. We don't know the exact reward, and we can't tell you what volatility you'll experience along the way.

All that said, the goal here is to learn low volatility investing. OK, fine, but just exactly what is that, and why should we do it? That's what this chapter is about. But instead of the formula you may have sought when you bought this book, we'll build a low volatility investing framework: a *thought process*. We'll do this first by further developing the reasons why a low volatility approach is important, then, by chapter's end, by laying out the major tenets of the low volatility investing thought process.

LOW VOLATILITY INVESTING AS A THOUGHT PROCESS

How, exactly, do you do low volatility investing? What formulas and betas and thetas and deltas and standard deviations and other statistical tools do you need to know? Give me a formula for trading off risk and reward and I'll give you a list of good investment ideas. You pick the risk and I'll tell you with 100 percent certainty what reward to expect. Or you pick the reward and I'll tell you the risk. Doesn't that sound nice?

Well, alas, the real world doesn't work that way. The risks aren't very predictable and, for that matter, neither are the rewards. While theory (and common sense) says they should go together—and they do—the precise quantification of the risk/reward trade-off is elusive.

And what about the combined volatility of your entire investing portfolio? What's the formula for that? There is one, but the bad news is that it's more complicated than all but the quants who once roamed the halls of MIT and Harvard can handle, or make work for a modest individual portfolio like yours or mine. And it wouldn't be anywhere near perfect, anyhow.

But you've also heard about so-called technical analysts—individual investors or traders who can apply a myriad of mathematical models and pattern analysis tools to a historical stream of prices of anything, and develop a prediction for the future. Can't they tell us what we need to know about risk and reward?

While the technical analysis approach is appealing, it doesn't help us make sound risk vs. reward decisions either. Technical analysis gives a good explanation of what has *already* happened, but it can't predict the future either. Why, if every signal flashed by a technical stochastic or MACD indicator worked, we'd all be doing it. Investing would be simple. The problem is, the models don't work perfectly. And if everyone did it, well, *someone* has to take the opposite side of a trade, and that wouldn't happen if that opposite side of the trade was wrong. So technicians can draw nice pictures, and they can reduce the probability of failure if they're really good and have a bit of luck on their side, but they can't predict the markets. They can't tell you how much reward you'll get for a given level of volatility, nor can they tell you how much volatility you'll get for a given level of reward.

Thus, because no model can predict the future and everything we know for sure happened in the past, and the past doesn't necessarily predict the future, we can't even rely on sophisticated tools that help us examine the past. It's not that these tools aren't useful; it's just that they won't give us the answer.

Low volatility investing, like any form of reason-based investing, really, is a thought process. It's a judgment on how to pick investments, looking at some numbers, looking at some charts, and applying some common sense to what we see. But beyond that, it's a look forward into the future: future scenarios and the myriad of external and internal intangibles that might affect those scenarios.

Expected volatility might be related to how volatile a company may have been in the past, or it may be a function of the strength of its brand, market leadership, and presence in the market. As a low volatility investor, you should keep an eye on both.

WHY IT'S IMPORTANT TO UNDERSTAND VOLATILITY

Understand volatility? How can we understand something we can't even measure, at least in a good enough way to project it into the future?

The truth is, we go through life understanding things conceptually without knowing precisely how they work. We can learn to cook pretty well with garlic and onions without knowing all the particulars, or how much of the active chemical ingredient allyl propyl disulfide those ingredients contain. We know about fire, how it starts, and what damage it can do, without knowing very much about the chemistry of burning and the physics of heat transfer and ignition. Whether it's fire or garlic, wholly without knowing how it works, we can embrace their existence, know a few things about what they do and *can* do, and respect their dangers. Once we do, we're ready to cook with garlic and fire.

We know about volatility without measuring it to the *n*th degree, and without doing a thorough investigation of where it came from. It's there, it has cause, it has effect, and it's likely to happen again. That's what we know, that's what we embrace, and that's what we can use in our investment cooking. But, how much effect? When will it happen again?

We know volatility can affect our investment performance. We also know it can affect our peace of mind, our comfort level, and our confidence. We know volatility, in subtle ways, can make us look bad, and it can create bad habits. If we ignore it, it can burn us. If we embrace it and bet on it, we can be wrong. We forget the fundamentals and focus on the twitter, to our demise.

Really, like garlic and fire, our imperative as investors is to embrace volatility and deal with it. As with fire, we don't want to avoid it and we don't want to spend too much time analyzing it, but we want to understand it enough to be able to use it safely, even productively. It's part of the cooking. It can be evil, but in our case, it's a necessary and tolerable evil once we learn its dangers.

Like fire, volatility presents a danger, and it can present discomfort. We need to know how much danger it presents, and we need to know what we are doing when we take on that danger. If we learn to accept it and heed its danger, we can learn to live with it. And, as investors, we can go on to live better lives—in this case, as successful investors—if we learn to deal with it.

Now we will examine some of the dangers of volatility and how they can affect your investing results.

UPSIDE, DOWNSIDE—NO, IT'S REALLY JUST THE DOWNSIDE THAT HURTS

One of the features of volatility that makes it so devilish to our investment results, and devilishly hard to measure, for that matter, is that we're primarily concerned about *downside* volatility. The price of an investment can jump around, but what we really care about—and are scared of—is how far and how fast something can *fall*. We don't mind falling up, we mind falling down. The measures of volatility we have available tend to measure movement in both directions, not just downward. We'd like to measure volatility, but we'd really like to measure the probability of going down, especially way down. That's what causes us to lose sleep. The upside? That's the fun stuff. The rewards, the justification that we're right; who doesn't love that? It's the downside, the feeling of being wrong, that really hurts.

THE HIGH COST OF A HARD HIT

As investors, we're all scared of the big dip. The downward plunge in the markets that can not only be expensive but can also shake our confidence as investors. That plunge may have a low probability, but it also has a big effect.

So we're scared of it for good reason. As will be shown shortly, a big down performance can take an even bigger up performance to recover. Once we're in a hole, it's hard to get out. Consider Table 3.1:

TABLE 3.1

Gain Required to Recover a Loss

Loss	Gain Required
−10%	11%
−20%	25%
−30%	43%
−40%	67%
−50%	100%
−60%	150%
−70%	233%
−80%	400%
−90%	900%

Suppose you have $1,000 invested in a particular investment. It goes *way* against you, and before you know it, your investment is worth $500: a 50-percent decline. Now, to recover the $1,000 originally invested, you need to earn back the $500 lost on a base of $500! To do that requires a 100-percent gain—a doubling—in the value of the investment to break even.

This example helps to illustrate several principles of volatility. First, as prudent investors, we can be tolerant of minor fluctuations and variations in the price of our stocks or the value of our portfolios. These minor variations—5 percent here, 10 percent there—don't take such a massive reversal or change in performance to correct. We can afford to lose 10 percent because it only takes an 11-percent gain to recover. Not so for the 30-, 40-, or 50-percent blowup; it takes far more to recover as you move down this scale. Hundred percent moves in anything are hard to come by!

That said, we cannot take 10 percent, or even 5 percent, losses ongoing and forever. Even if we underperform the markets by a few percentage points, as we'll see later in this chapter, we can lose out on considerable gains once the power of compounding sets in. Small hits are OK, so long as they aren't persistent or don't last forever.

Big losses are a different story. We can tolerate the 10-percent correction and even ignore the 10-percent twitter, but if we're exposing ourselves to 50-percent losses on individual investments—or worse, on substantial portions of our portfolios—look out! It will take a lot to turn that ship around and get it back to where it went off course. There's a big difference between fluctuation, minor corrections (considered to be 10-percent pullbacks by most market professionals), and an all-out bear market, usually considered a plunge of 20 percent or more. The prudent investor senses the difference between fluctuations, corrections, and the more destructive bear markets.

THE HIGH COST OF AN UNTIMELY HIT

There are dozens of reasons to invest—to build family wealth, save for college, afford and acquire other assets, or save for retirement, just to give a quick summary. Whether we apply short- or long-term strategies or some combination of the two to our investments, the goal is usually the long-term accumulation of wealth, usually accompanied by payouts of cash along the way. As financial planners describe it, we work for our money in the early years; in the later years we want our money to work for us.

Particularly when the principles and effects of compounding are considered, it makes a difference not just how much we succeed but also *when* we succeed in the markets. The general principle is that the more we can earn *sooner*—to unleash the power of compounding to a greater degree over a longer time—the better off we are. Conversely, if our investment capital takes a hit in the early going, as we've seen, it takes a lot just to get back to even, let alone to get ahead.

What that means, of course, is that volatility can be expensive, especially if it goes beyond normal investment noise into creating a significant downturn, especially at the beginning of an investing period.

Steady Gains, Early vs. Late

The examples we'll consider are a bit complicated but realistic in today's world of retirement planning. They start off with a conventional wisdom, researched and documented by financial planner William Bengen, with considerable supporting and follow-up research from others. He tested actual market performance over every 30-year period since the 30-year span of 1926 to 1955 and found that with a portfolio of 60 percent stocks and 40 percent intermediate-term U.S. bonds, you could afford to withdraw a little more than 4 percent of the value of that portfolio each year and still keep the nest egg intact.

The gains from the remaining portfolio would replenish the withdrawal, and over the course of what financial planners call the distribution period, you would lose nothing from the portfolio. Assuming the average return (inflation adjusted) for this portfolio ranged around 4 percent (plus or minus year-to-year volatility), this hypothesis made sense. Want $40,000 a year in retirement income to supplement Social Security and pension payouts? Simply build a nest egg of $1 million and let the rest take care of itself. You'll receive your income, and your nest egg will be left intact for your heirs. This is known as the "4-percent rule," and has served the needs of individuals and their financial planners well over the years.

The 4-percent rule generally works, so long as volatility stays normal and predictable and within reasonable bounds. But if the timing of good years and bad years starts to become less random, with sequences of good or bad years in the beginning, or worse, a market rout in the beginning, what happens to this rosy scenario? As many newly minted retirees in the 2001–2002 period and again in the 2008–2009 period found out, it can get pretty ugly.

As the next two tables show, even if returns match and come out even over the long haul, *when* they occur can make a difference. Tables 3.2 and 3.3 show what happens to a $100,000 nest egg that encounters 10 "good" years of 10-percent market gains and 10 "bad" years of market losses in a 20-year period (I used 20 years to shorten the presentation, but the principles apply to 30 years or any length of time). On top of that scenario, I overlaid a 4-percent payout each year, which, of course, varies in dollar amount depending on the base level of funds available.

TABLE 3.2

Timing is Everything: The Effect of Early vs. Late Gains

20-Year retirement, 4% annual withdrawals					
POSITIVE RETURNS, FIRST 10 YEARS					
Initial amount	Year	Annual return	Year-end total BEFORE withdrawal	4% Withdrawal	Year-end amount AFTER withdrawal
$100,000	1	10%	$110,000	$4,400	$105,600
	2	10%	$116,160	$4,646	$111,514
	3	10%	$122,665	$4,907	$117,758
	4	10%	$129,534	$5,181	$124,353
	5	10%	$136,788	$5,472	$131,317
	6	10%	$144,448	$5,778	$138,670
	7	10%	$152,537	$6,101	$146,436
	8	10%	$161,079	$6,443	$154,636
	9	10%	$170,100	$6,804	$163,296
	10	10%	$179,625	$7,185	$172,440
	11	−10%	$155,196	$6,208	$148,989
	12	−10%	$134,090	$5,364	$128,726
	13	−10%	$115,854	$4,634	$111,219
	14	−10%	$100,097	$4,004	$96,094
	15	−10%	$86,484	$3,459	$83,025
	16	−10%	$74,722	$2,989	$71,733
	17	−10%	$64,560	$2,582	$61,978
	18	−10%	$55,780	$2,231	$53,549
	19	−10%	$48,194	$1,928	$46,266
	20	−10%	$41,639	$1,666	$39,974
			TOTAL WITHDRAWN:	$91,982	
			ENDING AMOUNT:		$39,974

TABLE 3.3

Timing is Everything: The Effect of Early vs. Late Gains

20-Year retirement, 4% annual withdrawals					
NEGATIVE RETURNS, FIRST 10 YEARS					
Initial amount	Year	Annual return	Year-end total BEFORE withdrawal	4% Withdrawal	Year-end amount AFTER withdrawal
$100,000	1	−10%	$90,000	$3,600	$86,400
	2	−10%	$77,760	$3,110	$74,650
	3	−10%	$67,185	$2,687	$64,497
	4	−10%	$58,048	$2,322	$55,726
	5	−10%	$50,153	$2,006	$48,147
	6	−10%	$43,332	$1,733	$41,599
	7	−10%	$37,439	$1,498	$35,941
	8	−10%	$32,347	$1,294	$31,053
	9	−10%	$27,948	$1,118	$26,830
	10	−10%	$24,147	$966	$23,181
	11	10%	$25,499	$1,020	$24,479
	12	10%	$26,927	$1,077	$25,850
	13	10%	$28,435	$1,137	$27,298
	14	10%	$30,028	$1,201	$28,827
	15	10%	$31,709	$1,268	$30,441
	16	10%	$33,485	$1,339	$32,146
	17	10%	$35,360	$1,414	$33,946
	18	10%	$37,340	$1,494	$35,847
	19	10%	$39,431	$1,577	$37,854
	20	10%	$41,639	$1,666	$39,974
		TOTAL WITHDRAWN:		**$33,529**	
		ENDING AMOUNT:			**$39,974**

Table 3.2 shows what happens when the markets gain 10 percent in the first 10 years, then lose 10 percent in the final 10 years. Table 3.3 shows the opposite: 10 percent losses in the first 10 years, 10 percent gains in the final 10 years. Note how the math works out to provide the same ending balance of $39,974 in both scenarios, pretty much what you would expect with a net zero gain or loss over the 20 years. But look what happens to the total payout; when we earned a lot early, we got a total of $91,982 in withdrawals, while when we lost early and earned late, we netted out only $33,529 in yearly cash payouts from the portfolio.

This is a fairly low volatility scenario: really, almost no volatility, given the similar gains and losses each year. But the timing of the ups and downs, in this somewhat oversimplified example, definitely does make a difference.

Early Hits Hit Hard

Now we move to a relatively more straightforward example and comparison. Table 3.4 shows an ideal low (no!) volatility world, where we earn 5 percent each year on our portfolio and withdraw a steady 4 percent to serve our retirement income needs.

Table 3.4 shows a placid scenario indeed—a relatively steady annual withdrawal and an increase in net capital left over after the 20-year period. It's a scenario we all can live with, right? Especially if we enter the 20-year retirement with $1 million instead of $100,000: $40,000 per year, plus pension and Social Security entitlements, and a larger amount to leave to our kids or charity than we started with. Not bad. Should Congress pass a law guaranteeing 5-percent returns?

Won't happen. But the "steady state" serves as a good model, anyway, for what *could* happen, plus or minus a few percentage points of normal fluctuating volatility. Steady gains plus low volatility equals financial happiness.

So what happens when we kick off our retirement—our distribution period—with a big loss? Like what happened to those new retirees in 2001 or 2008? Consider what happened in Table 3.5:

TABLE 3.4

Timing is Everything: Steady State Returns

20-Year retirement, 4% annual withdrawals					
ALTERNATING +5%, −5% RETURNS					
Initial amount	Year	Annual return	Year-end total BEFORE withdrawal	4% Withdrawal	Year-end amount AFTER withdrawal
$100,000	1	−5%	$95,000	$3,800	$91,200
	2	−5%	$85,500	$3,420	$82,080
	3	5%	$102,600	$4,104	$98,496
	4	5%	$123,120	$4,925	$118,195
	5	−5%	$110,808	$4,432	$106,376
	6	−5%	$99,727	$3,989	$95,738
	7	5%	$109,700	$4,388	$105,312
	8	5%	$120,670	$4,827	$115,843
	9	−5%	$108,603	$4,344	$104,259
	10	−5%	$97,743	$3,910	$93,833
	11	5%	$107,517	$4,301	$103,216
	12	5%	$118,269	$4,731	$113,538
	13	−5%	$106,442	$4,258	$102,184
	14	−5%	$95,798	$3,832	$91,966
	15	5%	$105,377	$4,215	$101,162
	16	5%	$115,915	$4,637	$111,278
	17	−5%	$104,324	$4,173	$100,151
	18	−5%	$93,891	$3,756	$90,136
	19	5%	$103,280	$4,131	$99,149
	20	5%	$113,608	$4,544	$109,064
		TOTAL WITHDRAWN:		$84,716	
		ENDING AMOUNT:			$109,064

TABLE 3.5

Timing is Everything: Early Hits Hit Hard

20-Year retirement, 4% annual withdrawals					
−20% RETURNS, FIRST TWO YEARS					
Initial amount	Year	Annual return	Year-end total BEFORE withdrawal	4% Withdrawal	Year-end amount AFTER withdrawal
$100,000	1	−20%	$80,000	$3,200	$76,800
	2	−20%	$64,000	$2,560	$61,440
	3	5%	$67,200	$2,688	$64,512
	4	5%	$70,560	$2,822	$67,738
	5	−5%	$67,032	$2,681	$64,351
	6	−5%	$63,680	$2,547	$61,133
	7	5%	$66,864	$2,675	$64,190
	8	5%	$70,208	$2,808	$67,399
	9	−5%	$66,697	$2,668	$64,029
	10	−5%	$63,362	$2,534	$60,828
	11	5%	$66,531	$2,661	$63,869
	12	5%	$69,857	$2,794	$67,063
	13	−5%	$66,364	$2,655	$63,710
	14	−5%	$63,046	$2,522	$60,524
	15	5%	$66,198	$2,648	$63,550
	16	5%	$69,508	$2,780	$66,728
	17	−5%	$66,033	$2,641	$63,391
	18	−5%	$62,731	$2,509	$60,222
	19	5%	$65,868	$2,635	$63,233
	20	5%	$69,161	$2,766	$66,395
			TOTAL WITHDRAWN:	$53,796	
			ENDING AMOUNT:		$66,395

Suppose you take a 20-percent whack out of a portfolio for two consecutive years. Then everything reverts back to the steady state (unlikely, for so-called reversions to the mean happens faster, but let's do it this way for the sake of clarity and comparison). What happens to the total withdrawals? A lot of annual withdrawal figures start with a $2 instead of a $4. And what about the total? It's $53,414, instead of the far more generous $90,701 observed in Table 3.4. Not too surprising: lose 20 percent of $100,000 invested two years in a row and you'd expect a roughly 40 percent—$40,000— hit to your investment proceeds.

But it doesn't stop there. The compounding train isn't derailed, but it's forced onto a slower track. So now, instead of $117,276 to leave to your grandkids or your local SPCA chapter, they will only get $68,079.

You can see that even a brief period of volatility—in this case, really, a negative, bear-market performance—can slow down the financial train considerably, and turn security into insecurity in a mere two-year period. And it can be worse; the steady-state 18 years that follow aren't likely to be so steady state in real life.

What have we learned? First, big volatility (down volatility, really) is much worse than small, fluctuating volatility. Second, early volatility is much worse than late volatility. These principles should become part of your vocabulary, part of your thought process for assessing and dealing with volatility.

THE HIGH COST OF UNDERPERFORMANCE

OK, you say, you've got it. You understand the lessons of the early part of this chapter—of the first three chapters, really. Volatility, especially downside volatility, especially prolonged or sharp downside volatility, especially early prolonged sharp or downside volatility— are to be avoided. These forms of volatility can turn the most carefully planned investment and retirement income base sour in a few short years, at the blink of an eye.

You know how to deal with this! Let's just avoid volatility altogether! We'll buy investments, like Treasury bonds, that last

20 years, pay interest, and we can cash them back at full value at the end of the 20-year period. Or, if we can't stand the volatility in bond prices, which really don't affect us until we sell, and we aren't going to sell anyway, we'll just put money in CDs or something. We'll eliminate the volatility, and things like what happened in Table 3.5 can't possibly happen to us!

This is all logical. It's a logical thought process, so far as it goes. If we want to eliminate volatility completely, just invest in something like a CD or a U.S. government security that cannot (unless some grievous thing happens like a government default) lose value, especially if we wait until maturity.

But here's the problem, and we saw this coming—especially if the low-interest rate cycle we're experiencing at the time of this writing persists—we won't earn much return. A ship is safe in port, but that's not what a ship is for!

Sure, we can dramatically reduce or even eliminate volatility if we're willing to accept a lower return on our investments. While risk begets reward and reward begets risk, safety comes with a price. The price—or cost—is what you lose by accepting inferior returns, returns less than we might otherwise get, to reduce or eliminate volatility.

How much does this cost? Consider what follows.

The Compounding Machine

If you're reading this book, you're probably already familiar with the idea of compounding, which Einstein once called "the most powerful force in the universe." Set some money aside and let returns and time take over, where not only the original investment but the returns also generate returns, and you can build up a pretty big pile of cash:

You can see two things clearly: (1) time is money, (2) *more* time is *more* money, and (3) more time is *a lot more* money if the rate of return is higher (Table 3.6). It's little wonder Warren Buffett and his Berkshire Hathaway holding company has done so well with an annual return of about 30 percent for over 40 years. This is where billions in wealth come from.

TABLE 3.6

Compounded Growth of $100,000

Number of Years	1	2	5	10	15	20	25	30	40
2.0%	$102,000	$104,040	$110,408	$121,899	$134,587	$148,595	$164,061	$181,136	$220,804
3.0%	$103,000	$106,090	$115,927	$134,392	$155,797	$180,611	$209,378	$242,726	$326,204
4.0%	$104,000	$108,160	$121,665	$148,024	$180,094	$219,112	$266,584	$324,340	$480,102
5.0%	$105,000	$110,250	$127,628	$162,889	$207,893	$265,330	$338,635	$432,194	$703,999
6.0%	$106,000	$112,360	$133,823	$179,085	$239,656	$320,714	$429,187	$574,349	$1,028,572
7.0%	$107,000	$114,490	$140,255	$196,715	$275,903	$386,968	$542,743	$761,226	$1,497,446
8.0%	$108,000	$116,640	$146,933	$215,892	$317,217	$466,096	$684,848	$1,006,266	$2,172,452
9.0%	$109,000	$118,810	$153,862	$236,736	$364,248	$560,441	$862,308	$1,326,768	$3,140,942
10.0%	$110,000	$121,000	$161,051	$259,374	$417,725	$672,750	$1,083,471	$1,744,940	$4,525,926
11.0%	$111,000	$123,210	$168,506	$283,942	$478,459	$806,231	$1,358,546	$2,289,230	$6,500,087
12.0%	$112,000	$125,440	$176,234	$310,585	$547,357	$964,629	$1,700,006	$2,995,992	$9,305,097
13.0%	$113,000	$127,690	$184,244	$339,457	$625,427	$1,152,309	$2,123,054	$3,911,590	$13,278,155
14.0%	$114,000	$129,960	$192,541	$370,722	$713,794	$1,374,349	$2,646,192	$5,095,016	$18,888,351
15.0%	$115,000	$132,250	$201,136	$404,556	$813,706	$1,636,654	$3,291,895	$6,621,177	$26,786,355

What Happens When You Underperform?

Let's take a quick glance at the compounding formula:

$$FV = [PV * (1+r)^n]$$

where FV is future value, PV is present value, r is the rate of return, and n is the number of years of compounding.

You can see, from the numbers above and the mathematics, that the results are very sensitive to the n—the number of years, and even more sensitive to the r—the rate of return—that ultimately is raised to the nth power. Even a tiny change in r makes a big difference, especially if the n is also large. Even a single percent extra return, raised to the 30th power, is a big deal.

With that sensitivity in mind, we move to Table 3.7.

Suppose we invest to move with the market—not to be greedy, but to move with the market—for an annual return of 5 percent. In the top line, we can see the proceeds, which double in just under 15 years (see the Rule of 72, below). If our investing horizon is long enough, and especially if we add to this nest egg over the years, we'll do pretty well.

Now, what happens if we go conservative to avoid volatility? What happens if we keep the ship in port because we're afraid of the high seas?

The rest of the table shows what happens if we give up even small amounts of return. Our nest egg, especially after 20 or 25 or 30 years, declines considerably. If we settle for just a half a percent less in return over a 30-year time frame, that dings our nest egg by almost $58,000. One percent less (a 4-percent return rate)? We "lose" $106,000. Now what if we settle for the just over 2-percent return offered by 20-year U.S. Treasury bonds as of early 2013? Or the 1.85-percent yield offered by the "best" bank CDs?

It isn't even on the chart, but you can easily see how far short of the 5-percent nest egg we'd end up—it's in the hundreds of thousands—on a $100,000 investment.

The long and short of it: we can cost ourselves a lot of money if we bury our heads in the sand and chase only the safest investments to avoid volatility.

TABLE 3.7

What Happens When You Underperform the Market

Number of Years	1	2	5	10	15	20	25	30	40
5% Market Return:	$105,000	$110,250	$127,628	$162,889	$207,893	$265,330	$338,635	$432,194	$703,999
Underperform by:									
0.5 percent	$104,500	$109,203	$124,618	$155,297	$193,528	$241,171	$300,543	$374,532	$581,636
1.0 percent	$104,000	$108,160	$121,665	$148,024	$180,094	$219,112	$266,584	$324,340	$480,102
1.5 percent	$103,500	$107,123	$118,769	$141,060	$167,535	$198,979	$236,324	$280,679	$395,926
2.0 percent	$103,000	$106,090	$115,927	$134,392	$155,797	$180,611	$209,378	$242,726	$326,204
2.5 percent	$102,500	$105,063	$113,141	$128,008	$144,830	$163,862	$185,394	$209,757	$268,506

What Happens When You Outperform?

Maybe you're wondering what happens if you embrace volatility a little bit more, perhaps by accepting a few more aggressive investments into your portfolio. Table 3.8, constructed like the underperformance table above, shows what happens if you eke out just a few more percentage points of return:

If the market return is 5 percent, and you accept the volatility fire just a bit, perhaps by adding a few higher-return, higher-volatility investments to your portfolio, you can see how your overall performance improves. Juice it up to, say, an average of 7 percent across your portfolio and your prospective 30-year nest egg jumps from just above $432,000 to just over $781,000, a gain of almost $250,000. Another way to look at it: the 2-percent excess return netted an 81-percent increase in the nest egg over that time period.

You can see a lesson forming here. If you embrace some volatility, you can achieve much better investing performance. Conversely, if you give up too much return to hide from volatility, you'll end up far short of what could have happened – and, more importantly, what you may need to achieve financial security.

DECODING THE BUFFETT MAGIC

While most of us would rejoice in beating the market by 2 percent, Warren Buffett certainly creamed us all by enjoying 30-percent returns over 40 years. No doubt he embraced some volatility along the way. But at the same time, he managed to find ways to reduce or avoid the volatility by knowing what he was doing: making investments that were well understood and uniquely positioned to avoid the kinds of volatility normally associated with high-performance investments. He invested in paint, carpet, furniture, and insurance—not computer chips or software or networks or social networking sites.

Buffett found higher returns with lower volatility but was willing to accept the volatility inherent in his investments. He didn't hide from volatility or diversify away from it, he embraced it by making a few carefully chosen investments. He wasn't scared of it because he understood the businesses, what they were about, and the amount and kind of volatility that was likely to happen. He took as much volatility out of the equation as possible by being prudent and was comfortable with the volatility that remained. He gave himself a margin of safety by buying "cheap," and he always emphasized the look forward at what the investment *could* do, rather than worrying about what it *did* do in the past.

THE RULE OF 72

Buffett famously eschewed higher math in his investment appraisals, but he used the so-called Rule of 72 extensively to make quick calculations and to visualize reward with differing levels of risk and return. Most of you familiar with the principles of compounding are also familiar with the Rule of 72 calculation shorthand. It goes like this:

Divide the return rate during the investment time frame (expressed as an integer) into the number 72 and you'll get the number of years required to double your money. Invest at 8 percent: 72/8 = nine years; invest at 3 percent and the number of years to double balloons to 24 years (72/3).

Or divide the number of years you have to accumulate a nest egg or reach a goal into 72 and you'll get the rate of return required. Starting with $50,000, and needing $100,000 to buy a house in four years? You'll need to earn 18 percent on your investment, so you might need to kick more in up front or push out the house purchase.

For our purposes, the Rule of 72 is a handy way to quickly assess the trade-offs between risk and return in terms of portfolio performance. You won't have to go back to Tables 3.7 and 3.8 to realize that even small changes in your investment performance can double your investment much more quickly or much more slowly.

TABLE 3.8

What Happens When You BEAT the Market

Number of Years	1	2	5	10	15	20	25	30	40
5% Market Return:	$105,000	$110,250	$127,628	$162,889	$207,893	$265,330	$338,635	$432,194	$703,999
Outperform by:									
1 %	$106,000	$112,360	$133,823	$179,085	$239,656	$320,714	$429,187	$574,349	$1,028,572
2 %	$107,000	$114,490	$140,255	$196,715	$275,903	$386,968	$542,743	$761,226	$1,497,446
3 %	$108,000	$116,640	$146,933	$215,892	$317,217	$466,096	$684,848	$1,006,266	$2,172,452
4 %	$109,000	$118,810	$153,862	$236,736	$364,248	$560,441	$862,308	$1,326,768	$3,140,942
5 %	$110,000	$121,000	$161,051	$259,374	$417,725	$672,750	$1,083,471	$1,744,940	$4,525,926

VOLATILITY, RISK, AND YOU
AS AN INVESTOR

By now we've come to a decision point. You, as an investor, know something about volatility and risk, where it comes from, and how it can affect your investment performance. You also know that if you hide under a rock and avoid volatility altogether, you'll eventually be sorry in all but the most remote black swan scenarios.

What are you to do?

It becomes a matter of deciding how you feel about risk and how you want to go forward, knowing there are at least four things you can do about risk to *manage* it. What are those four things? We introduced them in the last chapter:

- *Avoid risk*: hide under a rock and accept risk-free returns of 2 percent or less

- *Retain risk*: know it's there, know its dangers, and deal with them

- *Reduce risk*: be smart about what you're doing by taking the necessary precautions

- *Transfer risk*: make contrarian investments or buy derivatives—another scary concept, but we'll get to that—to ensure your portfolio

You'll probably recognize the best investing approach overall is some combination of the four. Warren Buffett's strategy was primarily to reduce risk by knowing what he was doing, but we can't all be so masterful, though we can embrace a lot of what he has to say. We may want to avoid risk with certain portions of our investments, like an emergency or college fund as we approach our children's college years. We'll retain risks, knowing it's hard to quantify or measure just how much risk we want to retain. We'll reduce risks by being smart, which means knowing where the risks come from and taking steps, like doing smart, forward-looking research to reduce them. And, as we'll see in Chapter 9, there are ways to transfer some of the risks by buying and selling certain types of options to trade a relatively more volatile future for certain cash today, or to ensure a portfolio outright.

At the end of the day, it all depends on how much risk you want to take and how you feel about risk. It becomes a balancing act—a little more risk here, a little less risk there—until you achieve a balance you're comfortable with.

HOW DO YOU *REALLY* FEEL ABOUT RISK?

When you set out to do almost anything—go to school, get a job, learn to play a musical instrument, buy a house—you know there will be some unknowns. You know there is some risk of making a less-than-perfect choice or decision. You know unexpected events may happen along the way and that the outcome may not be exactly as you planned it. As they say, that's life.

The questions you ask yourself, more likely subconsciously than consciously, are (1) how much risk is involved, (2) is the outcome worth the risk, and (3) are you willing to take that risk? You may not have much choice in some of these matters; if you have to drive to work, you have to drive to work. You do it, and your MO switches to reducing the risk of the trip by driving slowly, safely, and so forth. You transfer some of the financial risk by buying insurance, and you retain some of the risk that something will happen to you. Perhaps, some day, you look forward to a day when you can avoid the risk altogether by tele-commuting.

While you may have to go to work, you don't have to invest. Well, really, you do, if you have any savings at all; even in a bank, you're investing in something; there's even risk involved with cash stuffed under the mattress. Plain and simple, if you have any money set aside at all, you have to invest. So, with whatever you do with that extra cash, the questions become the three mentioned above: how much risk is involved, is the outcome worth the risk, and are you willing to take that risk? What is your *risk tolerance*?

From experience, conditioning, and probably even genetics, we all have different risk profiles. We all look at different risks differently, and some of us embrace the risk snake well: we understand it and we know how to manage it, that is, to avoid, reduce, retain, or transfer it. We know snakes are a fact of life and there may not be as much to be afraid of as our instinct tells us. Our approach to risk may be rational and calculating or emotional and fear driven, depending on who we are.

It's important to know who we are and how we behave about risk, especially something as abstract as investment risk. It's especially important if you're working with a financial professional or advisor whose job is to find the right investments to achieve your goals while maintaining your comfort levels. To that end, researchers have devised some quasiscientific ways to measure your risk tolerance, which are examined in the box below.

Why such a risk tolerance assessment? Because, while you should know about these techniques, and maybe even put them to use and experience them, the amount of risk and volatility you should expose yourself to may come down to a few very fundamental and basic questions, which I'll share in a minute.

ASSESSING YOUR RISK TOLERANCE BY SURVEY

If you work with a financial professional or advisor one of the first things you'll probably do is take a short survey to try to capture your attitudes about risk and your investing time horizon. This is so the advisor can make recommendations suited to your personal goals and risk tolerance.

Most advisor will offer one of two surveys: the Ibbotson Associates Risk Tolerance Questionnaire or the FinaAmerica Risk Tolerance Questionnaire. Both dig into your investing time horizon and use a choice modeling approach—offering you choices, allowing you to pick your poison—to ultimately arrive at a time horizon and a rough risk score and grouping, like the conservative, moderate, growth, and aggressive categories served up by the Ibbotson survey.

Here are two sample questions from the Ibbotson Survey (2006):

Q. Historically, portfolios with the highest average returns have tended to have the highest chance of short-term losses. The table below provides the average dollar return of three hypothetical investments of $100,000 and the possibility of losing money (ending value of less than $100,000) over a one-year holding period. Please select the portfolio with which you are most comfortable.

Portfolio	Ending value	Probability of losing money	Point value assigned
A	$107,000	19%	0
B	$109,000	24%	9
C	$110,000	26%	14
D	$111,000	28%	17

Q. Historically, markets have experienced downturns, both short-term and prolonged, and market recoveries, both moderate and substantial. Suppose you owned a well-diversified portfolio that fell by 20% (i.e. $1,000 initial investment would now be worth $800) over a short period, consistent with the overall market. Assuming you still have 10 years until you begin withdrawals, how would you react?

a. I would not change my portfolio. (Point value 17)

b. I would wait at least one year before changing to options that are more conservative. (Point value 12)

c. I would wait at least three months before changing to options that are more conservative. (Point value 7)

d. I would immediately change to options that are more conservative. (Point value 0)

The final tally of point value shows your aversion to or acceptance of risk; the higher the score, the more you accept or even embrace risk. Note how taking what seems to be just a little more risk (option D in the first question instead of option a) gives a much higher risk score.

The downside of surveys such as these are (1) they're hypothetical; you're not under fire with your own money on the line, and (2) and somewhat related, you naturally have a tendency to answer with what you think you *should* do, not what you would *really* do. What you *would* do only comes out when you're in the heat of battle. Still, the surveys can provide some useful guidance regarding what volatility and risk you can accept. They are particularly helpful if you've already experienced the heat of a few actual downturns with your own money on the line. And they're helpful when you're doing this together with a partner, so that you can better understand one another's risk tolerance.

It's not hard to find these surveys. If you have an advisor or financial professional at your disposal you can probably source one through him or her; you can also find them online with a search.

RISK AT THE END OF THE DAY

In my view, you can measure risk and talk about risk all day, but it's really how you feel about risk that counts. Your aversion to risk may change over time—or even daily—based on what's going on around you. Only you can decide, and only you can tell, what you're comfortable with.

In my view, and I'm recommending this as a way to think about it, what's risky is what makes you lose sleep at night. It is anything that's psychologically upsetting or distracting that causes you not to be wholly focused or effective on the rest of what's going on around you. Here is a short risk checklist:

- If you can't sleep at night, you're taking too much risk.

- If you can't function normally without being distracted; if you're irritable or angry or pensive or withdrawn, you're probably taking too much risk.

- If you're risking something greater than you can afford to lose, you're taking too much risk.

- If you're truly worried about your long-term financial security, you're taking too much risk

- The converse is true, too. If you're truly worried about long-term financial security, you may not be taking *enough* risk: you're sacrificing too much return.

As suggested earlier, "take no risk" is not an option. If you have money, you will take risk. If you want your money to work for you some day, you have to take a little more risk, especially in view of long-term inflation. But, like everything else in life, if you embrace and manage the risk properly and stay within yourself, you won't lose sleep at night.

LOW VOLATILITY INVESTING DEFINED

Low volatility investing is the acceptance and management of some *investing risk to produce better-than-market returns while minimizing exposure to the sharp downturns that can have long-term effects on investing performance.*

Low volatility investing observes the past but bases most investing thought on reducing risk by understanding the investments and their risks and rewards, assessing what will happen to them in the future, and combining them in a way that allows growth while still furnishing some protection against catastrophic events.

In the next chapter we'll lay out a foundation of some of the key measures of volatility and how to speak the language and use them in real life. In Part Two we'll lay out the fundamentals of embracing volatility by looking forward, by avoiding, retaining, reducing, and transferring risk, and by building prudent investment portfolios.

KEY CONCEPTS

▶   The amount—and timing—of volatility can be very important.

▶   Normal volatility doesn't mean much, but a sharp, early down-turn is very destructive.

▶   Measuring risk and risk/reward trade-offs is elusive in practice.

▶   Past volatility doesn't predict the future; volatility is neither predictable nor random.

▶   Underperforming the markets by even a small amount can be costly in the long run.

▶   Risk profile surveys are helpful but don't capture your feelings under fire.

▶   Risk only what you can afford to lose.

▶   If you can't sleep at night, you're taking too much risk.

▶   If you can't function without being distracted, you're taking too much risk.

▶   If you're truly worried about financial security, you're taking too much—or too little—risk.

▶   Low volatility investing is the acceptance and management of *some* investing risk to produce better than market returns, while minimizing exposure to wealth-destroying sharp downturns.

CHAPTER 4

Volatility: With and Without the Math

Consider two clear, concise quotes you may or may not be familiar with. These quotes speak volumes. One concerns investing directly, the other is easily applied to it.

Fiction author Katherine Neville, in her spellbinding historical mathematical fantasy novel *The Eight* postulated through one of her characters, "What can be measured can be understood, what can be understood can be altered."

On the other hand, Warren Buffett, former newspaper-delivering teenager turned multibillionaire Oracle of Omaha, has stated a number of times over the years, about investing in general, "If this required calculus, I'd still be delivering newspapers."

OK, which way do we go? Given that the meaningful measurement and representation are going to require some calculus—actually, more statistics than calculus—what shall we do? How do we "measure" so that we can "understand" so that we can "alter"—that is, take or avoid action—based on what we measure?

FIRST, READ MY ESSAY

This obviously becomes an important question as we move forward. How do we reconcile these two notions, measuring everything so that we can understand it, yet staying above the labor-intensive, technique-intensive, and inherently imperfect world of volatility calculus? Obviously Mr. Buffett did it; he in all probability has never actually measured the standard deviation of anything or used it in any model for his investing. That said, I'm quite sure he understands the concept.

From the outset, *All About Low Volatility Investing* has been intended as a practical, actionable book, aimed at individual investors seeking decent returns beyond the risk-free rate while still being able to sleep at night. We want to adopt the thought processes and techniques of low volatility investing so that we can implement them effectively, given that investing is not our full-time occupation. The constraints of time, tools, and data—not to mention inclination—will probably steer us wide of a deep academic or technical approach to investing.

Measuring volatility has become a subject of considerable academic and technical exercise. Much has gone into the mathematical and statistical appraisal of volatility, and the effects of volatility on investments and investment returns. The academic community has supplied numerous important models, like *Modern Portfolio Theory* and the *Capital Asset Pricing* model, which are useful concepts to understand, but must we do the calculations?

For reasons discussed shortly, these models may work better in theory than practice. What we do know for sure is that (1) they emphasize the past, while we as investors should emphasize the future; and (2) they take a lot of time, tools, and data that we probably don't have at our fingertips.

So where does that leave us? The real question becomes: Do we need to measure everything to understand it? Can we get away with knowing the concepts and the relationships and how two investments compare on a calculated volatility value without knowing the specific formula and how it is calculated using what data? Can we get away without being able to do it ourselves?

The answer, in my view, is yes. As I've indicated before, it's the thought process that's important. Is an investment volatile? You probably don't need a fancy metric calculated with complex statistical formulas to figure that out. Look at a chart. Or think about the external, internal, and personal risks that might affect the investment. A new company, like Cree, Inc., trying to commercialize specialized semiconductor technology into commercially viable LED lighting products?

Sure, it will be volatile. You can look at the chart, and you'll see that it can be volatile. Do you need to measure this volatility? Probably not.

You may want to compare its volatility against another investment. Again, do you need to calculate its volatility? Again, probably not. Why? Because you can most likely find someone else to do it for you, like, in the examples I'll use, a major brokerage house. Even if you did calculate the volatility, there are many ways to do it, and many ways you can go wrong or measure it differently from someone else. The upshot: if you want to compare something, let someone else make the calculations, someone else with experts on board and the tools and the big data warehouse and the technique. Just be careful to use the same volatility measures when you make the comparison—that is, compare apples to apples.

At the end of the day, like so much else we talk about, it's all about return on investment. What is the return on investment for spending a day collecting historical data on a few investments and crunching through some massive statistical model to optimize and make the right choice for your portfolio? There is some value to doing it, but the marginal value, the marginal return on investment, may not be worth the cost, especially when you consider that focusing on these rearward-looking metrics might distract you from the things that are really more important, like whether or not the company you're investing in is gaining market share. It may help to measure and model volatility precisely, but how much help is it compared to the time and energy spent to do it?

So, the challenge in this chapter and the next is to learn about some of the ways volatility is measured and interpreted, not so much so we can do it ourselves but so that we can understand the useful measures that are out there and the thought processes they support. The goal is to apply them to our low volatility investing thought process. This chapter is about measurements; the next is a survey of popular measurements for individual securities and portfolios. The goal of these two chapters is to understand the measures and their strengths and weaknesses, not to calculate them, and not necessarily to even use them in an investment decision. Instead, they are served up to round out this thing we call our thought process.

End of essay. Now, on to the show.

BEWARE OF THE QUANTS

What are quants? You've probably heard the term, and you may have already classified this chapter as the quant chapter. But what do these quants have to do with investing, and what do they have to do with you?

Quants are quantitative analysts. According to Bing Dictionary, a quant is "an expert in quantitative data: somebody skilled in computing and the analysis of quantitative data, employed by a company to make financial predictions."

Let's take a closer look at two phrases in this definition:

- "Skilled in computing and the analysis of quantitative data"
- "Employed by a company to make financial predictions"

Does this describe you?

Are you "skilled in computing and the analysis of quantitative data"? Even if you are, we suspect you don't want to do it all the time for your investments. And are you "employed by a company to make financial predictions"? No, you're probably an individual investor, and even if you had the skill, you probably don't have the resources in the form of data and computing power—not to mention the time—to pull it off.

Perhaps I'm belaboring the point made in the essay in the chapter opener. Analysis is good, and with enough number crunching and the skill to interpret it, it can help us some, but it doesn't give all the answers. Stick to simple math but understand the "quant" concepts; you can apply them intuitively without building complex models it would take all day to source the data and build—and you won't run the risk of missing the point completely.

Remember, the past doesn't predict the future. And there are too many variables you can't quant, like human behavior and economic sentiment. Some of the models are pretty cool, but they're far from perfect, and they may sidetrack you from making the right decisions. Informed common sense will help you more in making the right decisions.

WANT TO GET IT RIGHT? JUST LOOK OUT THE WINDOW

We can put hours and hours of crunch time into measuring volatility and trying to quantify risk vs. reward: what the numbers tell us and don't tell us. Warren Buffett had a very clear-eyed view of risk without having to resort to calculations of standard deviations and covariances and beta to arrive at the right answer.

Again, it's not a formula. Buffett can—and most likely does—use the idea of standard deviation or beta intuitively without calculating the actual numbers. In his view, and mine as well, investing is not, and never will be, a formula. There are no equations to determine the best investments. There are theoretical approximations, but we can't depend on them 100 percent. For a host of reasons, they don't tell all, and they don't always work. The point is to be able to measure and conceptually understand what's going on.

For example, there are many measurable factors that can go into a weather forecast. Temperature, relative humidity, barometric pressure, wind direction and speed, topography, and cloud cover, just to name a few, all are factors in a weather forecast. We observe history and crunch lots of numbers using huge, complex algorithms developed at the University of Wisconsin or some such. But even with all the number crunching, they still don't get it right. Forecasters still don't know for sure it's going to rain just because the humidity hits one number. Weather is a combination of how all those factors work together. And if someone throws a number at you—75 percent relative humidity—you don't know what it means in the context of other numbers.

We all gripe and joke about the weatherman because we've all done a better job one time or another simply by looking out the window. There's a lot of truth to that! The data can help, but at the end of the day, a conceptual understanding—and *sense*—of how everything works together is what creates a good weather forecast. And weather is far less complex than investing in many ways. Why? Because there are far fewer unknowns and unquantifiable risk factors, like economics and emotions, that might come into play. In the end, some of your best investment calls will occur by simply looking out the window, but it helps to know something about the humidity, air pressure, and what's on the satellite image before you open the drapes.

Playing Quant Without Being (or Hiring) a Quant

Beyond developing your own conceptual understanding, the best way to take advantage of the quant stuff, if you really choose to make it part of your investing equation, is to hire a professional manager. Am I suggesting hiring your own personal quant? No, not at all. If you're really committed to a strong quantitative approach, the best way to get it is to invest in funds that have professional management, and a staff of statisticians at their disposal, with all the big-data databases and number-crunching machines they might need. Better yet, find funds that have low volatility in their investment objectives. You'll pay a percent or so, but it's much more efficient than trying to grind it out yourself. We'll introduce some of those funds in Chapter 8.

At this stage, you're probably better off knowing what questions to ask and making big-picture look-out-the-window risk/reward decisions than getting bogged down trying to calculate the risk yourself. You can look at the numbers, particularly *comparative* numbers, to get an idea whether an investment more or less accomplishes your objectives. You can also look at a chart to get a quick view or vision of the volatility without knowing the precise numbers within, much as you would look at a weather satellite map to get a sense of where the rain is and which way it's going. Complex data and equations lie behind what you see in the satellite image, but do you need to know them to interpret the image?

At the end of the day, quantitative measures are important mostly for comparison and, for the true quants, to go into more complex models to build portfolios or combinations of investments.

BUSINESS AND INVESTING 101: THE RISK/REWARD TRADE-OFF

So what are we trying to do, anyway? What are we trying to measure? It's really a good question, because as practical investors, we don't want to consume valuable time measuring something just for the sake of measuring—especially as complex as it can become in practice.

As we touched on earlier, where there's risk, there's reward. You could consider that the driving force, the zen, of investing, in particular, the force behind choosing or selecting investments. If you're seeking a greater reward, take more risk. If you want to take less risk, you'll generally sacrifice something on the reward side.

Figure 4.1 illustrates the idea. Risk is shown as the independent variable—that is, the variable you can control,really, by selecting it. Reward is the y axis or dependent variable. How much risk do you want to take? If you want to take zero risk, you move to the left side of the chart and accept the return afforded by the risk-free rate—which, in early 2013, was 2 percent at best based on the return of a two-year U.S. Treasury bond.

As you move to the right, taking more risk, the return starts to rise. Take a little more risk and the return rises proportionately. How much risk do you want to take? And how fast does the line rise? This is where it starts to get a bit theoretical—and difficult to measure. As discussed earlier, it's hard to say, "I want to take x risk to get y reward"; the measures aren't that simple.

FIGURE 4.1

Risk/Reward Trade-Off: Market Risk

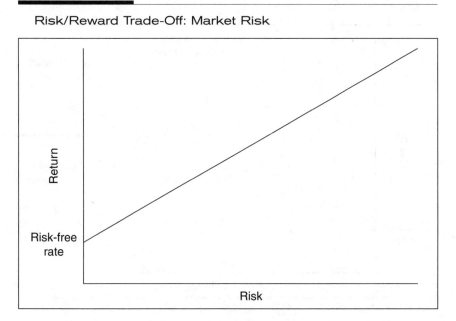

What's important here is to grasp the concept, then we'll get to a few measures to help assess risk/reward and especially to compare it. Standard deviation and beta are two common risk measures one might apply to the *x* axis. Both have their value and their imperfections but work reasonably well if used as comparative measures, as pointed out earlier.

The slope of the line is important to understand but also difficult to measure. How fast does the return rise as the risk "runs"? A measure called the Sharpe ratio measures this. The Sharpe ratio—and the slope of the line—roughly describe the riskiness of a given market environment, and how much the market pays to take more risk. In a volatile, high-risk environment, the market pays you relatively more handsomely to take more risk, and the slope is steeper. In a low-risk environment, you must take a lot more risk to get an additional increment of return. These lines describe a market environment; any particular investment you examine will put you at a different point on the line rather than defining a different line (Figure 4.2).

FIGURE 4.2

Risk/Return Trade-Off: Riskier and Less Risky Market Environments

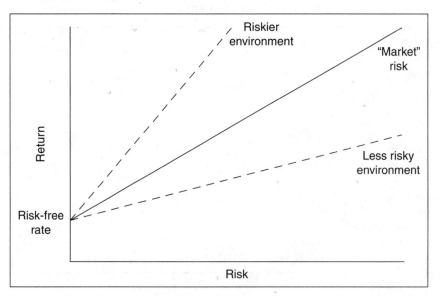

Another important concept to grasp: this risk/reward trade-off model represents a market but offers choices for a single investment or security. But what about two or more securities taken together? What about a portfolio, where investments are carefully chosen because they have different risk/reward profiles? Because the variations—the volatilities—of two or more investments taken together can cancel each other out, the risk/reward profile for a combination of investments changes a bit; in fact, it becomes a nonlinear *efficient frontier*, depicting risk/reward optimal combinations of investments, as we'll see in Chapter 5.

Like a lot of concepts described in this book, the conceptual framework is important, the math is difficult and not particularly productive to do in practice, and the source data are difficult to collect. You can't find the slope of the line listed anywhere in the *Wall Street Journal*, and most investors won't calculate the slope of the line, nor the x and y points along it to choose your investments. It gets worse when you look at a portfolio and try to mathematically approximate the efficient frontier curve and select the best investments to optimize it.

Finally—and you may have already grasped this—low volatility investing, as we define it, is venturing out from the risk-free level of return to take some calculated risk to achieve greater returns, without going out too far on the risk/reward limb. With the right combination of investments in a portfolio, you can actually jump slightly above the risk/reward line at the outset to get proportionally more return for the risk taken, as the efficient frontier line isn't linear at low levels of risk. Once again, it's easier to grasp in concept than to model it in numbers.

WHY THE MEASURES DON'T ALWAYS WORK

At the risk of beating this to death, you may have purchased this book looking for a formula to reduce risk while achieving a decent reward towards meeting your investment goals. As you've read along so far, you may be disappointed to learn that no such formula exists, and if it did, there would be many reasons why either it wouldn't work or it wouldn't tell you enough to make it worth going through the mathematical exercise.

In this section I'll more directly summarize the reasons why, especially as an individual investor lacking the quant capability and the big-data and computing resources to master the calculations, you're better off not going there or leaving it to the pros. Even the pros recognize these limitations and use the quant result as an input, but far from a final determinant, of an investment portfolio. Or at least they should, anyway!

In practice, there are two general categories of limitations on the data approach:

1. *The past doesn't predict the future.* No matter how much math you apply to how much data, you're still looking backward. Trying to say what's going to happen based on what has happened is a dangerous game, particularly with anything involving as many nonquantifiable variables as investing. The best thing you can do with the models is to gain a better understanding of what happened in the past, but you can't be sure it will happen again in much the same way; in fact, you can be pretty sure it *won't* happen the same way again

2. *There are too many moving parts.* External, internal, and personal factors all come into play, and no model can take everything into account. A stock may have played predictably in the past (and a company's earnings may have played predictably, too, thus the stock price predictability), but what happens when something changes? What happens when customers suddenly decide they don't like a product anymore or, for that matter, when investors decide they don't like a stock (or gold or corn or a bond or real estate) anymore, or as much as they did? You can't predict all the factors that influence the future. Nobody can. Again, if you could, who would take the other side of the trade?

Additionally, there are some more technical factors that make measures difficult to collect or to use meaningfully in practice:

- *Many models assume normal or predictable behavior.* If you're at all familiar with basic statistics, you know that much can be made of measuring the mean and standard deviation of random events; those measures can make some sense of that randomness, and we'll examine them shortly. But what if the behavior isn't random? What if the random twitter of our investments isn't so random; maybe a few bad days lead to a few more bad days because human emotions allow them to? Further, as we described in Chapter 2 (and Figure 2.1), so-called long-tail events some three to even six standard deviations from the mean happen far more frequently than a normal distribution would predict (hence, the fat tail). Such nonrandomness doesn't so much render the models useless as it requires use with an accompanying grain of salt.

- *Multiple variables magnify the problem.* Risk and volatility are a function of several factors. But it's hard enough to be certain the randomness or the pattern of one variable is meaningful and measurable and thus predictable. What happens when you mush a dozen variables together? A hundred variables? Statistically, some of the randomness, and some of the imperfections, cancel out. But how do you weigh all the variables? Do the weights stay the same? Or are there a normal distribution and standard deviation around the weights, too? You can see how it becomes fantastically complicated in a hurry.

- *Different base or period length or time frame.* If you choose to measure volatility with a given metric, there are several choices on which to base that metric. What is the time period? A month? A year? Several years? And what are the increments? Days? Weeks? Months? Years? Hours? Minutes? The answers you get will vary according to what you choose. If you measure monthly volatility, many of the variations within that month will cancel each other out, so you may lose a lot of sleep over an investment that appears calm when measured in monthly buckets. Or you could measure minute-by-minute volatility, but unless you're a minute-by-minute trader, what good is that measure? Most people would probably choose monthly or weekly volatility as a proxy for getting the most sleep and to separate the news from the noise. And the longer the better; but if volatility has ticked up recently, you want to know that, too, and avoid watering it down with periods of calm long past. As if this weren't a complex enough series of choices, if you grab your volatility metrics from existing sources, like broker websites, they're all calculated differently, too. Again, you need to compare consistent metrics calculated the same way, not standard deviation from one source against another, or even standard deviation for a fund vs. a stock vs. a commodity; all might be calculated differently.

- *Price vs. change in price.* Here's another to add to the growing list of bugaboos. Some metrics will calculate the volatility of a price, others the volatility of the *change in price*, sometimes described as the return or some such. The calculation of straight price volatility doesn't take into account any trend that might be occurring—if a stock is advancing by a steady 3 percent every month, that will look like volatility— while if you looked at a chart, everything would be moving smoothly up and to the right. So to capture this, many look at the volatility of the change in price; with the same example, now if you measured the volatility of the change every month (3 percent), you would indeed see very low volatility. But the volatility of this change can be a difficult concept to grasp and translate into sleep-at-night calm; still, it's probably better than a straight price volatility calculation.

- *Relationships change in times of crisis.* Finally—and this is the big bugaboo we all saw in the 2008 crisis—what seems to drive volatility and risk in "normal" times may have nothing to do with what happens when big, unforeseen events enter the picture. The conventional wisdom has always held that gold and other precious metals are a safe haven and store of value any time the value of money—currency— comes into question. Similarly, bonds are the safe haven when the value of stocks comes into question. But what

happened when Lehman Brothers went down and emotion took over? What happened when the Flash Crash of
May 2010 hit? *Everything* went down. Assets that had been
negatively correlated before became positively correlated
when the black swan landed. Every model for optimizing an
investment portfolio by picking noncorrelated assets went
out the window, at least for a while. Such changes in relationships happen even without a crisis; for most of 2011 and
2012, Apple stock rose persistently as the market fell, then
fell consistently as the market rose in early 2013, showing a
negative correlation. As 2013 unfolds and Apple becomes
more of a value and less of a growth stock, the correlation
and movement with the market is getting more positive.
Relationships change; even what's measured and understood may need to be measured constantly; nothing can be
depended on for too long. This shows again that there are
too many moving parts for any model to work successfully
in any given situation, especially the long tail risk situations
we want the most protection against.

- *The past doesn't predict the future*. Yes, you're right, this is
  repeated from above. But it's important enough to repeat.

Once again, the brightly lit conclusion remains: you can go
crazy trying to measure everything—and miss the point completely.
It'll rain on your picnic even when you thought it wasn't possible.

FINDING THE RIGHT MEASURES, MODELS, AND CHARTS ONLINE

As I alluded to earlier, many measures come prepackaged in today's
investing websites. They may be somewhat below the surface and
take a little doing to tease out. The beta measure appears readily
on most investing websites. Standard deviations are available on
some, but you may have to tease them out. Correlations between
investments are much harder to find, other than beta, which correlates investments to the stock market, usually the S&P 500 Index.

Once you find these measures, you have a set of apples-to-apples figures you can use comparatively, and that's probably the best way to use them: one standard deviation against another from the same site or source, one beta vs. another beta, etc. The more complex portfolio volatility measures, especially for a custom portfolio you might construct yourself, continue to be hard to find and mostly available to professionals only; thus, to get a statistically determined low volatility portfolio, you might be best off letting the pros put it together.

While it may still be hard to do measures using the tools available on the web, you can learn a lot about certain measures and how they are applied, especially if the math doesn't scare you away. A number of websites give more detailed explanations of these measures, including the standby Wikipedia. A search on a measure, such as "beta, investing," will return a lot of learning material. Some websites even provide Excel spreadsheets to help you build models yourself, but be careful: there are a lot of nuances in data collection and their actual use, and they get very complicated very quickly if you're doing anything beyond modeling, say, five or six investments.

Many websites, including Wikipedia entries, tend to give the math and mechanics but fall short on practical interpretation and tips on how to use them. Some, like Andrew Matuszak's Economist at Large (http://www.ecolarge.com) go through formulas and even help you build spreadsheets, but even if you succeed in building the spreadsheet, it's still a challenge (and enormously time consuming) to populate it with quality source data and interpret the result.

Finally, charts are another important tool in the low volatility investor's arsenal. While I would probably give the Internet as a whole a C or D grade in terms of providing volatility measures and models, it probably deserves an A- for charting tools. Financial portals like Google Finance (google.com/finance) and Yahoo!Finance (finance.yahoo.com) provide well-designed and easily configured charts for selected time periods and granularity, and allow an easy comparison of one security to another. It's a bit tricky to chart a stock against, say, the price of gold, but that can be done by using a straight gold-based portfolio, say, the SPDR Gold Trust ETF (GLD). Most brokerage sites also provide good charting tools; some start to add in some volatility measures to the mix, as we'll see in the next chapter with the Bollinger Bands chart on the Charles Schwab site.

For those who really believe a picture is worth a thousand words, StockCharts.com offers a very complete and detailed charting service, mostly for free, but there are more advanced pay-for levels. StockCharts allows the charting of some of the more complex statistical variables, like covariance, but stops short of true portfolio modeling. You can do this with or without StockCharts, but it can help to sharpen your analysis if you're so inclined. But remember: although pictures may be worth a thousand words, they still don't predict the future!

As we work through the measures and their application toward your own low volatility thought process, I'll work in several different web sources for key material as examples.

THREE PARTS COMMON SENSE

The short take: it's good to understand all this stuff, at least conceptually, but it's unlikely you'll apply it directly to your investing; you're better off with the practical, commonsense Buffett approach, which weighs in volatility intuitively without trying to measure it, and weighs in a lot more factors about the future, the quality of the investment and the internal factors around it, and builds in a margin of safety.

At the end of the day, it's a choice between backward-thinking number crunching vs. forward-thinking common sense. The best probable course for a low volatility investor is to understand the numbers but not necessarily do them; add them into the mix, a mix that might be one part numbers and three parts common sense. There's nothing sacred about that mix; I just put it out there; the reality is that each investor will mix his or her own drink to suit his or her own taste.

COMMON VOLATILITY MEASURES

By now, you should have a conceptual feel for what volatility is and for the practicality of measuring it and incorporating those measures into your investing thought process. At this point, we'll move forward to cover some of the specific measures you'll see or consider intuitively in Chapter 5. If you have no appetite for the math, or just can't see yourself grappling with it, that's probably OK. Beyond Chapter 5, we'll get into more practical approaches for evaluating investments and for incorporating them into a "smart" portfolio.

In Chapter 5 we'll examine seven measures and models that I feel are most useful to know about. The models go beyond specific measures and are really concepts developed around measures; the distinction is unimportant here, because what's really important is the concept in all seven cases.

The measures and models can be used to describe the volatility characteristics of an investment, a group or portfolio of investments, or the market as a whole. In practice—it bears repeating—the concept counts for more than the actual number or formula. And it also bears repeating: most of these measures are more useful as comparative measures, rather than as actionable numbers in and of themselves.

Here are my magnificent seven, which will be the subject of Chapter 5:

- *Variance and standard deviation*: a representation of raw volatility, that is, fluctuation around a mean or average, represented as a single figure.

- *Beta*: a single figure representing the correlation of volatility between a security or portfolio and a major market index, usually the S&P 500 Index.

- *Sharpe ratio*: a single figure estimating the return efficiency of a security or portfolio, evaluating the return against the risk taken as measured by standard deviation.

- *Correlation and covariance*: raw single-figure statistics representing the degree to which two or more securities move together (or not)

- *Portfolio correlation and the efficient frontier*: a concept, based on correlation and covariance, of how to evaluate the risk/reward profile of a group of securities; a portfolio.

- *VIX*—Volatility index: a fast-read, single-figure indicator of volatility for the broad stock market as represented by the S&P 500.

- *Black-Scholes model*: a complex mathematical model designed to estimate option prices based on volatility, time to expiration, and other measurable factors. While Black-Scholes models a single-figure option price, for us the concept and component measures of historical and implied volatility for a given security are most useful.

Of these measures, you'll most often see beta as a quick proxy or estimate of volatility, and for the most part it works, so long as you understand its shortcomings. You should become fluent in beta: if you choose to learn about and internalize just one of the volatility measures and models offered above, beta is probably the right one.

KEY CONCEPTS

▶ Understanding volatility measures and models is more important than "doing" them; they can help guide the low volatility investing process even without specific numbers.

▶ Measures and models analyze the past; they don't predict the future

▶ Without a big-data warehouse, complex math, and lots of computing power, most measures are impractical to do yourself.

▶ Other measurement and modeling problems include the assumption of normal or predictable behavior, the sheer complexity of hundreds of variables, many not quantifiable ("too many moving parts"), and the inconsistency of time periods and time frames between measures or models.

▶ Beta is the most dependable and readily available volatility measure.

CHAPTER 5

A Field Guide to Common Volatility Measures

This chapter is intended to provide a brief conceptual and mathematical overview of the seven measures and models I feel an investor like you, an investor oriented toward managing (and minimizing) volatility, should know something about.

Although the statistical formulas will make this resemble a textbook in many places, that isn't the intent at all. It isn't really important, nor is it the intent, for you to fully grasp or memorize these formulas or even to use them in your investing practice. Although I am an advocate and teacher of the do-it-yourself investor, building these formulas and models yourself presents considerable difficulties in practice, takes a lot of time, and isn't really recommended unless you have a lot of time, data, and computing power to devote to the task—and that you accept that these formulas and models still won't give you an exact answer.

Again, building the conceptual understanding and role in your thought process is most important, followed by knowing how to use these measures when you see them.

As we begin the journey, we'll cover a few points about source data and sourcing data. Then each of the seven key measures and models are described with examples or illustrations where they make sense. Some refinements and extended applications will also be noted where appropriate. The seven measures and models, again, are:

- Variance and standard deviation
- Beta
- Sharpe ratio
- Covariance and correlation
- Portfolio correlation and the efficient frontier
- VIX
- Black-Scholes model

So, if you're so inclined, get out your calculators and let's go!

A FEW WORDS ABOUT HISTORICAL DATA

As was introduced in Chapter 4, even the selection and acquisition of data to support volatility measures can be tricky. Historical data, especially set up to be easily downloaded into your calculations (which most likely will be done in an Excel spreadsheet or something similar) are hard to find. That's the first problem. The second problem is determining what buckets and increments of time to measure, and whether to measure a security or index price, the *change* in that price, or both.

Many investing sites have price histories. Many of these have only daily price histories. Do you want to measure or know about daily volatility? Probably not. It's too nervous; there's too much noise with the news, and you're an investor, not a rapid-fire trader, anyhow.

Historical Data from Yahoo!Finance

The best commonly available site I've found for historical data is Yahoo!Finance: specifically, its historical prices section. You can get prices for any security, and a lot of indexes, as far back as 1950, if the security or index has been around that long. You can get daily, weekly, and monthly prices as well as adjusted prices, which take into account splits and dividends.

You can easily download Yahoo!Finance data into a spreadsheet; however, you may have to do some processing and scrubbing to get it right for your own analysis. Conveniently for investors seeking to measure total return for an investment, Yahoo! includes dividends paid as line items in their data table; unfortunately you can't choose to exclude them, so they must be purged from your worksheet. For volatility analysis, most likely you're only interested in the far right-hand column, not the monthly highs and lows (although that can be interesting for building charts or examining volatility within a month). As such, you may have to do some editing after you pull the data.

Creating Data Tables

Once I have my scrubbed pull, I organize it something like what's shown in Figure 5.1. Note that I have also added calculations for the percent gain or loss, or percentage change for each period with a simple spreadsheet calculation $[(Price_n/Price_{n-1})-1]$. That's also why, for this 12-month analysis, 13 months of data were pulled, to provide a base for the change calculation in the first 12 months (–12 months from today). Figure 5.1 shows four data pulls: one for the S&P 500 Index ("^GSPC" on Yahoo!Finance); one each for two fairly volatile stocks, CREE, our LED semiconductor manufacturer and one for mobile handset maker BlackBerry (symbol BBRY); and one for the much less volatile paper goods maker, Kimberly-Clark:

So, Month –1 represents the end of the most recent month, and the result is 12 months of history of price and price change leading to the present. You can get a lot out of simply eyeballing these figures. You can also chart them easily, and they will become source data for some of your calculations.

How Much History?

Another question that quants and other investors have to wrestle with is "How much history should I use for the analysis?" It's a good question. Statistical models, especially those that try to make sense

FIGURE 5.1

Data for S&P 500 Index, CREE, BlackBerry, and Kimberly-Clark, 12 Months, from Yahoo!Finance

S&P 500			CREE			BlackBerry			Kimberly-Clark		
Month	Closing Price	% Gain/Loss	Month	Closing Price	% Gain/Loss	Month	Closing Price	% Gain/Loss	Month	Closing Price	% Gain/Loss
−1	$1552.48	2.5%	−1	$52.79	16.7%	−1	$15.03	12.5%	−1	$94.93	1.6%
−2	$1514.68	1.1%	−2	$45.23	4.8%	−2	$13.36	2.9%	−2	$93.46	5.3%
−3	$1498.11	5.0%	−3	$43.15	27.0%	−3	$12.98	9.4%	−3	$88.75	6.0%
−4	$1426.19	0.7%	−4	$33.98	5.2%	−4	$11.87	2.3%	−4	$83.72	−0.6%
−5	$1416.18	0.3%	−5	$32.31	6.6%	−5	$11.60	46.3%	−5	$84.26	2.7%
−6	$1412.16	−2.0%	−6	$30.30	18.8%	−6	$7.93	5.7%	−6	$82.03	−2.7%
−7	$1440.67	2.4%	−7	$25.51	−9.5%	−7	$7.50	12.1%	−7	$84.32	3.5%
−8	$1406.58	2.0%	−8	$28.20	17.7%	−8	$6.69	−6.4%	−8	$81.45	−3.7%
−9	$1379.32	1.3%	−9	$23.95	−6.7%	−9	$7.15	−3.2%	−9	$84.58	3.6%
−10	$1362.16	4.0%	−10	$25.67	2.4%	−10	$7.39	−28.5%	−10	$81.62	6.6%
−11	$1310.33	−6.3%	−11	$25.07	−18.9%	−11	$10.33	−27.8%	−11	$76.59	1.1%
−12	$1397.91	−0.7%	−12	$30.90	−2.3%	−12	$14.30	−2.7%	−12	$75.74	6.2%
−13	$1408.47		−13	$31.63		−13	$14.70		−13	$71.32	

out of random behavior, work best with more data. Statistically, any calculation involving 30 or more pieces of input data is probably more robust than one that involves fewer data points. But when you're looking at the volatility of an investment, does what happened two or two and a half years ago really count? Have things changed enough that such history is less meaningful that what's going on right now? Probably, but you won't know for sure.

Statisticians deal with this by making adjustments for smaller sample sizes and, in some cases, by creating weighted averages and moving averages that weight the recent past more heavily. It starts to get pretty complicated pretty fast. You can be your own judge of the robustness of a data stream. It helps, when you use a figure calculated by someone else, to know how it was calculated, but you'll find in practice that you won't always be told. A 6- to 18-month view is a good place to get started. More important is to compare apples to apples: don't compare a 6-month standard deviation to another that's been calculated over 5 years.

VARIANCE AND STANDARD DEVIATION

What is volatility, anyway?

Volatility can be defined as the movement or dispersion of any set of data around its average, or mean, value. A set of data that jumps wildly up and down, above and below the mean, is more volatile than a set of data that stays close to the mean. For our purposes, the mean and the volatility around that mean are typically based on the price or value of something (like a stock price or an index) or the price change (percent gain/loss or return) of something. You can learn a lot about something by knowing the mean and the variation around that mean.

But how do you get to that variation? One way is to simply look at the chart. If the scales are set up properly, you can easily assess whether stock A or stock B is more volatile. That's a practical approach, but it also helps to express that variation as a single number, both for comparison and as input into other measures and models.

So statisticians invented a measure called variance, which sums up and processes the deviations from the mean into a single number by totaling the mathematical squares of those deviations. Why squares? Because we want to understand the absolute variation—plusses and minuses—rather than having them cancel each other out. Plus 10, then minus 10, may cancel out, but for our purposes, it shows volatility.

Standard Deviation: What It Is and What It Does

Once the squares are processed into a singular variance figure, statisticians take the square root of the total, so that the units of measure in the resulting figure match the units of the original data (instead of the squares of the data). That square root value is called the standard deviation, and it gives us some important conceptual points, as well as feeding into models and measures we'll look at later in this chapter.

The Calculation

Formulas are fun, and you may wish to take them apart and understand them—or not. They are supplied mostly for your interest.

$$\sigma = \sqrt{\frac{1}{N}\sum_{i=1}^{N}(x_i - \mu)^2},$$

Where:

- σ is the standard deviation (sigma)
- x_i is the actual value for each i data point
- μ is the mean for your data

More likely, if you make this calculation, you'll use the STD-DEV function in Excel. If you go there, you'll notice that there's a STDDEVP and a STDDEVS function. The P is for a population, usually robust if there are more than 30 data points. Statisticians approximate the standard deviation for a sample using *(N – 1)* in the above example instead of *N*. The resulting standard deviation values will correspondingly be a little larger if the sample version is used, to allow for the possibility of greater variation if a full population were considered. For this exercise you don't need to worry about this much, except to be consistent.

Also important: what is the time frame and what time periods are being used? It makes no sense to calculate daily volatility if you're concerned only about weekly volatility, and it also makes no sense to compare a weekly figure to a monthly one. You should also avoid comparing five-year standard deviations to one-year standard deviations, except to see whether a security has become more or less volatile over time. Be careful here: different sources use different periods and time horizons.

Interpreting the Measure

Beyond the mathematics and standard deviation figures themselves, the standard deviation is a measure of what's called a normal probability distribution; that is, a picture of the dispersion of your data series. From that distribution and intrinsic to the math, we can estimate that

- Approximately 68 percent of all occurrences have been, and are likely to be, within one standard deviation of the mean
- Approximately 95 percent will be within two standard deviations of the mean
- Approximately 99 percent will be within three standard deviations of the mean.

Figure 5.2 shows a normal distribution bell curve and the one, two, and three standard deviation ranges around it. Note that this is the same figure is used in Chapter 2 to show the fat tails—the higher probabilities of events happening farther than two deviations away from the mean that seem apparent in real life.

FIGURE 5.2

Normal Distribution Dispersion Around the Mean, Measured in Standard Deviations

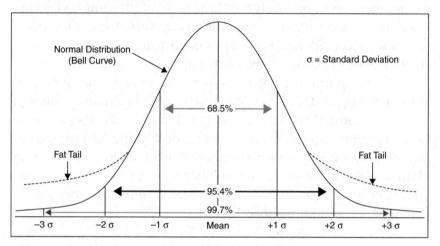

Now, back to the data for the three stocks and the S&P 500, this time with the means (averages) and standard deviations calculated in Figure 5.3:

So now, with some data and a few calculations in hand, you can see or infer that:

- From these data, you can infer that approximately 68 percent of all S&P 500 closes will be within plus or minus 62.43 points (one standard deviation) of 1425.02, 95 percent will be within 104.83 points (two standard deviations), and 99 percent will be within 187.29, or three standard deviations, of that mean.

- Similarly, monthly percent changes will, 68 percent of the time, be within plus or minus 2.8 percent; 95 percent will be within plus or minus 5.6 percent, and 99 percent will be within plus or minus 8.4 percent.

- The standard deviation for the S&P 500 price is much higher than the others. But the index price is also much higher; it will serve you well to think of the standard deviation as a percentage of the price.

FIGURE 5.3

Mean and Standard Deviation: S&P 500, CREE, BBRY, and KMB

S&P 500			CREE			BlackBerry			Kimberly-Clark		
Month	Closing Price	% Gain/Loss	Month	Closing Price	% Gain/Loss	Month	Closing Price	% Gain/Loss	Month	Closing Price	% Gain/Loss
-1	$1552.48	-2.5%	-1	$52.79	16.7%	-1	$15.03	12.5%	-1	$94.93	1.6%
-2	$1514.68	1.1%	-2	$45.23	4.8%	-2	$13.36	2.9%	-2	$93.46	5.3%
-3	$1498.11	5.0%	-3	$43.15	27.0%	-3	$12.98	9.4%	-3	$88.75	6.0%
-4	$1426.19	0.7%	-4	$33.98	5.2%	-4	$11.87	2.3%	-4	$83.72	-0.6%
-5	$1416.18	0.3%	-5	$32.31	6.6%	-5	$11.60	46.3%	-5	$84.26	2.7%
-6	$1412.16	-2.0%	-6	$30.30	18.8%	-6	$7.93	5.7%	-6	$82.03	-2.7%
-7	$1440.67	2.4%	-7	$25.51	-9.5%	-7	$7.50	12.1%	-7	$84.32	3.5%
-8	$1406.58	2.0%	-8	$28.20	17.7%	-8	$6.69	-6.4%	-8	$81.45	-3.7%
-9	$1379.32	1.3%	-9	$23.95	-6.7%	-9	$7.15	-3.2%	-9	$84.58	3.6%
-10	$1362.16	4.0%	-10	$25.67	2.4%	-10	$7.39	-28.5%	-10	$81.62	6.6%
-11	$1310.33	-6.3%	-11	$25.07	-18.9%	-11	$10.33	-27.8%	-11	$76.59	1.1%
-12	$1397.91	-0.7%	-12	$30.90	-2.3%	-12	$14.30	-2.7%	-12	$75.74	6.2%
-13	$1408.47		-13	$31.63		-13	$14.70		-13	$71.32	
Mean	$1,425.02	0.9%	Mean	$32.98	5.2%	Mean	$10.83	1.9%	Mean	$83.29	2.5%
Stddev	$62.43	2.8%	Stddev	$8.49	12.8%	Stddev	$3.03	18.7%	Stddev	$6.36	3.3%

- That construct breaks down when you measure the standard deviation of the percentage *change* of the price, because negative and positive percentage change figures cancel each other out, hence reducing the mean. The standard deviation of percentage-change figures, however, give the clearest view of which investments are the most volatile.

- On the basis of standard deviation of price change, and of standard deviation of price as a percentage of the price, clearly Kimberly-Clark is a little more volatile than the S&P 500. Cree is quite a bit more volatile, and BlackBerry was by a large margin the most volatile.

- Because the mean percentage change for Cree is considerably larger than for BlackBerry, you can infer that some of Cree's "volatility" is actually an upward price move. BlackBerry showed considerable volatility just to stay at almost the same price level over the 12-month period.

Strengths and Shortcomings

The principal advantages of standard deviation are:

- It is a fairly pure measure of volatility; it truly measures the ups and downs of a price or change in price.

- It provides a single figure.

- That single figure can be used (with care) to describe the future: 68 percent within one standard deviation, etc.

On the other hand, disadvantages include:

- Assumption of a random, or normal distribution: does the sequence of stock prices for BlackBerry, for instance, look random?

- It is hard to calculate, especially with sufficient data.

- It doesn't explain trends; growth or decline trends can be seen as volatility.

- It doesn't appear regularly as a measure for investment analysis (likely because of the other shortcomings).

Standard Deviation in Practice

In practice, like many of our metrics, standard deviation has more value as a concept than as a dependable investment analytic. It's difficult and time consuming to calculate meaningfully yourself, and it is only available on a few investing websites.

For example, Fidelity (https://www.fidelity.com) has one-, three-, and five-year standard deviation calculations in its database for individual stocks and funds, but they don't appear on any of the standard stock statistic pages. You can back into only them by doing a compare and by selecting performance and volatility measures or by using the stock screener. Further, they don't explain how they're calculated, and I haven't been able to duplicate their figures mathematically.

Like most measures, standard deviation is best for comparison, as you might do to compare Cree vs. Kimberly-Clark. Uses beyond that start to break down and become more cumbersome than they're worth. What can be helpful, and I'll show this in Chapter 7 on analyzing stocks, is comparing one standard deviation to another using the comparison page or to develop a screen selecting one standard deviation and other characteristics, like growth (risk/reward!).

A PICTURE IN TIME: BOLLINGER BANDS

As I have suggested before, looking at a chart or picture is sometimes the best way to capture and understand volatility. If sharp ups and downs—especially downs—worry you, you can plainly see them on the chart, recognizing, of course, that the chart is history, not the future.

Author and financial analyst John Bollinger gave us a neat visual tool to "see" standard deviation in action, particularly to see it as it changes over time. The tool, naturally, is referred to as Bollinger Bands, and is based on the standard deviation of the moving average of a price. The standard deviation defines a channel in which the price moves: that channel expands or contracts based on the standard deviation. An example is shown in Figure 5.4, from the Charles Schwab investment website:

FIGURE 5.4

Bollinger Bands, CREE, from Charles Schwab

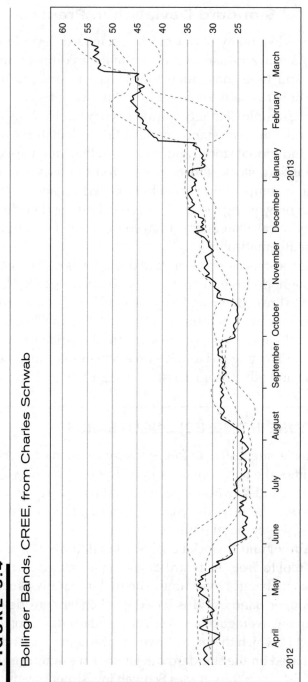

The chart shows the actual stock price with the dark heavy line, then three dotted lines. The center line is the moving average, and the two outside lines represent two standard deviations from the moving average at that point in time. Note the periods of increased volatility indicated by the wider bands.

BETA

By now you might be understandably frustrated at being almost halfway through a chapter before coming across a volatility measure you can really use, easily, effectively, and regularly, in your investing process. The good news: that's about to change with the introduction of beta to the low volatility thought process.

Yes, beta is a Greek letter (β) and, as such, may seem academically oriented and scary. But it isn't so scary in practice, and has been adapted for use and regular display by most investing websites. It is a popular and easy-to-find proxy for volatility.

Beta: What It Is and What It Does

Beta, as we'll see in a moment, correlates the price movement of an investment, usually a stock or a fund, with a benchmark: in almost all cases, the stock market as a whole. In theory, you could use beta to correlate anything with anything, but in practice, and as you'll normally see it displayed, it correlates the behavior of an investment with the S&P 500 stock index, using that index as the benchmark for market performance.

The Calculation

We're getting a little ahead of ourselves here, because the beta calculation is a correlation statistic we haven't discussed yet, and includes a component statistic we will also discuss shortly: covariance. But bear with me, it will make sense.

Beta is a correlation-based measure: that is, a measure of how two streams of data correlate each other, set up so that a perfect correlation comes out to a perfect 1. In most cases, and what you'll see in most investing portals, is the performance of an investment correlated to the S&P 500 Index.

The formula takes the statistically calculated covariance of the randomness of the return rate of the investment in question related to the randomness of the S&P 500 Index. Then it divides it by the variance of the S&P 500 Index to normalize the values to 1 for perfect correlation, or a linear deviation from 1. The formula:

$$\beta_a = \frac{\text{Cov}(r_a, r_b)}{\text{Var}(r_b)}$$

...where β_a is the beta of investment a, Cov (r_a, r_b) is the statistically calculated covariance between the return of investment a and the return of the asset class, in our case, the S&P 500, and Var(r_b) is the variance of the S&P 500. You can set up this calculation in Excel with two streams of return or period change data and the VAR and COVAR functions.

Interpreting the Measure

Beta starts to really make sense when you look at the actual values and what they mean (see Table 5.1). Since beta values appear in many websites, this is all you really have to do.

TABLE 5.1

Figure 5.5 Beta Values and What They Mean

β value	What It means	Volatility	Example
$\beta < 0$	Asset generally moves opposite to the benchmark	Inverse	Gold
$\beta = 0$	Asset movement is uncorrelated to the benchmark	Unrelated	Fixed asset, like CD
$0 < \beta < 1$	Asset moves in same direction, but not as much, as the benchmark	Low(er) volatility	Steady "staple" stock
$\beta = 1$	Asset moves in same direction, by same amount, as benchmark	Same volatility	Market performing stock
$\beta > 1$	Asset moves in same direction, and more so, as benchmark	High(er) volatility	Riskier stock

So, a stock like Kimberly-Clark, according to Google Finance, most recently had a beta value of 0.32. Cree has a beta of 1.05, and BlackBerry has a beta of 1.69. What do these tell us?

First, Kimberly-Clark moves in the same direction as the market, but not nearly as much. If the market (as measured by S&P) goes up 10 percent, Kimberly is likely to rise 3.2 percent. Same on the downside: if the market goes down 10 percent, Kimberly is likely to drop by 3.2 percent. So, Kimberly-Clark is less volatile than the market.

Cree, with a beta of 1.05, moves pretty much in line with the market, at least so far as percentage changes are concerned. When the market is up 10 percent, Cree is likely to be up 10.5 percent. You get the idea. BlackBerry? A 10-percent drop will likely see a 16.9-percent drop in the BlackBerry price.

So what about gold? In most times it is normally negatively correlated with the market. Markets are down, gold is up as a safe haven. But the most recent beta of the SPDR Gold Trust EFT (GLD) shows a value of 0.15, so it is very weakly positive correlated. That's a change from years past. But again, you get the idea; you can search for, and select, investments that have low betas—low correlations or even inverse correlations—to dampen the volatility of your investment portfolio.

Strengths and Shortcomings

Strengths include:

- Easy to use, common, and available on most investing websites, including Yahoo!Finance and Google Finance.

- Shows relative volatility with the market as a whole, a handy indicator of an individual security's volatility. Relative volatility measures are usually more meaningful than absolute ones.

- Easy to compare one stock or fund with another. Cross comparisons between stocks and funds work, too, but it's better to use a single source, as the data unit and time frame can vary.

Shortcomings:

- Beta is not an absolute but rather a relative measure of volatility; this can also be a shortcoming. Beta correlates with the stock market, regardless of what it's doing. A strong correlation with the market may mean high volatility—and lost sleep at night—because the markets are volatile. Or it might suggest low volatility when the markets are calm, even if your investment is inherently volatile.

- False indications are possible. A low beta can still mean high volatility. Suppose your investment is wildly volatile, but its ups and downs don't correlate with the market. It may show a low correlation with the market and a low beta but still be highly volatile. This does not happen very often. And, as just stated, a high beta can mean low volatility if the markets are calm.

- Most public beta measures compare to S&P 500, and nothing else. If you want beta between your investments, and, say, gold, you'll have to do it yourself, calculating the correlation coefficient, as shown below. But the S&P comparison is very useful for most purposes.

- You generally don't know the calculation details with public figures: what data units and time periods were used.

Using Beta in Practice

Beta is a handy and fast single-figure indicator for volatility, easy to find and easy to use as a search parameter. You can usually find a beta figure for any stock or fund.

In low volatility investing, low or mildly negative beta investments are used to avoid volatility in a stock and to reduce volatility in a portfolio. With the exceptions noted above, high beta investments are generally more opportunistic but also more risky, and low beta means low volatility.

Beta, because of its simplicity and availability, is the best single measure to use for low volatility investing.

SHARPE RATIO

As an investor, wouldn't it be nice to have a simple measure that goes beyond just measuring risk or volatility to measuring that holy grail of investing, the risk vs. reward profile of an investment?

That's what Professor William Sharpe was thinking in the mid-1960s, as he was working on some rather complex models of price and value securities in the context of risk and reward. An academic at heart, he came up with something he called the "reward-to-variability ratio." The ratio was simpler than the academic-sounding name implied; ultimately it just came to be called the Sharpe ratio.

Sharpe Ratio: What It Is and What It Does

The Sharpe ratio simply measures the reward gained by a security over a time period (or more often, these days, a portfolio of securities) and compares that to the risk taken over that period. One portfolio manager might earn the same gains as another, but if he or she took twice as much risk to get there, isn't the second portfolio manager doing a better job? In this framework, yes. And, as a low volatility investor, don't you seek the same gain with half the risk (or twice the gain with the same risk)? If so, this measure is right up your alley.

The Calculation

The Sharpe ratio measures the excess return over a time period: that is, the return generated above and beyond the risk-free rate. The risk-free rate is what you could earn without taking any risk; you could invest in U.S. Treasuries, for example, and incur no risk at all. By measuring excess return, the Sharpe ratio gets you to a pure measure of what a security or portfolio manager is really earning by taking the risk.

The formula takes actual returns, subtracts the risk-free rate, and divides that by the standard deviation incurred over the time period:

$$S = \frac{E[R_a - R_b]}{\sigma}$$

- S is the Sharpe ratio result.
- E is the expected value or mean of the observations over the units of time in a time period
- R_a is the actual rate of return over each unit of time.
- R_b is the risk-free rate of return, usually a U.S. Treasury bond for a comparable time period.
- σ is the standard deviation over the time period.

Interpreting the Measure

As you would suspect, the higher the Sharpe ratio, the better: that is, the more excess return per unit of risk taken.

Figure 5.5 shows the Sharpe ratio calculated for the three stocks used as examples above:

So, which investment is best, from a pure risk-to-reward viewpoint? First, you'll notice the negative Sharpe ratio for BlackBerry; that's bad, because the only way you can get a negative ratio is to have negative returns. So, rule that one out. Now, between the other two, we have Kimberly-Clark, which has a lower standard deviation but still lower returns, and a Sharpe ratio of 0.141. Cree has a higher risk profile with a standard deviation of 12.8 percent, but a far higher average excess return, yielding a Sharpe ratio of 0.247.

So a positive Sharpe ratio is good, and a higher Sharpe ratio is better. We've earned more return per the amount of risk taken.

FIGURE 5.5

Sharpe Ratio Examples, Risk-Free Return 2 Percent

	CREE			BlackBerry			Kimberly-Clark	
Month	Return (R_b)	Excess Return	Month	Return (R_b)	Excess Return	Month	Return (R_b)	Excess Return
−1	16.7%	14.7%	−1	12.5%	10.5%	−1	1.6%	−0.4%
−2	4.8%	2.8%	−2	2.9%	0.9%	−2	5.3%	3.3%
−3	27.0%	25.0%	−3	9.4%	7.4%	−3	6.0%	4.0%
−4	5.2%	3.2%	−4	2.3%	0.3%	−4	−0.6%	−2.6%
−5	6.6%	4.6%	−5	46.3%	44.3%	−5	2.7%	0.7%
−6	18.8%	16.8%	−6	5.7%	3.7%	−6	−2.7%	−4.7%
−7	−9.5%	−11.5%	−7	12.1%	10.1%	−7	3.5%	1.5%
−8	17.7%	15.7%	−8	−6.4%	−8.4%	−8	−3.7%	−5.7%
−9	−6.7%	−8.7%	−9	−3.2%	−5.2%	−9	3.6%	1.6%
−10	2.4%	0.4%	−10	−28.5%	−30.5%	−10	6.6%	4.6%
−11	−18.9%	−20.9%	−11	−27.8%	−29.8%	−11	1.1%	−0.9%
−12	−2.3%	−4.3%	−12	−2.7%	−4.7%	−12	6.2%	4.2%
$E(R_a - R_b)$		3.2%	$E(R_a - R_b)$		−0.1%	$E(R_a - R_b)$		0.5%
Stddev		12.8%	Stddev		18.7%	Stddev		3.3%
Sharpe		0.247	Sharpe		−0.006	Sharpe		0.141

Strengths and Shortcomings

Strengths include:

- Simplicity
- Measures what we really want to know: risk vs. reward
- Easy to find for mutual funds and ETFs

Shortcomings include:

- Assumes normal distribution, like standard deviation, and doesn't separate good from bad (downside) volatility.
- Single number by itself doesn't mean much; must be used comparatively.
- Not clear whether a high number is because of high return or low risk.
- Not easy to find for single securities or investments other than funds.

Using the Sharpe Ratio in Practice

The Sharpe ratio can be thought of as the bang-for-the-buck ratio. It is most often used for measuring a portfolio, especially the performance of a packaged portfolio: that is, a fund. How good a job did the fund manager do? How well constructed is the ETF or other index investment? How much risk was taken to achieve a given reward? The ratio helps us figure that out, and is especially useful when used as a comparative tool. As you build a low volatility portfolio, you'll want to seek funds and other investments with a high Sharpe ratio, especially if that ratio is built on a low—lower than market—standard deviation.

You'll also want to add investments to a portfolio that have a high Sharpe ratio. While it's not easy to find this as a calculated value on many investing websites, you can do it intuitively; the Sharpe ratio will become part of your thought process.

COVARIANCE AND CORRELATION

Correlation, as the name implies, measures how two streams of data "correlate," or correspond, with each other. It is based on another similar concept called covariance. Covariance is a raw measure; correlation takes that raw measure and normalizes it to something easier to understand.

Covariance and Correlation: What They Are and What They Do

You have two stocks. They move in lockstep with each other. One is up 50 cents for a day, and the other is up exactly the same amount. Then it's down 25 cents the same day. The other stock follows in lockstep.

The two stocks are said to be perfectly correlated and, as you might already surmise, you don't need one of them; invest in one or the other, and you'll get the same performance.

But the world doesn't work that way. Very seldom are two assets perfectly correlated. For that matter, we wouldn't *want* it to work that way, because there would be no way to defend ourselves against the vicissitudes of the markets. We get further—and get there more safely—by spreading our eggs across many baskets. What we're really trying to do is to avoid too high a correlation; we want different investments to perform differently in different scenarios. If something bad happens to one investment or investment class, we want to own another one that is less affected, or that might even be affected in the opposite direction.

Covariance is a pure statistical measure of to what degree two investments move in lockstep with each other. Correlation, as mentioned above, normalizes the covariance to give a quick, single-digit readout that makes sense. If two assets are perfectly correlated, the correlation coefficient will be 1. If they are absolutely, perfectly negatively correlated—that is, they move in exact opposite directions by the same amount—the correlation coefficient is –1. If they aren't correlated at all—that is, there is no statistical relationship between how each moves—the correlation coefficient is 0.

All other decimal values in between—which is what we usually get—give us a useful indication of how two assets are correlated. These values can be used to build a portfolio by mixing assets more or less correlated with each other to achieve different purposes. Covariance and correlation feed other models designed to optimize the total level of risk and reward based on how assets move or don't move with each other. The calculations are incredibly complex but produce something we call the efficient frontier, discussed in the next section.

The Calculation

The calculations of covariance and correlation are really beyond the scope of this book; you can research them separately if you want. Useful Excel functions will allow you to perform them. As an introduction, here is the formula for the covariance of two variables, x and y (expressed as the combined standard deviation of the two), where E is the expected value or mean of the measures. Typically, covariance is applied to the change or percentage change in values:

$$\sigma(x,y) = E\left[(x - E[x])(y - E[y])\right]$$

or

$$= E[xy] - E[x]\,E[y]$$

The calculation returns a number that is difficult to comprehend except to say that a positive covariance reflects a positive correlation and a negative covariance represents a negative number (you can use the COVARIANCE function in Excel to play with this). Take the mean of one data series and the mean of the other, multiply them, and subtract them from the mean of each element in the data series multiplied (got that?). Again, the number isn't important, but the concept is, and we'll make the number mean something by normalizing it into a correlation coefficient:

$$Correl\,(X,\,Y) = \frac{\sum (x - \bar{x})(y - \bar{y})}{\sqrt{\sum (x - \bar{x})^2\,\sum (y - \bar{y})^2}}$$

In Excel, this is calculated rather simply using the CORREL function in the statistical function set.

Note that this calculation involves only two variables, x and y. You can imagine how complex the formula becomes if you're trying to calculate the correlation coefficient among numerous investments in a large portfolio. That's what the efficient frontier and its models do, with matrix algebra way beyond the scope of this book.

Interpreting the Measure

The best way to explain the interpretation of the measure is by example. Figure 5.6 shows four examples of correlation between Asset A and four other assets, Assets B, C, D, and E. The data show percent changes for each asset for a six-month period.

First, you can see that Asset C moves exactly in lockstep with Asset A, while Asset D moves exactly the opposite to Asset A. The correlation coefficients are 1 and –1, respectively. This doesn't happen too often in the real world. Asset B is somewhat correlated with Asset A; that is, it moves *to a degree* in the same direction, but not as precisely—in fact, it may even occasionally move in the opposite direction. It is said to be positively correlated, but not perfectly correlated. Asset E, on the other hand, moves generally in the opposite direction, so it would be negatively correlated.

If there was an Asset F, with a correlation coefficient of 0.14, how would you interpret that? It is positively correlated, but not very correlated, to Asset A. If something happened to Asset A, would you expect the same response from Asset F? Maybe a little, but not much. Asset F would likely lower the volatility of the portfolio. Asset E, being negative, as you may recognize, would lower the volatility still further, but the returns would likely cancel out as well: you might sleep better at night but not gain very much market value.

When complex math and sufficient histories are available, portfolio management becomes a matter of crunching these correlations for a variety of investment possibilities. The math is beyond what most individuals can handle, but the principle is important.

FIGURE 5.6

Correlation Coefficient Examples

Month	Asset A	Asset B
-1	10%	2%
-2	8%	3%
-3	-5%	1%
-4	4%	-1%
-5	5%	3%
-6	15%	4%
Correl:	0.59757039	

Month	Asset A	Asset C
-1	10%	10%
-2	8%	8%
-3	-5%	-5%
-4	4%	4%
-5	5%	5%
-6	15%	15%
Correl:	1	

Month	Asset A	Asset D
-1	10%	-10%
-2	8%	-8%
-3	-5%	5%
-4	4%	-4%
-5	5%	-5%
-6	15%	-15%
Correl:	-1	

Month	Asset A	Asset E
-1	10%	-2%
-2	8%	3%
-3	-5%	1%
-4	4%	-4%
-5	5%	-1%
-6	15%	-2%
Correl:	-0.2531	

You might notice that our friend beta is similar to this correlation measure, except that the measure isn't allowed to exceed 1 or go below −1. With the standard correlation coefficient, 1 is as good as it gets; there can be no better than a 1:1 correlation. With beta, of course, stock prices can move more in a given direction than the S&P 500. Still, correlation is used in much the same way, to find securities that move in the same direction as a baseline (or each other) or not. You can start to see how a very quantitatively minded portfolio manager, with the right set of tools and data, could start to blend portfolio components that were not perfectly correlated to reduce volatility.

Strengths and Shortcomings

As you might guess, the primary strengths pertain to the value and simplicity of the resulting figure; the shortcomings align to the complexity and difficulty of calculation.

Strengths:

- Single-figure correlation coefficient tells a lot
- Good source data for building diversified portfolio model

Shortcomings:

- Complex math, tools, or statistics generally not available online
- Extraordinary or long-tail events can disrupt calculation

Using Covariance and Correlation in Practice

It's helpful to understand covariance and correlation conceptually but difficult to put them into practice mathematically; both are more suited for deep quantitative analysis beyond our scope. Aside from Excel, there are no tools to simply enter two investments—or an index—and out pops a correlation coefficient. With Stockcharts. com, you can not only calculate a correlation coefficient but plot its movement over time. But it's pretty hard to get there, and once you finally do, you've measured only the correlation between two investments; evaluating several investments would be a big task; evaluating several together wouldn't be possible.

Again, it's all about the thought process: how much do the ups and downs of something occur together? You can use comparative charts, which stop short of giving actual numbers, but can give you an idea. And, if you use professionally managed funds, you can be fairly certain correlation models are deployed to optimize them, especially if they're marketed as low volatility funds.

WHAT ABOUT *R*-SQUARED?

In your attempt to understand and apply volatility measures, you may have already come across a measure called R-squared, often denoted as R^2. R-squared is a sibling in the covariance and correlation measures family just explained but isn't quite the same thing.

R^2 is known as the coefficient of determination, is calculated by regression, and is designed to explain how much Variable B's movement is explained by Variable A. If Variable B moves in exact lockstep with Variable A, the R^2 will be 1; if there is no relationship, the R^2 will be 0. R-squared attempts to measure the dependence of Variable B on Variable A, that is, how much the change in Variable B is accountable to changes in Variable A.

Most often this is used to explain the performance of a mutual fund or ETF and how much the fund changed in conjunction with the change in a base index (almost always the S&P 500). So for Fund A, you might find an R^2 of 0.77, meaning 77 percent of the fund's movement was explained by the S&P 500 movement: a 77 percent match. Compared to another fund with an R^2 of 0.23, it moves more in tandem with the S&P 500. The low R^2 for the second fund suggests that it moves on its own, or that its movement correlates more strongly with something else, although what that might be is left a mystery.

THE EFFICIENT FRONTIER

In an ideal world, as a low volatility investor you would like to find a safe, stable security that paid high returns with little to no risk. Buy it, bank it, and hold on to it forever.

But you know the real world doesn't work that way. There is no such thing as a high-paying investment with little to no risk. If there were, everyone would buy it, driving the price northward, and it wouldn't be so high-paying anymore.

So, as a practical low volatility investor, your goal is to build a portfolio of securities that gives you the most bang for your buck—a portfolio that provides the most return possible for a given level of risk; better yet, one that optimizes the amount of return you get per unit of risk deployed. You want the mostest for the leastest: the most return possible for the least amount of risk taken.

Unfortunately, the task of figuring out just which securities to mush together to get to that optimal point is daunting, especially when you get up to large numbers of securities. We'll leave that mess to a good-sized computer and database, and to the quants who know how to run it. For now, that optimal point can be conceptualized as being along an efficient frontier, as originally conceived by portfolio theorist and statistician Harry Markowitz in the 1950s. Here, we'll describe the efficient frontier as a concept.

How the Efficient Frontier Works

The efficient frontier, like most of what we've talked about, is about risk and reward. Recall Figure 4.1, where risk and reward are related by a straight line moving upward and to the right. Each point on the line represents a choice among rewards for a given level of risk taken. Take more risk, get more reward. Or, to reduce risk, you can accept a security with a smaller reward.

This all works well, but interesting things start happening when you combine securities in a portfolio. When two securities are taken together, what happens to the risk/reward profile?

Unless they are perfectly correlated—that is, the correlation coefficient is 1—there will be some difference in how their prices
behave. Some of the movements will cancel each other out and,
as a result, the combined risk, or standard deviation, of the two
securities will be a bit less, sometimes a lot less, than the sum
of the individual standard deviations taken separately. The
smaller the covariance between the two securities—the more out
of sync they are—the smaller the standard deviation of a portfolio that combines them.

If you combine several securities, this effect can be even more
pronounced, to a point. At some point, an additional security will
not change the risk/reward profile; the reward is optimized for that
level of risk.

You may not have followed all of this, and indeed the math
is too complex for anything other than a good-sized computer.
But the result, when combining securities into a portfolio, is a
curvilinear line representing the risk/reward trade-off for a
series of tested portfolios, replacing the traditional straight line
used for evaluating a series of single securities. The conceptual
picture is shown in Figure 5.7.

FIGURE 5.7

The Efficient Frontier

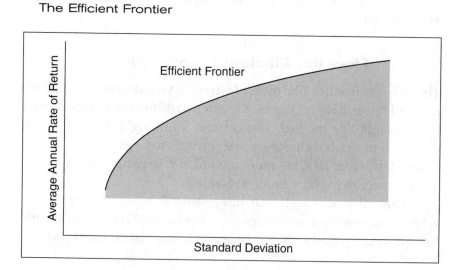

The Calculation

The calculation? Don't worry about it. It defies a simple explanation, especially when portfolios of more than two securities are evaluated. Essentially, calculated covariances between each security are placed in a table with weights corresponding to their weighting in a portfolio. A portfolio with six securities would require 36 covariances to be calculated: each security with another security. These covariances are placed into a matrix to determine a combined portfolio standard deviation given the investments, the expected return and standard deviation of that return for each investment, and the weighting of each investment. The investments—or the weighting of each investment—are varied until the highest return level is achieved for a given increment of standard deviation. If standard deviation starts to increase faster than the return, the mix of securities has moved beyond its optimal point.

SO YOU STILL WANT TO DO THE MATH?

An optimized matrix of weighted covariances. Got that? You weren't really expected to. It's a fascinating process, but in practice the calculation is beyond what most of us can do with limited data and computing tools. There are a few resources available to walk you through the calculation and you can even download Excel-based models to use yourself, possibly to construct a portfolio for yourself, more likely just to understand the process better. The best I've found, a site that includes both models and a good explanation of the models, is fellow Indiana University graduate and financial consultant Andrew Matuszak's Economist at Large, specifically the portion of it that covers Modern Portfolio Theory. The site has a sequence of lessons that starts at http://www.economistatlarge.com/portfolio-theory.

Interpreting the Model

Unlike the other measures we've discussed, the efficient frontier model doesn't produce a single quantifiable number for us to digest

FIGURE 5.8

The Optimal Portfolio on the Efficient Frontier

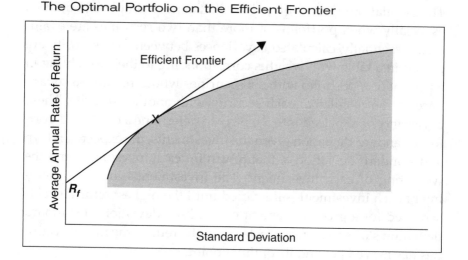

unless we dig deep into the math. The lesson is conceptual; as an investor, you want to find a portfolio that maximizes the return given the level of risk taken. Modern Portfolio Theory describes a line that connects the risk-free rate of return (R_f) through its tangent on the efficient frontier; the slope of this line is the Sharpe ratio $[(R_p - R_f)\,\sigma$, as described earlier]. Figure 5.8 shows the concept. This chart goes well beyond mathematical comprehension at this level, but conceptually, what you're looking for in a best portfolio is the combination of securities and weightings that gives best return for the risk deployed; that best portfolio appears at point X.

Strengths and Shortcomings

The strengths and shortcomings of the efficient frontier model aren't hard to guess:

Strengths include:

- Scientific, quantitative process to achieve diversification by maximizing return for a given level of risk.
- Can mathematically—or intuitively— assess the effect of adding one security to a portfolio or changing the weight of that security

Shortcomings:

- Calculation out of reach of the average user
- Standard deviation based, assumes normal random behavior; other problems cited with normal distribution assumption described above

Using the Efficient Frontier in Practice

As we've noted, the math and data requirements of the efficient frontier model are beyond most mortal investors. But the concept is important: what portfolio mix gives you the greatest return per incremental unit of risk taken? This is where the rubber meets the road in becoming a low volatility investor.

When you invest in a security, ask yourself: "Does this security, combined with the other securities I own, add more to my return than my risk?" If you already own one leading-edge semiconductor company, adding another may increase return, but you probably aren't reducing your risk, as the returns are probably strongly correlated. Isn't it better to add a company that makes consumer staples and paper products? It will increase your returns but will reduce the combined standard deviation of your portfolio, as the correlation of those returns to the semiconductor stock isn't very strong.

That's the thought process. You can think it as you invest. If you still prefer the quantitative approach to solving this problem, you may find it with actively managed funds, which have the resources and know-how to run these models. The 1-percent fee they might charge may be worth it. But even if you go this way, it's never certain whether they run enough possibilities and make good use of the results, or whether the results are impaired by imperfect statistical assumptions.

VIX

VIX stands for Volatility Index, an empirical—crowdsourced, really—measure of the aggregate volatility at any point in time of the S&P 500 Index. As such, it serves as a general proxy for the volatility of the stock market. VIX is used as an indicator and as a tradable security through various funds and derivatives that use it as a base.

How VIX Works

To understand VIX, you need to understand options, and we might as well start that discussion here, because in addition to being the basis for the VIX and the Black-Scholes model that follows, options are part of the low volatility investor's tool kit as described in detail in Chapter 9.

An option is the right to buy or sell something, usually a security, at or before a specified time in the future (the expiration date) at a specified price (the *strike price*). That right sells for a price, called a *premium*, and option contracts are bought and sold on a wide variety of securities and indexes on a daily basis on specialized option exchanges—for instance, the Chicago Board Options Exchange, or CBOE.

So, what determines the price of an option? Well, if you guessed the supply and demand of players in the market, like stocks, gold, or any other investment, you're right, but only so far as that goes. What an investor will pay for an option depends on how close a security is to the strike price, the time to expiration, and—you may have guessed it—the volatility of the underlying security.

Suppose you were thinking about buying three-month call options (options to buy; options to sell are known as *puts*) on two stocks. One was a high-flying tech stock, like Cree, Inc., described above, while the other was a staid, stately consumer staples stock that wasn't likely to change much in the short term. Which stock would command the higher option price? Which option would you be willing to pay for, assuming both stocks were trading, say, at a dollar below the current strike price?

The simple answer—the one with the greater volatility—is the tech stock. Why? Because with higher volatility there is a wider range of possible outcomes between now and the expiration date. Think about it: if Cree stock is up or down one or two points a day, while KMB barely ekes out a 25-cent gain or loss, which option would you pay more for?

You can see how volatility influences price. The next step, and the crux of the VIX matter, is to work backward to understand how option prices can reflect volatility.

VIX is an index created by the CBOE to measure aggregate volatility of the S&P 500 Index. How does the CBOE do that? By looking at the option prices for options traded on the index, the index makers can impute the volatility for the index—the *implied volatility* of that index. If option prices are high, that's empirical evidence that traders believe the markets are volatile, that they are feeling and anticipating volatility as the buy and sell option contracts. If option prices are low, traders are sensing a low volatility period.

Thus, the VIX is a handy single-figure indicator of overall stock market volatility. It is an indicator of the investing climate at any given point in time. While useful as a single indicator of current volatility, changes and patterns in VIX are important indicators, too.

Figure 5.9 shows VIX over the past six years. Note the peaks during the 2008 meltdown and lesser peaks during more recent periods of volatility due to budgetary stalemates, problems in Europe, and so forth.

The Calculation

The calculation, as described earlier, is based on a composite calculation of actual prices for options on the S&P 500 Index. The calculated figure roughly translates to the expected movement in the S&P 500 Index over the next 30-day period, which is then annualized.

For example, if the VIX is 14, this represents an expected annualized change of 14 percent over the next 30 days. To convert that to a monthly expected change in percent, divide the annualized figure (14 percent) by 3.46 (that's the square root of 12; the numerator is based on a standard deviation, which is a square root; you must also take the square root of the denominator). You get 4.04 percent. You can infer that the index options are priced with the idea that 68 percent (one standard deviation) of S&P movements over the next 30 days will be within plus or minus 4.04 percent; 95 percent of movements will be within plus or minus 8.08 percent (two standard deviations). That may or may not actually happen, but that's what the crowd of option traders and the price they're willing to pay are telling us.

Interpreting the Measure

A high VIX means volatile markets, at least in the short term; a low VIX indicates relative calm, at least until the next event that stirs up volatility. The dividing line between high and low is at about 20.

FIGURE 5.9

VIX Index, 2007-Present

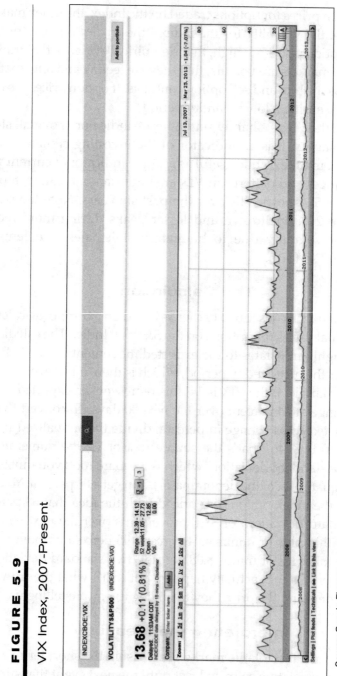

Source: Google Finance

Strengths and Shortcomings

VIX is a good high-level single figure estimate for current market volatility but doesn't help us much with individual investment decisions.

Strengths:

- Simplicity, single figure, quick view of the climate and incoming bad weather.

- Has a leading element; it is based on options, which are a trader's view of the future.

Shortcomings:

- Doesn't help us make individual investments. Only covers S&P 500, not other markets, indexes, or individual securities.

- Doesn't distinguish upward vs. downward volatility; not a pure risk measure.

- Doesn't tell anything about future more than 30 days out

- Crowdsourced; crowds aren't always right.

Using VIX in Practice

VIX should be used as a handy gauge for the overall volatility of a market; it's an indicator of climate. Changes in VIX are worth watching, too, as one would watch changes in the weather. If VIX starts to rise, it is like gathering storm clouds; they indicate a possible volatility increase on the horizon. As an investor, you might want to trim riskier investments to reduce how wet you get or to avoid the rain altogether.

BLACK-SCHOLES MODEL

By now it's probably clear that, in the world of finance, if something can be measured, modeled, or quantified, someone has probably already done so. What is the price of an option? It's what someone is willing to pay it for and what someone is willing to sell it for. What *should* the price be? That's a function of a several moving parts—a number of variables—and, not surprisingly, there's a model to calculate it. That model can be used to understand implied and actual volatility for individual securities, much as VIX can be used to capture implied volatility for the entire market.

Black-Scholes: What It Is and What It Does

In 1973, economists Fischer Black and Myron Scholes introduced the Black-Scholes model for pricing options and other derivative instruments. The Black-Scholes model calculates a theoretical option price that is based on six measurable factors, one of which is volatility. The price of the option thus reflects volatility, and the volatility component—the *implied volatility*—as well as the actual component measure historical volatility appear on some financial websites. These figures can give us a fast indication of an individual security's volatility much as VIX does for the entire market.

Factors included in the Black-Scholes model include:

- Current price of the underlying stock or index
- Strike price of the option
- Volatility, standard-deviation based, of the underlying stock or index
- Time until expiration
- Risk-free interest rate
- The stochastic drift rate of the stock price: a measure of the pattern of price changes

The result of Black-Scholes is the price of an option. If two options have the same relationship between the underlying stock price and the strike price, and the same time till expiration—say, both are $1 below strike with 30 days left until expiration—the one with higher volatility will have a higher option price, and the one with a higher option price will have a higher strike price.

The Calculation

The math is exceptionally complex, and you don't want to go there. It is a decay function, where the price decays slightly as you get closer to the expiration, but the pattern of the decay depends on the six variables noted above. For a sampler, the formula below calculates the price of a call option:

$$C(s, t) = N(d_1) S - N(d_2) Ke^{-r(T-t)}$$

$$d_1 = \frac{\ln \dfrac{S}{K} + \left(r + \dfrac{\sigma^2}{2}\right)(T-t)}{\sigma\sqrt{T-t}}$$

$$d_2 = \frac{\ln \dfrac{S}{K} + \left(r - \dfrac{\sigma^2}{2}\right)(T-t)}{\sigma\sqrt{T-t}} = d_1 - \sigma\sqrt{T-t}.$$

Interpreting the Measure

An option price—including a theoretical price calculated by Black-Scholes—can tell you a lot about the volatility of a security. If an option price is high relative to the stock price, and high compared to like options on comparable securities, you can get a pretty good idea of the underlying volatility. If a call option price for a 30-day expiration, $1 below strike option for Stock A is 10 percent of the stock's price, and the option price for Stock B is 2 percent of the stock price, Stock A must be considerably more volatile.

Perhaps more useful, where you can find it, are the actual readings of implied and historical volatility found in conjunction with the Black-Scholes calculation. Implied volatility (IV) for the future is estimated in a manner similar to VIX, where actual option prices are fed backward through the Black-Scholes model to capture the implied volatility used in the model. Actual historical volatility (HV) used in the calculation may also be shown. The options research section of Fidelity Investments' website provides excellent tables under IV Index—if you're an account owner. Figure 5.10 shows an example for Cree, Inc.:

FIGURE 5.10

Implied and Historical Volatility, Cree, Inc., from Fidelity Investments

Fidelity.com   [   ] Search   [   ] Quotes   Customer Service

| Accounts & Trade | News & Insights | Research | Guidance & Retirement |

Research >   Content and da

Options

| Overview | **Quotes & Tools** | Trading Ideas |

Enter Symbol
[CREE] [Search]
Find Symbol

CREE CREE INC
$54.34 ⬇ -0.94 (-1.70%)
AS OF 4:00:00PM ET 03/25/2013

Bid 54.14 X 3   IV30 40.44
Ask 54.30 X 3   IV60 51.01
Vol 2,028,897   IV90 47.33

Details
Key Statistics | Option Chain | **IV Index**

Tools
Option Quote & Chart | Probability Calculator | P/L Calc

IV INDEX

Implied Volatility Index 🔲

Term	Current IV Index				1 Week Ago		1 Month Ago	
	Call	Chg.	Put	Chg.	Call	Put	Call	Put
30 Days	42.80%	2.78%	43.13%	2.28%	36.88%	37.73%	36.07%	37.55%
60 Days	50.23%	0.95%	50.64%	0.57%	41.94%	42.93%	36.08%	37.79%
90 Days	46.85%	0.67%	47.51%	0.62%	44.09%	45.16%	39.54%	41.46%
120 Days	45.96%	0.61%	47.03%	0.46%	43.92%	45.25%	41.17%	43.17%
150 Days	45.42%	0.55%	46.75%	0.32%	43.45%	45.01%	40.64%	43.03%
180 Days	45.04%	0.49%	46.55%	0.23%	43.13%	44.85%	40.24%	42.90%

Historical Volatility ❷

Term	HV	1 Week ago	1 Month ago	52-Week High		52-Week Low	
10 Days	25.02%	71.01%	19.05%	99.72%	01/24/2013	10.94%	10/11/2012
20 Days	53.20%	54.28%	70.76%	79.50%	01/23/2013	19.56%	02/21/2013
30 Days	45.53%	44.73%	59.36%	70.62%	03/05/2013	21.49%	09/21/2012
60 Days	55.59%	55.51%	50.83%	55.88%	03/08/2013	28.34%	10/16/2012
90 Days	49.30%	49.19%	46.70%	52.36%	03/22/2012	32.81%	10/15/2012
120 Days	46.22%	47.52%	43.42%	63.10%	03/22/2012	32.67%	01/03/2013
150 Days	43.67%	43.84%	41.02%	64.28%	03/22/2012	35.03%	01/17/2013
180 Days	42.03%	42.51%	41.60%	66.89%	04/18/2012	36.69%	01/04/2013

The charts show the IV from 30 to 180 days ahead working backward from actual option prices, just as the VIX model did. The daily change and week ago or a month ago columns, which show you whether the implied volatility is increasing or decreasing, are handy things to know. At the bottom is actual historical volatility, which is one standard deviation of actual price change over the indicated period. Also shown is a nice breakdown of the history of that volatility.

These are very high percentages for a single standard deviation (68 percent expectation) range; as a comparison, Figure 5.11 shows the same table for Kimberly-Clark:

FIGURE 5.11

Implied and Historical Volatility, Kimberly-Clark, from Fidelity Investments

Enter Symbol	**KMB** KIMBERLY CLARK CORP	Bid 94.44 X 1	IV30 18.47
kmb [Search]	**$94.54** ↓ -1.12 (-1.17%)	Ask 94.90 X 2	IV60 16.85
Find Symbol	AS OF 4:00:00PM ET 03/25/2013	Vol 2,852,990	IV90 15.67

Details
Key Statistics | Option Chain | IV Index

Tools
Option Quote & Chart | Probability Calculator | P/L Calcula

IV INDEX

Implied Volatility Index ❷

Term	Current IV Index				1 Week Ago		1 Month Ago	
	Call	Chg.	Put	Chg.	Call	Put	Call	Put
30 Days	18.88%	1.94%	18.50%	1.39%	17.52%	17.63%	14.97%	14.89%
60 Days	16.93%	1.61%	16.47%	1.21%	15.97%	15.82%	14.76%	14.32%
90 Days	15.77%	1.42%	15.38%	1.10%	15.20%	14.90%	13.96%	13.36%
120 Days	15.20%	1.35%	14.84%	1.07%	14.79%	14.42%	13.55%	12.85%
150 Days	15.08%	1.28%	14.73%	1.06%	14.53%	14.23%	13.30%	12.56%
180 Days	14.99%	1.24%	14.65%	1.06%	14.36%	14.12%	13.42%	12.89%

Historical Volatility ❷

Term	HV	1 Week ago	1 Month ago	52-Week High		52-Week Low	
10 Days	13.18%	11.38%	10.19%	24.74%	08/06/2012	4.04%	08/31/2012
20 Days	12.62%	15.01%	11.65%	18.98%	08/09/2012	6.32%	10/18/2012
30 Days	14.06%	13.28%	10.26%	16.41%	08/09/2012	7.23%	04/19/2012
60 Days	13.99%	13.99%	12.98%	14.14%	08/10/2012	8.36%	04/19/2012
90 Days	13.35%	12.99%	12.75%	13.76%	03/07/2013	9.48%	04/19/2012
120 Days	12.84%	12.49%	11.89%	13.62%	03/26/2012	9.72%	06/18/2012
150 Days	12.16%	11.89%	12.67%	14.13%	03/26/2012	10.31%	07/16/2012
180 Days	12.80%	12.70%	12.58%	15.39%	03/29/2012	10.89%	10/12/2012

You can see the difference between a high and low volatility stock. These figures are available for any security with options traded on it, which includes most ETFs; you can get an implied and historical volatility for gold using the SPDR Gold ETF (GLD) as a proxy, for example.

A somewhat less complete version of these tables is available for free—that is, without having an account—from the CBOE website at http://www.cboe.com/TradTool/IVolMain.aspx; then enter the IV Index free services tab.

Strengths and Shortcomings

Strengths:

- Robust model incorporates many factors, has tested well in practice.
- IV and HV data are interesting and gives a complete and easily compared view, past, present, and future.
- Good research sites do much of the legwork for you.

Shortcomings:

- Complex math, difficult to comprehend, impossible to do on your own.
- Do we really need this much information?
- IV is crowdsourced like VIX—and crowds can be wrong.
- Free tools on the web are difficult to find; CBOE is probably the best. Excel spreadsheets are available for the model itself.

Using Black-Scholes in Practice

Low volatility investors might use options as we describe in Chapter 9 to transfer risk and enhance income. Even if they don't buy and sell options, an investor with time and access may want to track option prices over time to detect shifts in volatility. Of course, that can also be done by watching the IV and HV tables, if access is available. Option prices, IV, and HV are good tools to characterize volatility and to compare one security to another.

At last: we're done with the math and other thought process builders. Whew. Now it's time to move to Part Two, where you'll find practical tips to build your very own low volatility portfolio.

KEY CONCEPTS

▶ Standard deviation is the purest measure of volatility, but it has some drawbacks and is not commonly available on investing websites.

▶ Particularly for stocks, beta is probably the best and easiest to use single volatility measure.

▶ The Sharpe ratio is useful especially for portfolios—funds—but you need to look at both the ratio and its components to fully understand it.

▶ It's possible to measure the expected volatility of a complete and customized portfolio by creating a matrix of covariances, but this task is well beyond the average user.

▶ In theory, the efficient frontier optimizes the risk/return profile of a portfolio; in practice, the calculation is difficult and best left to professionals.

▶ VIX and Black-Scholes give a crowdsourced glimpse into the volatility expectations of the market.

▶ Formulas can help measure and interpret volatility and can help you build a portfolio, but they don't give the complete answer.

Becoming a Low Volatility Investor

PART TWO

Becoming a Low Volatility Investor

CHAPTER 6

Building a Low Volatility Portfolio

If you've been reading *All About Low Volatility Investing* in sequence—Chapters 1 through 5—you would be altogether justified in wondering just when you were going to learn how to do low volatility investing! Until now you've seen lots of numbers, read lots of theory, and sampled the math. You've read that low volatility investing, for most of us, is a thought process, not a formula. You've read that some formulas exist, but they're mostly beyond the realm of ordinary individual investors, and they don't get it all done anyhow.

So now we'll switch gears a bit. We'll fasten our seat belts (or take them off, if the math was particularly scary) to embark on a journey of technique. Part One covered low volatility investing theory and introduced the thought process; now Part Two will expand on the thought process and add some technique.

In Part Two we'll move forward to what's practical and actionable to construct a low volatility portfolio that enhances your returns modestly while reducing your risk. Now, I realize this may seem out of order: should we really talk about building a portfolio first, then about evaluating investments? Isn't that like creating the package before deciding what's inside? Perhaps. But I think it's easier to start with a strategic framework; once you have that under your belt, it will be helpful when examining individual investment choices.

Part Two starts with a look at traditional diversification and asset allocation., In most cases, diversification and asset allocation are done first in the interest of investor safety, and only secondly to enhance returns, if at all. From there we do a different construct for diversifying a portfolio, what I call a tiered approach, which takes into account both risk/reward scenarios and the time devoted to managing different parts of your portfolio.

The *tiered* portfolio, which will become familiar by the end of this chapter, serves as the strategic framework as we move forward to cover stocks, funds, alternative investments, so-called inverse investments, and the risk-transferring derivative investments known as options. These topics are each covered in Chapters 7 through 9. Finally, in Chapter 10, we'll assemble the puzzle pieces into a useful and actionable low volatility investing style.

IS DIVERSIFICATION THE ANSWER?

Listen to any financial talk show these days, read most books on investing, or listen to most financial advisor, and you're bound to hear a lot about diversification. If diversification is the answer, what is the question?

Diversification is often given as the necessary medicine to reduce portfolio volatility. If you avoid putting all your eggs in one basket, you won't suffer so much when that basket is tipped over. If one stock or one fund takes a big hit for any reason, the other investments you own aren't likely to suffer the same fate—at least not as much. If oil giant BP has a spill, it will hit that stock but, in concept, will leave most of your other investments alone. In some cases, those other investments, like gold or even alternative energy, might even go up.

It's true: diversification insulates you from events—particularly internal risks, or risks intrinsic to the company or invest-ment itself—because that company or investment is only part of your portfolio. Diversification can help reduce external or personal risks, but as we've seen especially lately, bad news casts a wide net.

SMART DIVERSIFICATION IS THE KEY

Warren Buffett said it best: "Diversification is for people who don't know what they're doing."

Now wouldn't you think, with what you've read and heard over the years, that the world's most successful investor would, in fact, depend a lot on diversification? That Buffett would want to cover all bases and reduce the risk of a cataclysmic blowup in his portfolio?

Well, apparently not. He is, in fact, so good at this that he feels he doesn't need to diversify just to reduce risk. Most of us mortals can hardly claim to be that good, so we do feel the need to diversify some, to not put all our eggs in one or a series of risky baskets. And, in fact, he does too; he owns several companies in different industries with different risk profiles.

But he also would say that diversification for diversification's sake is more likely to water down your returns than improve them and can be more likely to make financial planners and others who make money off your money more successful than it will make you.

Which brings us to the topic of *smart* diversification. What is smart diversification? It means taking some steps to reduce risk (remember our four choices: avoid, reduce, retain, transfer)—strategically—without simply giving up returns. Sure, you can diversify a lot of the risk out of a portfolio by buying a fund with 600 stocks in it, but how will you beat the market? You're essentially *buying* the market. If you have one stock that loses 100 percent of its value, you won't feel the pinch, because it's only 1/600th of your portfolio. But the same thing happens in the upside; you may have one or even 100 stars in your 600-stock fund, but the returns will be watered down by the subpar performance of the rest.

The trick is, then, to invest prudently to have as many of those good 100 stocks in your portfolio as you can without also having the bad ones. I'm not saying not to diversify." What I'm saying is that you shouldn't diversify just for diversification's sake. I'm also saying that you shouldn't overdiversify just to avoid risk, because you'll almost surely avoid above-market returns, too, in the process. If you're willing to give up above-market returns just for safety's sake, you're best off buying an index fund that simply tracks the market and heading for the garden or the golf course.

Smart diversification means:

- Not buying a mutual fund or exchange-traded fund with as many as 1,800 holdings (yes, there are some), which will inevitably—mathematically—only produce market returns or something less after management or transaction costs are deducted. Funds with 50 or fewer handpicked or well-targeted investments are better. Don't bring the bad and ugly in with the good.
- Not buying too many stocks yourself for much the same reason.
- Not just diversifying by asset class (stocks, bonds, cash, or commodities) but smartly *within* the class.
- Not buying overlapping funds where the holdings are similar.

So, diversifying smart means reducing risk by spreading the eggs around, but also paying attention to how many eggs you have and to each one to make sure it really fits in the nest. Does it spread your risk? Does it enhance your portfolio's return? If the answer to both questions is yes, you're on the right track.

THE DIVERSIFICATION PARADOX

The typical diversification principle you hear goes something like this: The prudent investor will always look for ways to diversify his or her portfolio by buying multiple stocks or funds in different industries. That way, risk is minimized, and there is a greater chance of achieving market rates of return.

OK, not bad. Most investors are satisfied with something at least close to market rates of return, and most of them want to sleep at night. The part about a "greater chance of achieving market rates of return" is actually true. But the sheer mathematical fact is that the more stocks or other investments you put into your portfolio, the less the odds of beating the market.

Think of the old probability models you studied in high school. If you toss a penny into the air, it comes down heads or tails, 50:50 probability. Toss a few more pennies in the air, say six total, and the odds are you'll get three heads and three tails, maybe two and four, maybe one and five, maybe even all six heads. Probabilities decrease as you go to the extremes, but these outcomes are all plausible. Now throw 100,000 pennies into the air. What are the chances of all 100,000 coming up heads? Desperately small. This is an extreme case, but the point remains: The more stocks you have, the more likely your winners and losers will cancel each other out.

Additionally, suppose you hit a home run and score a 50 percent gain on a stock. If it's one of four stocks in your portfolio and all others break even, the portfolio gains on average 12.5 percent. If it's one of 10 stocks, with all the others breaking even, the gain is only 5 percent. Holding too many stocks dilutes the gains of the winners. Combined with transaction costs and management fees, this phenomenon helps explain why some two-thirds of stock mutual funds underperform the markets, as measured by the S&P 500 Index. But what about reducing risk? True, the more pennies you throw, the lower the odds that they will all come up tails. If the performance of your stocks is really random, then owning more stocks reduces the chance of beating market returns. The converse is also true: owning many stocks reduces the chance of dramatically underperforming the market.

Remember, true investors aren't random stock pickers. They take out the risk by understanding the investments and their intrinsic value, rather than by spreading the risk across more companies. Smart investors are focus investors who drive toward deep understanding of their investments without diluting possible returns through diversification. They see danger in owning too many investments, which may be beyond the scope of what they can manage or keep track of. Here's the paradox: Instead of reducing risk through diversification, risk may actually increase as it becomes harder to follow the fortunes of so many businesses. That's why Buffett and others reject diversification per se as an investment strategy. They prefer to reduce risk by watching a few companies and investments more closely.

WHAT'S WRONG WITH TRADITIONAL ASSET ALLOCATION MODELS?

Diversification, naturally, gives rise to the idea of asset allocation (see Table 6.1). You don't want all your eggs in one basket. So, financial advisors and many in the investment community, instead of focusing on nests and eggs, focus on pies. Pie charts, that is: charts that show how much of your investible worth should be in stocks, bonds, real estate, etc. Better pie charts with more detail, breaking stocks down into large-cap, mid-cap, small-cap, international, emerging market, etc.

TABLE 6.1

Typical Asset Allocation Choices

As of 2/28/2013	Standard deviation	1-Year return	5-Year return	10-Year return
STOCKS				
Large-Cap Stocks	15.2%	13.3%	4.9%	8.1%
Mid-Cap Stocks	18.1%	13.9%	8.1%	11.5%
Small-Cap Stocks	20.0%	15.3%	8.5%	12.3%
International Stocks	20.1%	10.1%	1.2%	9.1%
Emerging Market Stocks	21.9%	0.0%	0.2%	16.5%
FIXED INCOME				
Intermediate Bonds	3.8%	2.5%	5.2%	5.0%
Short–Term Bonds	1.0%	0.7%	2.1%	3.0%
OVERALL MARKET				
Vanguard Total Stock Market Index	15.9%	13.4%	5.5%	9.0%

Source: American Institute of Individual Investors

These pies aren't all bad; they just don't go far enough, as we'll see. The chart below shows some of the numbers that might be used to construct a pie. Actually, this is a better than average table, because the standard deviation of each asset class is listed next to the returns for one, five, and ten years.

These figures show the trade-offs between risk and reward for at least some of the major asset classes. You can make some decisions or at least guide your thought process through them: "I want to stay with large-cap stocks for most of my portfolio to reduce standard deviation, and I'm willing to accept the lower return" or "I want to boost my return approximately 3 percent for a good chunk of my portfolio, and I'm willing to accept the incremental 3-percent standard deviation."

As suggested, this is all good, as far as it goes. Such a pie doesn't really tell you what to invest in, except for funds aligned with these major asset classes. Also, it's hard to put the returns and standard deviations in dollar terms, and we already know about the assumptions and faults of standard deviation. You're pretty much getting market return for the different sectors of the market.

This isn't so bad if you really don't want to spend much time on it and don't really care to beat market return. You can simply buy a U.S. mid-cap ETF or an emerging market ETF or an intermediate bond ETF to capture these segments, if you trust the funds—the indexes or the managers that guide them. It's a hands-off approach, sometimes the only one available for employer-sponsored retirement plans, so again, it's good as far as it goes. It's not wrong; it just doesn't go far enough.

Remember what we're trying to do. We're trying to actively manage volatility and risk—avoid, reduce, retain, or transfer risk, as described in Chapter 2, and in the Chapter 5 efficient frontier framework, you're trying to add investments at the frontier, that is, at the highest possible return level for the amount of risk taken. You want to select investments carefully to eke out those one, two, or three extra percentage points of excess return. You want the most bang for your buck.

FOUR ALTERNATIVE WAYS TO DIVERSIFY

Diversification is important. You don't want all your eggs in one basket, no matter how good that basket is or looks to be. External, internal, and personal risk factors can change. Business can change, competition can change, a company can lose a CEO or run afoul of accounting rules; there are big rocks out there that can scuttle even the most secure investment. The smartest way to think of diversification is multidimensionally; that is, you want to diversify across several dimensions, not just asset class (e.g., stocks, bonds, cash). Some of those dimensions include:

- *Industry*: To reduce volatility, you should avoid concentrating too much in one industry. Even solid industries like energy or healthcare can change, and what is bad for the group almost always hurts all the players in that group. Even Buffett diversifies across industries: insurance, paint, utilities, transportation, and home furnishings. It's best to diversify across at least four or five industries. A good example of industry diversification thinking can be found nightly on CNBC's *Mad Money*, on which Jim Cramer reviews five stock caller portfolios during the show.

- *Risk profile*: For low volatility investing, risk-profile diversification is a really good idea. It's sort of what some pros get to by diversifying across large-cap, mid-cap, and small-cap companies. The idea is taken a step further by specifically choosing conservative and more aggressive investments as parts of a complete portfolio. We'll examine shortly how a portfolio can be segmented, or tiered, to diversify by not only risk but also the amount of time spent managing the different portfolio segments.

- *Time horizon*: Diversifying by time horizon—that is, how long it will take an investment to achieve a return objective—is a variation of the risk profile diversification theme; really, it's just another way to think about it. You can think of it as pay me now vs. pay me later. You may want some stocks or other investments that pay a current and regular income, balanced with others, perhaps more aggressive growth stocks that promise a larger payback later on. Having some of both—not all now stocks, not all later ones—is a smart way to diversify.

- *Type of investment: fund vs. individual stocks:* As mentioned above, I don't really think the choice of stocks vs. bonds vs. cash vs. commodities and real estate or other really gets to the point of diversification, although smart investors should probably own all of these or their equivalents. However, in the interest of time and focus on the really important parts of your portfolio, some diversification between funds and individual stocks makes sense. Manage some if it yourself, and let the pros manage some of it for you. You'll get a balance of your ideas and those of others; moreover, you'll find yourself with more time, as suggested, to do a really good job managing what you do manage.

BUILDING A TIERED PORTFOLIO

With these diversification ideas in mind, the next step is to describe an effective method to diversify a portfolio to manage volatility and return. The idea behind the tiered model is to think of your investment portfolio as a tiered pyramid of investments, with each tier receiving different amounts of attention and designed to achieve different risk/reward objectives. The goal is to optimize the risk/reward trade-off for each investment and to make the most effective use of your time, operating under the assumption that you're not a professional investor.

What and Why

The tiered approach segments your portfolio into three distinct tiers, which I call the *foundation,* the *rotational,* and the *opportunistic* portfolios. We'll get to what each of those tiers is, and how they work, in a moment.

The tiers suggested here aren't based just on the type of assets; they're also based on the amount of activity and attention you want to pay to different parts of your portfolio. You'll spend more time on certain segments and less time on others; you'll take more risk on certain segments to get more return while reducing risk on others while, hopefully, still earning a decent return. It's a strategic portfolio approach similar to one you might use if you were managing a small business: put most of your focus on the products and customers who might bring the greatest new return to your business; let the rest of your slow, steady customer base function as it has for the long term. Figure 6.1 illustrates the main idea:

FIGURE 6.1

Standard Portfolio Tier Model

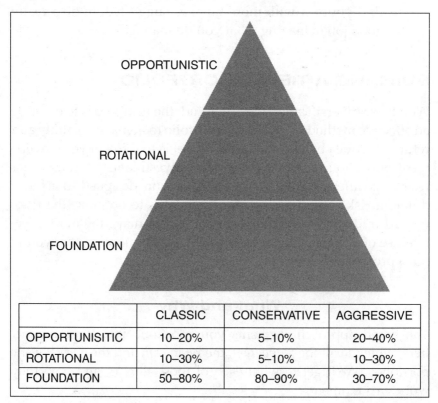

	CLASSIC	CONSERVATIVE	AGGRESSIVE
OPPORTUNISITIC	10–20%	5–10%	20–40%
ROTATIONAL	10–30%	5–10%	10–30%
FOUNDATION	50–80%	80–90%	30–70%

In this figure, you can see the three segments. You'll diversify within each of the three as you choose the specific investments. These segments can be set up as distinct or specific investment accounts (i.e., brokerage accounts) if you want; that part isn't as important as the thought process.

The table below the pyramid shows the three segments, which roughly correspond to risk profile—the "foundation" investments being the least risky and probably the largest portion of your portfolio; the "opportunistic" investments being more risky but also geared to generating more and a more short-term return. The "classic," "conservative," and "aggressive" columns show how these groups of investors might divide their tiers.

The idea will come together as we examine each of the tiered segments.

FOUNDATION INVESTMENTS

In this construct, each investor defines and manages a cornerstone foundation portfolio, which is long term in nature and requires relatively less active management. In this part of the portfolio, the goal is to produce a decent but probably not market-beating return, while lowering volatility by spreading risk through lower-correlated (low beta, low standard deviation) investments. Stock and bond funds, bonds held to maturity, and solid, low beta or standard deviation, dividend-paying stocks belong in a typical foundation portfolio.

Frequently, the foundation portfolio includes retirement accounts (the paradigmatic long-term investment) and may include your personal residence or other long-lived personal or family assets such as trusts, collectibles, and so forth. A foundation portfolio may also contain some long-term plays in commodities or real estate to defend against inflation, particularly in energy, precious metals, and real estate trusts. The foundation portfolio is largely left alone, although as with all investments, it is important to check at least occasionally to make sure performance—and any professionals who might be involved, like fund managers—are keeping up with expectations for both return and reduced volatility.

ROTATIONAL INVESTMENTS

The second segment—the rotational portfolio—is managed more actively to keep up with changes in business cycles and conditions. It is likely in a set of stocks or funds that might be rotated or remixed occasionally to reflect business conditions or to get a little more offensive or defensive. The portfolio is managed to redeploy assets among market or business sectors, between aggressive and defensive business assets, from domestic to international plays, from large-cap to small-cap companies, from companies or industries in favor versus out of favor, from stocks to bonds to commodities, and so forth. Sector-specific ETFs are a favorite component of these portfolios, as are cyclical and commodity-based stocks like gold mining stocks.

While the idea isn't new, the advent of *low-friction* ETFs and other index portfolios makes rotation much more practical for individual investors. What does low-friction mean? They trade like a single stock, with all the commission discounts and simplicity of a single stock trade. You don't have to liquidate or acquire a whole basket full of investments to follow a sector. We should note that it's been possible to rotate assets in mutual fund families for years with a single phone call, but most funds in these families are less pure plays in their sector, and most families do not cover all sectors.

The Inverse Triangle

The rotational portfolio is where many of your defensive plays might occur. Defensive plays can be very low correlated or negatively correlated assets: assets designed to hold their own or even go up when the markets go down. Such assets inoculate your portfolio against those swings, and having a small portion of your portfolio designed to go the other way can not only make you feel better when things go south, they can turn an otherwise sharp loss into something more palatable.

For example, suppose you have a $100,000 portfolio, all of which is invested long: that is, toward price appreciation. A large negative external event occurs, and the portfolio drops 20 percent and you're left with $80,000 and a bad taste in your mouth about investing.

Now suppose you had put 10 percent of your portfolio in a defensive, negatively correlated—an inverse—asset that actually *moved up* 20 percent as the market dropped 20 percent. You would lose 20 percent on 90 percent of your portfolio and gain 20 percent on 10 percent of it. If you do the math, you'll see you end up with $84,000 instead of $80,000: only a 16-percent drop, not the 20 percent everyone else experienced. (Of course, your upside potential would be similarly limited, but this result is consistent with the idea of reducing volatility.)

Some leveraged negative investments actually go 3× against the markets, so it might have appreciated 60 percent during the market drop. By the way, if you had invested in the 3× inverse investment, the total loss would come out to only 12 percent: only half the loss for consigning only 10 percent of your portfolio to the inverse asset.

We'll discuss inverse assets, which include short and leveraged funds, shorting stocks, and using options, further in Chapters 8 and 9. In the overall scheme of volatility management, such investments become a way to transfer risk away from your portfolio.

Figure 6.2 shows how the inverse triangle might be tucked into your tiered scheme. The triangle is usually part of the rotational portfolio but can also become a slice of your opportunistic portfolio: say, if you see a stock that just seems ridiculously overpriced and you want to take advantage in the short term.

Opportunistic Investments

The opportunistic portfolio is the most actively traded portion of an active investor's total portfolio. It is the risky right if you think about the traditional risk/reward trade-off chart. In the opportunistic portfolio look for stocks or other investments that might be riskier, and might seem to be notably under (or over) valued at a particular time but are geared to produce above-average returns.

FIGURE 6.2

Portfolio Tiers with Inverse Component

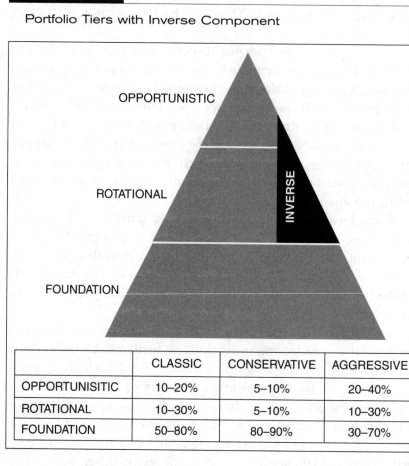

	CLASSIC	CONSERVATIVE	AGGRESSIVE
OPPORTUNISITIC	10–20%	5–10%	20–40%
ROTATIONAL	10–30%	5–10%	10–30%
FOUNDATION	50–80%	80–90%	30–70%

These might be high beta stocks or investments, investments that move more than the markets and return relatively more than market performance.

The opportunistic portfolio also may be used to generate short-term income through covered option writing (which we'll cover in Chapter 9). Options are essentially a cash-based risk transfer mechanism whereby a possible but low probability investment outcome is exchanged for a less profitable but more certain and very short-term cash return scenario. A fee or premium is paid in exchange for transferring the opportunity for more aggressive gain to someone else. You collect this fee. Effectively, you, as the owner of a stock, can convert a growth investment into a shorter-term income investment, paying yourself a dividend for the ownership of the stock by selling an option. Is this risky? Actually, in most situations it is less risky than owning the stock *without* selling an option, and converts a long-term investment into a short-term cash generating opportunity, transferring some risk in the process.

Curiously, beyond generating above-average returns, one primary objective of the opportunistic portfolio is to generate income, or cash. Most traditional investors look at the long-term, more conservative components of a portfolio to generate income through bonds, dividend-paying stocks, and so forth. In this framework, the short-term opportunistic portfolio might be used for short-term trades or to sell options to generate cash. These swing trades usually run from a few days to a month or so, and may even be day trades if things work out particularly well and particularly fast. It should be emphasized that day trades are not the low volatility investor's typical practice.

ARE RETIREMENT ACCOUNTS *ALWAYS* PART OF THE FOUNDATION?

The long-term objectives and nature of retirement accounts suggest normal inclusion as part of the foundation portfolio. In fact, retirement assets can be deployed as part of either the rotational or opportunistic portfolio. In fact, it might make a lot of sense. Why? Because returns generated are tax free, at least until withdrawn. Tax-free returns can compound much faster. Because of the importance of these assets, one should commit only a small portion to an actively managed opportunistic portfolio, but it can be a good way to juice the growth of this important asset base.

The tiered portfolio approach is presented as a framework; of course, what you put into each of the tiers is just as—if not more—important. These contents will be covered over the next four chapters, starting with stocks, then funds, fixed income and other investments, then the inverse universe, and, finally, options.

KEY CONCEPTS

▶ Overdiversification consigns you to market returns—less fees and/or commissions—and that's all. This can be OK if chosen consciously, but you're not likely to beat the market even by a few percent. Avoid packaged portfolios with anything more than 50, maybe 100 component investments.

▶ There's nothing wrong with asset class diversification; it just doesn't go far enough. Consider diversifying by industry, risk profile, time horizon, and type of investment.

▶ Another way to diversify is to know what you're doing (Buffett's principle): research your core investments carefully; use funds or highly correlated market performing investments for the rest.

▶ A tiered portfolio approach can help you manage risk/reward profiles of individual investments and tell you where to spend the most time.

▶ Within a tiered portfolio, foundation investments like dividend-paying stocks produce market (or better) returns with relatively less risk, rotational investments (mostly ETFs and inverse investments) add some defense and sector diversification, and opportunistic investments employ a little more risk to boost returns. The net result should be a portfolio that generates above-market returns with below-market risk.

CHAPTER 7

Low Volatility Stock Investing

When most people think about investing, they think first about investing in stocks. Stocks still represent one of the most diverse and straightforward ways to buy into the growth and substance of the global economy. By buying stocks, you're giving a chunk of your capital to a business that makes and markets and sell products and services. In doing so, a return is generated on that capital: more return if the company is more successful, and more return as the economy grows.

Obviously, there are thousands of companies to choose from and, just as obviously, each has a different risk/reward profile. You can choose from a steady manufacturer of consumer staples, like Kimberly-Clark, or from a company deeply vested in the latest technologies, such as gallium arsenide semiconductor components for LED lighting, like Cree, Inc., introduced in Chapter 2. Low risk, low-to-moderate reward. High risk, high reward. The choices are all over the map.

You can buy shares in a company directly, or you can buy a fund that in turn buys a selection of companies. When you use a fund, as we'll see in the next chapter, you're buying a package that includes elements of diversification, professional know-how and management, and access to difficult investments like emerging-market stocks. Such a packaged product typically reduces risk and volatility through diversification and a degree of professional know-how, but it also typically reduces the return.

People who choose to buy individual stocks seek to do better than the packaged products. They seek to avoid fees and other downsides of investing in a fund. They may know more about certain industries, or may have a different view of risk and reward than a fund manager does. Or they, like Warren Buffett, may simply have a keen business sense that rises above the stoic methods of quantitative models and the tried-and-true tactics of ordinary Wall Street.

Or they may simply enjoy the intrigue and interest and self-determination of stock picking. Too, they might be pretty good at it.

Whatever the reasons, they—and you—are looking to build a portfolio to generate short-term income and long-term financial security. Especially if you're reading this book, it's safe to assume you want at least a major portion of that portfolio—the foundation—to be built up with at least some low volatility stocks. Those stocks have relatively stable prices with returns that at least match—preferably beat—the market by a modest amount.

We can't predict the future, and we can't precisely predict a stock's volatility or its return into the future. Most of the available tools are rearview-mirror looks at stock price history, standard deviation and other volatility measures, and financial results. This is part of the picture, but I think there's more to it than that. The best way to pick low volatility stocks is by blending what we know about the past with factors that might make the business more successful, or at least less prone to failure. Both work together to reduce future risk.

So how does this work in practice? We'll look at a few current core indicators, then blend them with a list of key future-looking value-investing principles. Those value-investing principles reduce the future risk of the business and provide a margin of safety. So this chapter is divided into two main parts: the first covers core indicators and stock screens you can use to select candidates based on them; the second offers a 14-step checklist for future value and margin of safety.

This approach is neither theoretical nor comprehensive but rather a practical guide to narrowing down choices and selecting stock investments, mainly for the foundation portfolio. You're looking for factors that indicate tailwinds to your investments from both a volatility and growth perspective. You seek to avoid characteristics suggestive of headwinds. No single stock will successfully pass all criteria. But if you find an abundance of these characteristics, you'll improve the odds of it being a solid low volatility performer. And, after all, improving the odds is what low volatility investing is all about.

CORE INDICATORS: FINDING LOW VOLATILITY STOCKS BY THE NUMBERS

One of the toughest jobs as an investor is to narrow down the selection of investments among a range of thousands. As we said, there are no formulas or secret searches that will tease out the small handful of absolute best investments to achieve your objectives, whatever they might be. But there are ways to narrow the search so that you can add other criteria, and a measure of intuition and gut feel, to arrive at your final choices.

To select low volatility stocks—stocks with lower-than-average market volatility and better than average returns—I believe in five practical indicators that are easy to understand and easy to find and construct searches for on most investing sites. These five indicators are beta, dividends, company size, price-to-earnings ratio, and growth. Again, these five indicators suggest tailwinds but won't give you absolute answers.

Low Beta Is Best

As we learned in Chapter 5, beta, which correlates a stock's price movements with the movement of the stock market as measured by the S&P 500 Index, isn't perfect. But it's pretty good, it's simple, and it's available almost everywhere.

Granted, market correlation isn't always what you want when markets are bad, and less-than-market correlation isn't so good either when the markets are going up. That said, beta can tell us a lot. As a rule of thumb, any stock with a beta less than 1 (the stock moves less than the market moves) is probably a good low volatility pick.

Stocks with a beta between 0.20 and 0.80 are usually safe and steady, especially if they're big companies. As the beta approaches 1, the volatility starts to move with the market, which usually isn't so bad but increases exposure when the markets correct. A beta greater than 1 indicates a higher volatility, and if other factors are right, higher returns, too; these stocks may be better for the opportunistic portfolio. Note, too, that stocks of companies with high internal risks may have high betas; they tend to correct even more than the markets when the tide goes out; bank stocks are a good example.

Negative betas may be found with a few stocks, especially gold mining and similar stocks, but these are typically speculative in their own way and should be used carefully. For our purposes, beta is the quick test of volatility. If you search for betas in that 0.20 to 0.80 range, you'll be off to a good start.

WHY NOT STANDARD DEVIATION?

As a pure measure of volatility, didn't we suggest that standard deviation is better? If a stock moves with the markets, but we can't sleep at night because of what the markets are doing, have we accomplished anything by using beta? Why don't we use standard deviation instead?

In theory, it's a good argument, but in practice, a lot of people don't understand standard deviation, because it can be measured in many ways. Further, as we learned, the measure suffers from other ills, notably the assumption of normal and random behavior. It's hard to find online, and if I tell you that a stock has a standard deviation of 0.44, what does that mean, anyway? Is that the variation in the stock price? Or the annual or monthly *change* in that price?

All that said, if you can find it (it's buried deep in the Fidelity investing website, for example) it's good if and when used as a comparative measure: one stock or fund against another stock or fund from the same source. Use the two standard deviation framework—95 percent of possibilities—to set a boundary; if that boundary isn't too far from the current stock price, it's a pretty safe bet. If you can find standard deviation, and better yet know how it's calculated, yes, it does hold up as a search, too.

A Bird in Hand: Dividends

If a company pays a healthy and growing dividend, two things happen: volatility typically declines and current return typically increases, both of which line up with our low volatility goals.

Attention to dividends is based on the principle that a bird in hand is better than two in the bush. Dollars that are paid to you today are yours and not subject to any future volatility (unless you want them to be), while dollars retained in the company and not paid out to you are still subject to all the risks of the company. Additionally, a management team paying dividends is looking out for your interests and shareholder returns in general rather than keeping everything in the business for an uncertain future or, worse, their own gain.

While a solid yield—one exceeding the 2.3-percent S&P 500 average in today's markets—is typically a good thing, it should be noted that dividends aren't contractual, and a company that reduces or eliminates its dividend may do so as a last-ditch measure; this can increase volatility considerably. A stock with an unusually high payout—say, 5 percent or more in today's markets—should also be looked at as suspect, because it isn't clear it can maintain such a payout. Beyond simply looking at the yield percentage, some due diligence on whether the company earns enough cash to pay the dividend is worthwhile.

Beyond that, it's a good idea to look for companies that raise their dividends consistently. It's like giving you a raise, and is a strong indication of ongoing business success and commitment to shareholders. I will sometimes do a search with a lower limit of 1 percent; then, if the company has a strong track record of dividend increases, especially recent ones, it can still be a good pick. Dividend history can be hard to find; my favorite source is the *Value Line Investment Survey* (see below).

To reduce volatility, search on stocks with steady and growing dividends—in today's markets, say, between 1 and 5 percent—and a look behind the scenes at the dividend track record also helps.

Size Matters

For the most part, bigger companies are more stable and can afford the setbacks that might happen on a handful of products or in a handful of geographies. Small companies, on the other hand, are usually more vulnerable to hiccups—external and internal risk factors—and may be based on less-proven technologies. When trying to avoid volatility, big is usually best; so-called large-cap companies—greater than $1 billion in market capitalization—are best. That said, I'll often lower that size criterion just to pick up a few more up-and-comers or small players that might dominate a niche (covered in the next section) and be solid low volatility picks on that basis.

Does the Price Make Sense? A Peek at the Price-to-Earnings Ratio

Price-to-earnings ratios (P/E) can be fickle indicators, but they can tell you whether a stock is overpriced relative to the market, relative to its peers, and relative to its history. A stock with a high P/E can be vulnerable to volatility, whereas one with a lower P/E has a greater margin of safety and resilience to the next hiccup.

Keep in mind that earnings streams can be fickle with extraordinary charges, restructurings, and so forth, so P/E on some companies may be overstated or not reflective of what's really going on. A stock with a P/E somewhat less than market average or, even better, less than industry average, is bound to be safer. Don't go too low here, though; a stock with a P/E of 4 in a market with an average P/E of 16 probably has something wrong with it, likely a large drop in the E anticipated for the future. A look at how P/E has changed over time—again, something available through Value Line—doesn't hurt.

Given today's market average P/E around 16, a search on P/Es between 8 and 16 is likely to bring back lower volatility stocks with decent returns.

A Little Growth Doesn't Hurt

We've said all along that our main goal is to reduce volatility and to sleep at night, but at the same time we also want to beat stuffing cash in a mattress, so we're concerned about returns, too. I always look for a measure of growth, at least in the first pass. Growth can be measured in many ways: earnings growth, cash flow growth, or simply the recent growth in the stock price. If you have a historical resource like Value Line, it also helps to double-check the persistence of that growth.

THE VALUE OF VALUE LINE

I've mentioned Value Line several times. Value Line produces the best one-page reports available (to individual investors, anyway) for a wide range of stocks, published as the *Value Line Investment Survey*. They show the numbers and, better yet, analyze them and project the future on a wide range of well-selected and important criteria. The reports are updated quarterly.

Among all Value Line offers, two things stand out for low volatility investors: history and stability or predictability measures. Value Line reports show history all on one page for up to 17 years for such matters as stock price, earnings, cash flow, dividends, revenues, profit margins, share counts, debt, and a number of other factors, each of which, and all together, can give you a sense of past volatility and persistence, much of which can be projected into the future.

Value Line also gives four helpful single figure indicators:

- Financial Strength: a grade showing overall financial wherewithal, the higher grades, of course, indicating more stability and less volatility
- Stock Price Stability: a percentile rank of how stable the stock price has been compared to other stocks they analyze; a score of 100 is the most stable
- Price Growth Persistence: same idea, except applied to growth, not just the stock price, so a 100 here and a high score in stability mean steady growth, up and to the right
- Earnings Predictability: another percentile indicator obviously relevant to both steady and growing stock prices and cash returns in the form of dividends

Value Line (http://www.valueline.com) has a number of packages available for subscription. The most basic is the Value Line 600, available in 2013 for $296 a year for a print and online subscription. The *Investment Survey* covers 1,700 stocks and runs about $600 for an annual subscription. Other related products are also available. The *Investment Survey* can often be found in a good local library, but if not, these tools are worth having access to for the serious low volatility investor.

CONSTRUCTING A LOW VOLATILITY STOCK SCREEN

There is no formula and you can't get to the answer just by looking at numbers and doing the math. But you can get a lot closer if you screen the stock universe for the factors just discussed. That's what we'll do here.

Using the screener on Google Finance (google.com/finance), you can screen all the factors we just mentioned: beta, dividend yield, size (market cap), P/E, and growth. You can add any criteria; for instance, industry, if you want to narrow your choices. To add search criteria, just hit the Add Criteria button and look for the one you want. For example, beta is found under the Stock Metrics category under Add Criteria.

Really nice is the set of graphic histograms offered up on the screen setup page. You can isolate a particular band within the range of the stock universe, and you can see how wide or narrow (how many stocks) that band turns out to be. You also get a quick indication of the number of stocks selected when all criteria are applied. You'll get the idea as you play with it, deciding where you want to be and how to reduce or expand the size of a search.

Figure 7.1 was done much as outlined in the core indicators discussion above:

FIGURE 7.1

Google Finance Stock Screener Setup

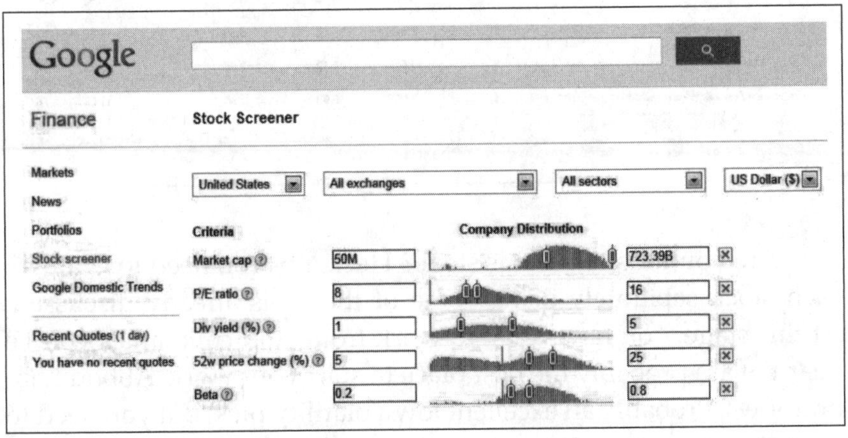

This low volatility screen returned 61 results, the first page of which is shown in Figure 7.2:

FIGURE 7.2

Google Finance Stock Screener Results

1 - 20 out of 61

Company name	Symbol	Currency	Market cap	P/E ratio	Div yield (%)	52w price change (%)	Beta
ACE Limited	ACE	$	30.04B	11.21	2.20	19.88	0.72
ACNB Corporation	ACNB	$	98.55M	11.07	4.52	15.86	0.66
Abbott Laboratories	ABT	$	56.47B	9.60	1.55	23.27	0.36
Activision Blizzard, Inc.	ATVI	$	16.25B	14.54	1.29	14.90	0.56
Associated Banc Corp	ASBC	$	2.45B	14.51	2.15	7.28	0.70
BCE Inc. (USA)	BCE	$	35.83B	13.83	4.88	14.55	0.74
BOK Financial Corporation	BOKF	$	4.20B	11.95	2.44	10.36	0.79
Baldwin & Lyons Inc	BWINB	$	354.93M	11.08	4.20	6.11	0.76
Bank of Commerce Holdings	BOCH	$	81.94M	13.29	2.34	15.28	0.73
Bank of SC Corporation	BKSC	$	54.64M	14.89	3.91	7.33	0.51
Bar Harbor Bankshares	BHB	$	140.67M	11.27	3.41	7.71	0.60
Cal-Maine Foods Inc	CALM	$	1.03B	11.77	2.85	9.37	0.59
Center Bancorp, Inc.	CNBC	$	199.29M	11.57	1.81	19.84	0.34
Central Valley Community Bancorp	CVCY	$	82.21M	11.54	2.36	20.08	0.37
Century Bancorp, Inc.	CNBKA	$	189.26M	9.93	1.42	19.29	0.29
Chevron Corporation	CVX	$	228.79B	8.84	3.03	9.88	0.77
Cullen/Frost Bankers, Inc.	CFR	$	3.79B	15.99	3.09	5.92	0.66
Dr Pepper Snapple Group Inc.	DPS	$	9.43B	15.62	3.26	14.82	0.72
Edison International	EIX	$	16.51B	11.12	2.66	18.72	0.58
Endurance Specialty Holdings Ltd.	ENH	$	2.06B	15.99	2.68	17.89	0.76

Show rows: 20   1 - 20 of 61 rows

Are you finished at this stage? Heck, no! You need to evaluate each stock separately using some of the tools already discussed. At this stage, you have a list to work from, and companies you've heard of are probably the best place to start your work. Abbott Laboratories? Probably an excellent low volatility pick, but you need to go further to get really comfortable with it.

The Google Finance screen is pretty effective, and it's fun to play with. Other screeners are available, especially on brokerage websites, and they can offer a richer assortment of selection criteria. Fidelity (www.fidelity.com) has a screener that can include standard deviation, earnings and cash flow growth, and several other volatility and return factors. Most features and selection variables are available free to outside investors; having a Fidelity account will gain access to more.

WHEN ALL ELSE FAILS, LOOK AT THE CHART

When chasing low volatility facts and figures, you can drive yourself nuts with numbers. Don't forget that when it comes to volatility, a picture can tell more than a thousand words, especially about past volatility. You can measure beta, stock price growth, and so forth, or you can just look at a graph. The graph doesn't tell everything either, particularly about the future, but it can give you a good sense of what you're really seeing in the figures.

Good charting tools exist on almost all investing portals and brokerage websites, and many allow you to get fancy with comparisons and tools, like Bollinger Bands (see Chapter 5). I would never settle on a low volatility investment without looking at a chart. But that said, I would never think the chart would tell me everything I needed to know about the future; there's more work to do. That's what we'll get to in the next section of the chapter.

CORE INDICATORS OF FUTURE VALUE

You've looked at some numbers like beta, growth, dividends, and P/E that may indicate tailwinds, or at least the absence of headwinds, in achieving your low volatility investing objectives. You have a few candidates worthy of a closer look. You're on the right track.

But all of the indicators described in the last section are rearward looking, right? They tell us what has happened, and how the stock price has behaved, but they stop short of telling us what will happen in the future and, in particular, the underlying qualities of the company you're buying stock in.

That's where the core principles of value investing come in: principles that can tell us how good the company is, and how good of a value its stock is. If you invest in companies with solid value fundamentals and intangibles, you lessen the chance of a looming business hiccup or failure. Which is to say, you reduce your risk.

The premise of value investing starts with the notion that you aren't buying stocks, you're buying a business. What the stock has done in the past is of little importance; what you care about right now is whether or not it's overpriced. But beyond that, you're looking at the entity as a business, trying to assess whether that business has the merits and qualities of a good business going forward. Among many tenets held by the Buffett school of value investing: (1) buy a stock like you're buying the entire business; (2) buy the business only if you understand it, and (3) buy it only if it is a good business, good enough that you'd like to own it outright.

The philosophy and principles of value investing, treated in their entirety, are the subjects of entire books. I've written a couple of them, by the way: *Value Investing for Dummies 2nd ed* (Wiley, 2007) and *The 25 Habits of Highly Successful Investors* (Adams, 2012) among them. These books may be worthwhile reading, for I believe that if you incorporate the principles of value investing, you'll reduce your risk.

The best approach is to boil these principles down into a short checklist of features to look for in a business. These items break down into *fundamentals* —measurable facts and trends—and *intangibles*—not so easily measured qualities of a company that really make things work. The fundamentals tend to be financial and operational measures, and these measures tend to look at the past, and tend to be internally focused. The intangibles tend to be marketplace qualities, like brand and customer loyalty, that tend to be external, and tend to look toward the future.

So, marketplace intangibles are about the future and financial fundamentals are about the past. Moreover, in my view, marketplace intangibles are a better indicator of future financial performance than past financial fundamentals. So in looking at future performance and volatility, marketplace intangibles stand out, but we can't ignore the financials. Or—consistent with the theme of this chapter—good marketplace intangibles indicate tailwinds; bad marketplace intangibles indicate headwinds.

What we're looking for, in essence, is excellence in marketing and in the operational and financial characteristics. In the interest of space, time, and simplicity, I will present a shopping checklist of seven Marketplace Excellence factors, mostly intangible, and seven more Financial/Operational Excellence characteristics a value investor would look for in a business, and that, I believe, will reduce volatility if they align. Again, no single company will score 100 percent on all; you're looking for tailwinds to improve your odds, not perfection.

MARKETPLACE EXCELLENCE

As suggested, marketplace excellence factors are the most leading indicators of the success of a business and, if executed consistently, will lead to future financial success. A company with an excellent, sustained position and face in the marketplace is less vulnerable to competition and can control price and cost. The business is more likely to be steady and growing, in contrast to a commodity producer with few marketplace differentiators, which will always be subject to the whims of competition and cost. Unless a company operates as a monopoly in the marketplace, a strong marketplace presence will be the difference between stable growth and unpredictable results; translation: volatility.

How do you research these marketplace factors? This is a challenge, and investors must be creative and willing to do some homework. The first and most obvious is simply taking it to the street (or online, or wherever the company does business): check out the presence, customer volumes, customer flows, strength of the message, price competitiveness, ease of doing business with the company, and so forth.

For years, Starbucks has stood out as an investment simply because of its understanding of customer desire for an attractive "third place," and it's easy to see just by walking into one how many customers there are, how loyal they are, and so forth. Everything else—the brand, the coffee, the service (in most cases, anyway)—supports this notion. An investor tuned into what's going on in the marketplace would determine Starbucks to be a winning business, but the high stock price relative to earnings might suggest some volatility might still be in store.

Smart investors read the financial news—and, if reading the *Wall Street Journal*, they start with the Marketplace, not the financial section. Why? The Marketplace contains stories about what companies are doing in the marketplace, what works and what doesn't work, new trends, new ideas, new products, new campaigns, or new competitors. Again, these will lead to future financial success (or not); it's the right place to start digesting financial news. Investors may also want to concentrate on an industry and read the stories and news on the industry or keep tabs through their own employment or smart friends employed in the industry. There are dozens of ways to keep your finger on the pulse of the marketplace.

Even if you don't buy or sell companies very often (and low volatility investors may not), you should keep up on the marketplace pulse if you're investing in individual businesses outright. The following seven factors, presented briefly, offer a checklist of what to look for.

Does the Company Have a Wide Moat?

The term *moat* comes from the Buffett school of investing and refers pretty much to the analogous image of a waterway around a castle. The waterway protects the castle.

In a similar way, you should look for factors that protect your investment from invaders, in this sense, competition. You want to avoid commodity producers who compete on nothing but price, and instead give the nod to companies that have a high degree of competitive advantage and value add. These companies have advantages in technology, products, brand, location, or even size or first-mover advantage: anything that makes them difficult to compete with or difficult for other companies to move into their market. Microsoft has a wide moat because few can duplicate its technology or its reach easily (although that's starting to erode as technology changes). Starbucks has a narrower but still good moat in brand, size, and customer loyalty; others have tried but few have come close.

When you size up a company, think about what its competitive advantages are, whether they're sustainable, and how the base technology (like computing) is changing. Companies with a wide moat are less subject to competitive (and price) invasion, and are less likely to be volatile—so long as the moat remains intact.

Does the Company Dominate a Niche?

Niche domination is a special case of the wide moat idea. If the company is the largest player in a well-defined and steady market, it's likely to be able to control price, save on marketing costs, and generally earn steadier profits, all leading to a steadier stock price with a decent return.

A good example is offered by the Pall Corporation (ticker symbol PLL). This $2.5-billion company dominates the global market for filtration and purification devices sold to industrial, medical, research. and other users. No other company comes close. It's not a huge company, but it's a huge player in a steady market.

Is Market Share Steady or Increasing?

Companies with a strong and steady—and better yet increasing—share of their markets are likely to be winners over the long term, again so long as they can sustain their shares. Market share gains—especially when based on factors other than price—indicate customer loyalty and, ultimately, pricing power, not to mention higher volumes and lower per unit costs.

It's not easy to get a number for market share, although this is where reading the news and analysis can help. You can also get an idea on the street: at many airports, for example, the Southwest counters and gates are booming with traffic, while others are relatively quiet. Apple's recent success is largely due to market share gains, tied to the domination of the personal digital device niche, which has grown big enough to nearly redefine the personal computing market.

You can see that a lot of these—market share, niche power, moats—go together; that idea will persist throughout this list.

Does the Company Have an Excellent Brand?

Few things can match a strong, dominant, and preferred brand in the marketplace. We've certainly seen it with Apple, and there are others that are obvious and not so obvious to the general public. As semirational, semiemotional creatures, we respond to the promise, trust, image, quality, and aura of a brand, often with loyalty, often by paying a higher price and being willing to put up with other negatives to get and stay on board.

Look for companies with strong brands: brands that mean something, brands that are appreciated by customers. Are you willing to pay more for a good brand, in, say, food or detergent? Then it's a good brand. If a company owns good brands, and does the right things to preserve and grow those brands, it's a good indicator of stability and healthy returns.

Does the Company Have Loyal Customers?

Loyal customers are good customers and, most importantly, repeat customers. A company doesn't have to spend marketing or sales dollars to get them to buy. Beyond that, loyal customers spread the word, a more important factor in today's socially networked world. Loyal customers preserve moats and niche dominance; when customers become disloyal, or are loyal only because of price, look out.

This, too, can be difficult to sniff out in the marketplace. Brand excellence usually begets customer loyalty. Customer reviews, comments in the trade press, and other commentary can tip you off to loyalty, as well as crowds, long lines, busy websites, and any casual conversation you might hear about a company or its products. Starbucks clearly has loyal customers. Walmart does, too, while Kmart, not so much. Apple: definitely loyal; HP: going downhill. It's not something to be easily measured, but you can pick up clues.

Is There a Channel and Supply Chain Advantage?

Here, we move a little more toward the operational characteristics of the business. Unless a business is its own channel—as in retail or distribution—it's a good idea to appraise how good its channels are, and how good its relationship is with its channels, particularly compared to the competition. Is your company a preferred supplier among its retailers or other channel partners? Are the company's products getting more floor space? Online space? Promotion? Are they being touted by the floor salespeople? Does the company have a strong online presence? Do the online selling channels work?

A bit more operational, but based on the same concept, is the supply chain. Does a company have a sustainable competitive advantage with its suppliers? Its location? Manufacturing locations? Distribution networks? Price or cost advantages with inputs and ingredients? Labor costs? These signs can be hard to pick up, because companies don't have to report much about costs and efficiencies other than total costs. But a look at the company's geography and what it says about their supply—and its consistency of supply and raw material costs—can tell a lot.

Companies like Procter & Gamble have done well—and reduced volatility—not just by building strong brands but by achieving excellence in both channels and supply chains

Does the Company Have International Exposure?

This last factor is a bit of a wild card because it can behave differently in different economic times and has behaved differently of late. Most companies that have a strong international presence have a degree of insulation from volatility at most times. The idea is simple: when the U.S. economy is in the tank, overseas economies can be strong, and vice versa.

That balance was tipped to a degree in the 2008–2009 recession, during which all economies suffered and, as a result of increased debts, particularly in Europe, the old order has been slow to recover. In recent years, companies with less international exposure have done better, particularly as the dollar has strengthened (which has been a double whammy to U.S. companies with high overseas sales). My premise remains unchanged: U.S investors should invest in U.S. companies with a good mix of exposure to all global economies: U.S., developed markets, and emerging markets. Buying U.S. companies that sell overseas is a better—or at least less volatile—way to play international exposure; there are no inconsistencies in accounting rules to worry about, and you're closer to the news that might affect the business. If you're a non-U.S investor, again, it probably makes sense to stay at home but invest in your global players.

Table 7.1 is a summary of Marketplace Excellence factors indicating volatility tailwinds:

TABLE 7.1

Summary of Marketplace Excellence Factors of Volatility Tailwinds

Marketplace Excellence Factors
Does the Company Have a Wide Moat?
Does the Company Dominate a Niche?
Is Market Share Steady or Increasing?
Does the Company Have an Excellent Brand?
Does the Company Have Loyal Customers?
Is There a Channel or Supply Chain Advantage?
Does a Company Have International Exposure?

OPERATIONAL AND FINANCIAL EXCELLENCE

Operational and financial excellence, of course, refers to the internal characteristics and results that indicate business success and, ultimately, high returns with low volatility. These excellence factors are inherently more quantifiable than marketplace factors, since we're mostly talking about dollars, cents, and *per*cents, not vague concepts like brand equity. Because they are quantifiable, it is also interesting to analyze the trends. Are things improving? Or not? Getting worse? That, more than anything else, can signal impending volatility, other things being equal.

This isn't a book about financial analysis, and I won't attempt to capture everything you need to know to assess a company's financial health in the next few pages. Again, we're looking for tailwinds: signs of excellence, signs that things are right with the company near and long term. We're looking for signs of health in profitability, cash flow, profit margins, capital and business structure, and share price. We are also looking for signs of strength in the face of headwinds, which do come from time to time in any business.

As the complexities of financial analysis are beyond the scope of this book, so are most of the sources of information. You can go nuts looking top to bottom at financial statements and especially 10-K annual reports, although knowing your way through these documents can help, and a stop at the 10-K can be far more revealing than a stop at the company's website. Financial portals like Google Finance and Yahoo!Finance are helpful, but for most of this analysis (and a good bit of marketplace analysis), I turn to Value Line once again. Their reports show not only most of the key facts and figures identified below, but also trends and, in a few cases, metrics like Earnings Predictability that help guide the volatility and return appraisal.

Here are the seven Financial and Operational Excellence factors:

Are Cash Flows and Earnings
Steady and Predictable?

This one is almost self-explanatory; with good financial reports and especially with Value Line reports, it's not too hard to tell whether earnings are predictable and stable. The Value Line Earnings Predictability score, mentioned above, is helpful. With Value Line you also get a good indication of cash flow and cash flow trends per share—earnings plus or minus (usually plus) a few noncash items like depreciation. As a general rule, a company that has steady and growing cash flows, well ahead of earnings (to allow for capital expenditures and equipment replacement) is destined for better performance and lower volatility than one that doesn't.

I also like to look at the Statement of Cash Flows over a few years to see whether the company is generating enough positive "Cash Flow from Operations" to more than cover "Cash Flow from Investing" and "Cash Flow from Financing." "Cash Flow from Investing" is a bit of a misnomer, mostly representing capital expenditures and asset replacement, and is typically a negative number. Cash flow from financing represents flows out for dividends, share buybacks, debt retirement, and similar. A company with a positive cash flow after subtracting investing and financing is producing capital; a negative balance, especially over time, tells us the company is consuming capital. The analysis of Statement of Cash Flows is a bit more complicated than this, but you get a good idea, and my two books on value investing mentioned above explain further.

Are Margins Steady and Growing?

Businesses are in business to earn profits, and gross, operating, and net profit margins tell a lot about whether a company is getting better or getting worse at doing that. The details of how these figures are calculated are beyond the scope of this book.

Looking at trends in margins (again, Value Line, data from company reports are more limited) can be very revealing. First, are the margins consistent? If not, the company may be subject to fierce competition, expensive marketing campaigns, fluctuating material costs, or all of the above. Second, comparing margins to industry competitors can be helpful, too, although as a predictor of volatility and long-term performance, I think trends are more important.

Are Dividends Steady and Growing?

This one was covered earlier, but I believe it's important to repeat that a company that pays a solid, steady dividend is less prone to volatility; your total returns will be enhanced, as they have been in the early 2010s, as payouts from most investing alternatives have suffered. A steady and growing dividend greatly strengthens the case, and again, Value Line is the best single fact-sheet source.

Some investors like to dig deeper to see how adequately the dividend is covered by earnings and cash flow. A company that pays out 90 percent of its earnings as dividends (another Value Line measure) is generous to shareholders, but what happens during the next downturn? Will the dividend be covered? A solid dividend reduces volatility, but a vulnerable dividend can dramatically increase it, especially if a wide band of investors has bought the stock for the dividend, as many did with bank stocks before 2008.

THE FLIP SIDE OF "PAY ME NOW…"

What about companies that pay no dividends? If a company performs well in other categories—marketplace excellence, earnings predictability, and so forth—the absence of a dividend doesn't necessarily increase volatility or even reduce shareholder returns, as Apple stockholders could attest, at least until mid-2012.

But retaining all those earnings in the business gives less room for error. If a high-flying company reinvests everything in itself and runs into a wall, look out! Again, a bird in hand is better, but a few solid growth stocks can enhance your returns without a huge volatility consequence.

Does the Company Have a Low and
Flexible Cost Structure?

You've heard the old expression, "It's hard to turn a battleship on a dime." Imagine owning a bunch of steel mills or railroad tracks, compared to a bunch of coffee shops; which company is more likely to be volatile? The one with the higher fixed costs and more intense capital structure, because it can't change quickly to adapt to business or marketplace conditions. And when it can't adapt, it can quickly lose money when things change.

Similarly, a company with a high employee count (per dollar of revenue or profit, as it's sometimes measured) or high capital replacement requirements, like an airline, is usually more subject to volatility. It's not necessarily that these are bad businesses or businesses to be avoided; it's just that their business structure makes them more vulnerable to change, and hence more volatile.

Is There Too Much Debt?

Many consumers have this problem, and so do many countries. Your financial situation is more volatile if you're deeply in debt and, as we know from reading the headlines about Europe, it's also true for countries. So why wouldn't it apply to businesses? Well, in fact, it does.

The analysis of appropriate debt levels for a business is, again, a more complex subject than can be dealt with completely here. Suffice it to say that a company with more debt is generally more volatile than one with less debt, particularly when comparing it within an industry. Like a high fixed-cost structure, more debt makes a company more vulnerable to headwinds because it can't tap that resource anymore to make change or invest in the business. It's harder to turn the battleship.

Evidence that debt is increasing is pretty easy to find. You can look at total debt levels—once again, Value Line is a good source of history—or persistent debt financing showing up in the Statement of Cash Flows under Cash from Financing Activities. Either way, it's a bad sign. Higher debt exposure usually means more volatility.

Share Count: Friend or Foe?

Just based on the statistical principles of large numbers, it seems intuitive that a company with large numbers of shares outstanding (and high trading volumes, or liquidity, in the markets) will be less volatile. Why? Because it's less likely that a single event will shake loose the thousands upon thousands of owners to do the same thing—sell—all at once.

With greater numbers of shares, and greater numbers of share-owners, it's more likely that the differences of opinion between those who are positive and those who are negative, or those who choose to do nothing, will prevail, and that any dip (or rise) is less pronounced. Companies with very large numbers of shares—say, over a half billion—are more stable, at least in my observations, than those with a low share count—say, under 100 million. If you choose a company with less than 100 million shares outstanding, a big hiccup or change of sentiment has more effect simply because there are fewer shareholders, and it's more likely they'll all run the same way at the same time.

The share count itself is not the only factor to consider. I also like to know the trend, that is, whether the share count is increasing or decreasing. A decreasing share count means that management may have the inclination—and has the means—to buy back shares to reduce the share count and to ultimately return some value to shareholders by raising the earnings per share. It's like a dividend, except that the remaining shareholders don't actually get the cash; they get more valuable shares, while the selling shareholders get all the cash.

Share buybacks have become a huge part of corporate returns in recent years, with some $400 billion bought back in 2012 alone. In my book, if a company is buying back a lot of shares—say, 1 to 5 percent of its float annually and regularly—it's a sign of stability in the business (else the company wouldn't have the means) and solid management acting in shareholders' interest (else they wouldn't have the inclination). Both are signs of reduced volatility going forward.

Of course, if the company issues a lot of debt to do the buybacks, and drives share counts down low enough to make them more vulnerable, this premise of reduced volatility goes out the window. By the same token, a company increasing share counts regularly over time is also suspect unless solid, organic expansion—that is, not by acquisition—is the result. A company that depends on acquisition for growth will be more volatile, both because of the uncertainties and costs of acquisitions and because of the underlying truth that it isn't able to grow its existing business, although it may take some time for those chickens to come home to roost.

Bottom line: seek companies with medium to large share counts and a predisposition to reduce them to reduce volatility. There are a lot of exceptions to this rule, but again, we're looking for tailwinds.

Does the P/E Compare Favorably?

Over the course of stock market history—at least as measured by the S&P 500 Index—the price-to-earnings ratio has centered at about 17.5. What does that mean?

First, it suggests that the market expects a return to shareholders of about 5.7 percent on a stock investment. How did we get that? Simply take the reciprocal of 17.5 percent, or 1 divided by 0.175, to calculate the expected yield implied in the figure. If you recall the annual inflation rate of 2 to 3 percent and the longer annual growth in GDP at a similar rate, the 5.7 percent return expectation isn't too surprising when taken as an average across all stocks.

Now, what does it mean when a stock has a P/E of 25? Does it mean that investors expect only a 4 percent (1/0.25) return on the stock? Maybe, but it's more likely that they expect the earnings to grow to the point that the P/E would revert to 17.5 and have priced the stock high now in advance of that occurrence. So, if the earnings per share of a stock were $1.00, investors on average would price the average stock at $17.50. To reach the $25 price level and to have the market P/E of 17.5, earnings would have to rise to $1.42 per share: a 42-percent increase.

Of course, many companies are capable of such an increase, especially if, like most, investors are willing to allow enough time for that to happen. But if the growth train derails, look out! If the earnings don't correct upward to meet investor expectations, the price will correct downward; translation: volatility.

This is a roundabout way to explain the premise that stocks with a higher-than-market P/E are likely to be more volatile, while stocks with a lower P/E are likely to be less volatile. Low P/E stocks are implicitly returning more to investors and aren't so much priced for future expectations (and hopes) that may not become reality.

Many investors choose to divide P/E by the earnings growth rate as experienced or forecast for the company, arriving at something called PEG—the price to earnings to growth rate. A PEG of 1 (P/E of 25 with a growth rate of 25 percent) is considered reasonable, while a PEG in excess of 3 is considered risky and speculative: the price has gotten ahead of current earnings and the projected growth rate.

Bottom line: to enjoy volatility tailwinds, look for P/Es less than the market and PEG readings of 1.0 or less.

Table 7.2 presents summarizes financial and operational tailwind factors:

TABLE 7.2

Summary of Tailwind Factors of Financial and Operational Excellence

Financial and Operational Excellence Factors
Are Cash Flows and Earnings Steady and Predictable?
Are Margins Steady and Growing?
Are Dividends Steady and Growing?
Does the Company Have a Low and Flexible Cost Structure?
Is There Too Much Debt?
Is Share Count a Friend or Foe?
Does The P/E Compare Favorably?

PROVIDING A MARGIN OF SAFETY

When value investors evaluate the purchase of a stock, they look at a number of fundamental and intangible factors to come up with an appropriate intrinsic value for the business and its share price. The calculations aren't perfect and are beyond the scope of this book (see my *Value Investing for Dummies* for a more formulaic approach). But whatever they determine as a fair price for the business, one enduring principle then deployed is to build in a margin of safety.

There is no formula, and any assessment you make of a company's value is, to a degree, subjective. So you build in an extra buffer, usually by seeking to buy the stock at a lower price than you or the market thinks it might really be worth. I can't give you any formula for doing this, but if you buy cheap, you take less risk (you reduce risk) down the road.

Buying at a relatively low P/E when looking at history (Value Line, again) is one measurable way to incorporate a margin of safety. However, you need to beware of substantial business changes that might be changing future expectations and growth rates, and thus lowering P/E for the moment. Similarly, extraordinary adjustments (down or up) to earnings can affect P/E calculations. If you can eliminate these factors, buying at relatively low P/Es can help reduce volatility.

HOW DO I CONSTRUCT A PORTFOLIO AROUND LOW VOLATILITY STOCKS?

This chapter has been concerned mainly with identifying and buying low volatility stocks, primarily as a component of the foundation portfolio outlined in Chapter 6. It doesn't go into the evaluation of more aggressive stocks that might be part of the opportunistic portfolio, but you can easily see that enhanced returns, not reduced risk, are the objective, and what you're looking for are companies with better-than-average growth prospects, not just low volatility. If you're lucky, you'll find companies that combine the two, but your bias is toward growth, not the reduction of volatility.

Almost any stock you buy is more volatile than a fund constructed of a number of similar stocks because of the diversification and canceling out features we've already discussed. So while individual stocks have their place in your foundation portfolio, they will (even if you're Warren Buffett) probably be more volatile than equivalent funds but should, if chosen right, enhance your returns. What this really means is that an ideal low volatility portfolio, at least for most investors, should have a mix of funds and stocks: funds to dampen volatility just a bit more and add a measure of professional management and stocks to enhance returns and avoid bringing in the losers with the winners, as most funds do. You'll find your right mix over time.

Chapter 8 gives insight into the selection of low volatility funds and other investments to complement stocks, and Chapter 10 gives more insight on how to put it all together.

TIME OUT FOR A BRIEF COMMERCIAL MESSAGE

So far you've watched (and hopefully enjoyed) this commercial-free broadcast of *All About Low Volatility Investing*. That's about to change.

Especially if you intend to build individual stocks—companies—into your low volatility portfolio, the first question you may be asking is something like "Where do I start?"

It's a good question, because there are a lot of companies out there. I have a resource that should narrow down your selections somewhat: my annually updated *The 100 Best Stocks to Buy*, written with my good friend and colleague Scott Bobo, and published by my good friends at Adams Media. These best stocks are selected using all the principles outlined in this chapter: marketplace excellence, dividends and dividend growth, low beta, and so forth. Our list of *100 Best Stocks* continually beats the markets, in both up and down markets, which is what you want to do.

So follow the cars (or the mouse clicks) and pick up a copy. Bet you'll be glad you did.

KEY CONCEPTS

▶ Low volatility stocks make sense for most foundation portfolios.

▶ Dividends, beta, size, and growth are core indicators of low volatility.

▶ Stock screeners can easily narrow down candidates using these core indicators.

▶ Forward-looking characteristics can be divided into two categories: Marketplace Excellence and Financial and Operational Excellence.

Beyond Stocks: Funds and Other Stuff

"A ship is safe in port. But that's not what a ship is for."

This prescient quote, borrowed from the Introduction, sums up the feeling low volatility investors may have when they shy away from buying stocks in favor of funds or other investments, professionally managed or otherwise. They want the security, safety, and techniques of the professionals. They want diversification. They want the price stability of fixed income investments. They want to have lots of eggs in a lot of different baskets. But they still want to sail the high seas of investment returns, because they know they must get somewhere financially. They want to achieve better-than-market returns in calm seas or rough, beating the market in an up market and losing less than the market when the going gets tough.

This chapter is all about deploying funds and other stuff, the other stuff mainly being bonds and other fixed income investments, real estate, commodities, and currencies. However, it's not just about playing defense, although we do seek a more secure portfolio in tempestuous times. It's also about generating a little offense, some market return for the entire portfolio. We may have some of our investing ships in port from time to time, but we recognize that ultimately the fleet must sail.

Funds and other stuff will give you greater diversification and, in almost all cases, lower volatility than picking stocks alone. When funds are used, the law of large numbers and the inevitable fact that some component investments will cancel each other out almost guarantee lower volatility. But that guarantee comes at a price—two prices, really. The first is the direct cost of the fund or alternative investment: funds in particular aren't free. Then there is the likely sacrifice of potential gains, as a fund is mathematically more likely to converge toward market performance, while the other stuff is more defensive and less likely to achieve substantial returns.

All that said, as a fund investor you may be quite willing to pay this price, often minor, to achieve greater stability and to spend less time analyzing and worrying about your investments. And some funds, and especially the other stuff, actually may hedge a portfolio by moving in the opposite direction; it's nice to have at least a few green arrows in your portfolio while everything else is falling hard around you. Thus, funds and other stuff are important components of a low volatility portfolio, especially foundation and rotational investments. You may even decide to use funds entirely, especially some of the new low volatility funds designed specifically to achieve our low volatility objectives.

There are two points to this chapter. One is to give a healthy perspective on just what funds and other stuff do and how they fit into the low volatility investing framework. The second is to share a few tips about how to pick good candidates. What this chapter does not do is go into a lot of detail about how funds and other stuff work: how to buy and sell them or how to do a full-blown evaluation. That subject is left to other books or the numerous websites operated by brokers, fund managers, and other industry players. The emphasis here is more on strategy, less on tactics.

Funds and other stuff includes:

- Mutual funds and exchange-traded funds (ETFs)
- Bonds and other fixed-income investments
- Real estate
- Commodities
- Currencies

Again, this is kind of a field guide approach to these invest-ments for those with a low volatility set of binoculars. It is not a zoology textbook.

USING FUNDS AND OTHER STUFF TO MANAGE RISK

At days' end, the main reasons to use funds and other stuff are to reduce volatility by diversifying, to add a layer of professional management and technique, and to save some time. If you recall, the main strategies to reduce volatility, borrowed from the insur-ance industry, are to avoid, reduce, or transfer risk, or to simply accept and absorb it.

With these choices in mind, funds and other stuff can do the following:

- *Avoid risk*: A stock fund can help you avoid internal or unsystematic risks, like the BP disaster or some major man-agement goof, which might kill a single company. You can avoid stocks altogether by perhaps buying real estate, gold, and other commodities or currencies. Don't like interna-tional stocks? European stocks? U.S. stocks, for that mat-ter? Funds can be chosen to avoid risk in certain markets, small-cap stocks, or even certain industries like technology, the First Trust NASDAQ 100 Ex-Tech ETF being an excellent example.

- *Reduce risk*: Funds do it through diversification and safety in numbers, professional management, professional tools, and access to information. Other investments, like gold or real estate or, to a lesser degree, bonds, reduce your exposure to external, internal, and personal risks, particularly those posed by government policy, economic cycles, and imperfect markets.

- *Retain risk*: Funds, in particular, can help you absorb risks more easily by better quantifying the risks you'll take. The sheer size and history of most funds make it relatively easier to project both volatility and returns going forward than with individual investments. The certainty gained and the hand-holding of professional management make the risks easier to take—to *absorb*—going forward.

- *Transfer risk*: Most of the investments in this chapter stop short of allowing you to transfer risks to someone else, although the inverse universe of negatively correlated funds allows you, in a sense, to transfer the risk of market failure to someone else. The idea of options offered in the next chapter is a far purer risk transfer.

FUND STUFF

Funds are investment products designed to package an assortment of investments into a single security you can buy and sell. Risking a dramatic oversimplification, the fund universe can be divided into two main camps: traditional mutual funds and exchange-traded funds, or ETFs. Both types of funds are professionally managed investment companies designed to pool investor assets into the purchase of a portfolio of securities to accomplish a stated objective. The value of the investment changes according to the value of the component investments.

Traditional mutual funds are the legacy and have been a primary investment vehicle for individual investors for over 50 years. There are about 14,000 such funds holding about $13 trillion in assets, and their purposes and stated objectives run from soup to nuts, as you might imagine. Most are managed by large investment companies like T. Rowe Price, Franklin-Templeton, Vanguard, and other more-or-less household names, and they might cover broad swaths of the market or be more of the boutique variety. Most but not all have professional management with a head fund manager and a staff of analysts supporting what is chosen for the fund.

Traditional mutual funds offer the advantage of professional management and a diverse selection. Disadvantages have crept in over the years, including high expenses (you have to pay for those managers and provide a profit margin for the fund company, as well as marketing, euphemistically known as 12b-1 fees to recruit new investors) and a kind of unwritten but often observed need to follow the institutional imperative: fund managers follow other managers so as not to be perceived as taking excess risks.

Both of these factors have led to a measured underperformance of traditional mutual funds as compared to the markets they're aligned with, typically the S&P 500 Index. Translation: you would be better off buying a simple index fund (tracks the market, far lower expenses). Traditional mutual fund packages function more as a tool for professional financial advisors to deploy for individuals than something for the individual to buy and sell themselves, although there are notable exceptions to that, especially the funds dominating most company-sponsored retirement plans, notably 401(k) plans and similar.

As such, I will focus this discussion on ETFs. ETFs are packaged single securities trading on stock exchanges (rather than directly with mutual fund companies) that create a basket of securities not by professionals making decisions but rather through tracking the composition of specially designed indexes. These indexes started out broad, bland, and obvious; the first ETF, the SPDR S&P 500 ETF, has tracked the S&P 500 Index since 1993. But the ETF idea has caught on, and since that inception, hundreds of new indexes have been created to track everything from broad baskets of stocks to the price of certain commodities in Australian dollars.

As of early 2013, there are some 1,391 exchange traded products, of which 1,234 are ETFs and 157 are so-called exchange-traded notes or ETNs, which are actually fixed income securities adjusted in value to track an index without actually owning the components of that index. The ETF space is growing by more than 100 funds every year and has amassed about $1.6 trillion in assets: about a tenth of the traditional mutual fund space, but this is where the puck is going in investment products. There are generalized and specialized ETFs covering stocks, bonds, fixed income investments, commodities, real estate, currencies, and the so-called leveraged and inverse funds designed to achieve specialized investing objectives. Within each of those groups, the segments available could fill a chapter in and of themselves, with divisions by market cap, style (growth vs. value), industry, sector, strategy, country, and region, just to name a few.

In a nutshell, this is why I'm choosing to focus on exchange-traded products:

- They're where the puck is going.
- Designed more for individual investors: easy to understand, screening tools work better.
- Low fees, low cost: typically 0.10 percent for the most generic index funds to 0.2–0.80 percent for more specialized funds, about half of the typical figures found in traditional mutual funds.
- Liquid, easy to buy and sell, easy to rotate investments or buy and hold forever.
- Better transparency, easier to know what they own at any given moment.
- New funds are available specifically adapted to the low volatility style.

You can't (and shouldn't) avoid traditional mutual funds. They have professional managers and can deploy a lot of the quantitative portfolio management tools described in Chapters 4 and 5. They appear as main selections in many retirement plans. Many of the same criteria I'll describe apply to the selection of traditional mutual funds, but you may need some help (or a more specialized portal) to assist you with the selections. I'm not ignoring traditional funds but simply using ETFs as my example.

The most popular new strategies in the fund space today are low volatility, dividend-oriented, commodities in local currencies, active management, specialized strategies (like insider buying, rising dividends), and a shift from Europe to Asia in the international funds. ETFs come with general and specialized objectives and large, medium, and small sizes, with about 82 percent of all ETF assets concentrated in 100 funds. The largest ETF providers are State Street (branded SPDRs), Invesco PowerShares and BlackRock iShares, but there are dozens of others, many operating in small corners of the market.

SELECTING LOW VOLATILITY FUNDS

Admittedly, the last two sections gave only a high-level overview of funds, the selection of funds, the advantages and disadvantages of funds, and how to use them. If you're a beginner, I recommend a longer learning phase before you invest in funds, one that includes financial portals, wiki entries, fund provider sites, and books on the subject. I wrote one of these books, *The 100 Best Exchange Traded Funds You Can Buy 2012* (Adams Media, 2012), which is a bit out of date but can help breed familiarity with some of the best ETFs out there and how they were selected.

With that in mind, I will walk you through some of the important selection criteria to identify ETFs consistent with low volatility objectives. These criteria work well in an ETF screen I constructed using Fidelity's stock screener, available to Fidelity account holders, but similar screeners are available elsewhere.

As with stock selections, my low volatility fund selections are based on a blend of fundamental and intangible factors. Since we're talking about funds here, we aren't looking at forward-looking marketplace factors like brand and customer loyalty as we would do for individual businesses, since funds are an aggregate of many businesses. The selection lies more in measurable fundamentals, but we do take a look at the list of stocks or other investments in a fund to get an intangible sense of the composition of the fund (and the underlying index) before moving forward.

The most important selection criteria include (using the Fidelity example):

- *Fund type*: a basic selection of stock, bond, commodity, currency, or blended funds, simply pointing to the type of fund you want to select.

- *Return to price performance*: shows the gain or loss of the fund, in one year, three years, or five years in Fidelity's case. Be flexible on this one; five-year performance is nice, but if a fund has been around for only four years, the screener will exclude it. I usually run long- and short-term versions.

- *Volatility*: not surprisingly, we get here early on—the typical volatility measures. Again, these measures might be looked at in one-year, three-year and five-year contexts to select in or select out funds with relatively less history:

  o *Sharpe ratio* is best for funds because it examines the performance of the entire portfolio. But you shouldn't look at the Sharpe ratio in a vacuum; you should also understand the components, performance, and standard deviation separately. Because a high Sharpe ratio can be a consequence of a high return or a low standard deviation, you might select a ship in port that gives up a lot of return to get the low volatility.

  o *Standard deviation*: a measure that in our case isn't described formulaically by Fidelity but appears to be the standard deviation of monthly price changes.

  o *Beta*: As described in Chapter 5, beta compares performance to the market, which doesn't necessarily mean it signals low volatility. In the Fidelity screen, the fund beta is compared to the S&P 500 Index if a stock but a bond index if a bond and an international index if an international stock, a nice feature.

- *Expense ratio*: Expenses can directly impact long-term returns, as covered in Chapter 3; good fund choices are available with expenses less than 0.50 percent; many are lower.

- *Number of holdings*: Low volatility investors should avoid overdiversification (too many holdings watering down returns and incorporating the bad stuff), as well as putting too many eggs in one basket. A number between 20 and 120 holdings is best; most solid low volatility choices are in this range.

- *Percent top 10 of total (concentration risk)*: Depending on how the underlying index is constructed, you might end up with an excessive concentration of assets in a handful of stocks even if there's a larger number of holdings. For example, so-called market-cap weighted indexes were overloaded with Apple when that stock recently far outperformed the general market. This criteria can't be selected on (although a related but unexplained concentration risk is available), but it's good to observe when looking at the portfolio composition page.

- *Actual holdings:* Less tangible than the other metrics is the list of actual holdings in the portfolio, which can again be accessed at the portfolio composition page. Look at the holdings (there is a top 10 list and a view all holdings button). It's good to judge whether the portfolio is consistent with what you would be comfortable holding if buying individual investments.
- *Dividend yield:* As with individual stocks, some current return is desirable.
- *Portfolio turnover*: A portfolio that changes a lot may suggest fund volatility and may also generate tax consequences through capital gains if not kept in check. This is more important with actively managed portfolios in traditional funds, as indexes that underlie ETFs don't change that frequently. A portfolio that changes more than 20 percent each year may be suspect.
- *Inception date*: finally, it can help to see experience—how long a fund has been around. If used as a selection criteria, however, you may miss out on some newer (or older) ideas that make sense.

A LOW VOLATILITY ETF SCREEN EXAMPLE

Sometimes the best way to explain something is simply to show an example. Here, I'll go through the setup of a stock screen to capture a set of qualifying ETFs with low volatility characteristics for further analysis. Note: the further analysis part is important!

Fidelity Investments, at www.fidelity.com, has the best ETF screening tool I've found, but there are many others. The Fidelity screener, under the Research and ETF tabs, offers extensive screening variables and ways to qualify those variables—equal to, greater than, less than, top 20 percent, bottom 20 percent—and statistical guides to show you how your selection criteria compare to the median or norm for a particular variable. The screener also shows the number of funds selected for any given set of criteria before it returns the list, helpful in determining whether your screen is too fine or coarse to be useful. You can save the screens for future use. One drawback: you have to have an account to get the most complete set of screening features.

For this low volatility ETF example, you can follow along with Figure 8.1, below. I didn't use all the criteria listed above, only those I felt were most important. I centered the search on the Sharpe ratio: the measure of return divided by risk, as expressed by the standard deviation. I added a one-year return and a one-year standard deviation measure to cross-check the Sharpe ratio components, so that I didn't land on something that had a very low return but also a very low standard deviation. (I used the one-year figures to avoid excluding new funds). I selected stock funds, not leveraged or inverse (explained later under Inverse Universe). I selected expense ratio to avoid high-cost funds, setting the expense ratio at 0.50 percent or less, and added the number of holdings figure to avoid over out overdiversification or underdiversification. Finally, I added dividend yield as a search criterion but did not qualify it to have that figure displayed on my report for all other qualifying ETFs.

You can use this set of criteria, or, of course, set up your own. As you set up your own search, it's interesting to look at market medians to help you define criteria (i.e., set the Expense Ratio to be less than the median), and look at the number of qualifiers at the right to see how selective you've been. This screen returned 19 candidates in early 2013, a nice number for further analysis. If it had returned 300 candidates, I probably would have tightened my criteria. If it had returned two candidates, I would have loosened them. It's interesting to look at market medians so you can position yourself to be lower, higher, etc. The number of candidates returned is also interesting; you can manage up to the number of results you want to evaluate further.

The 19 screen results are shown in Figure 8.2:

FIGURE 8.1

Low Volatility ETF Screen Setup

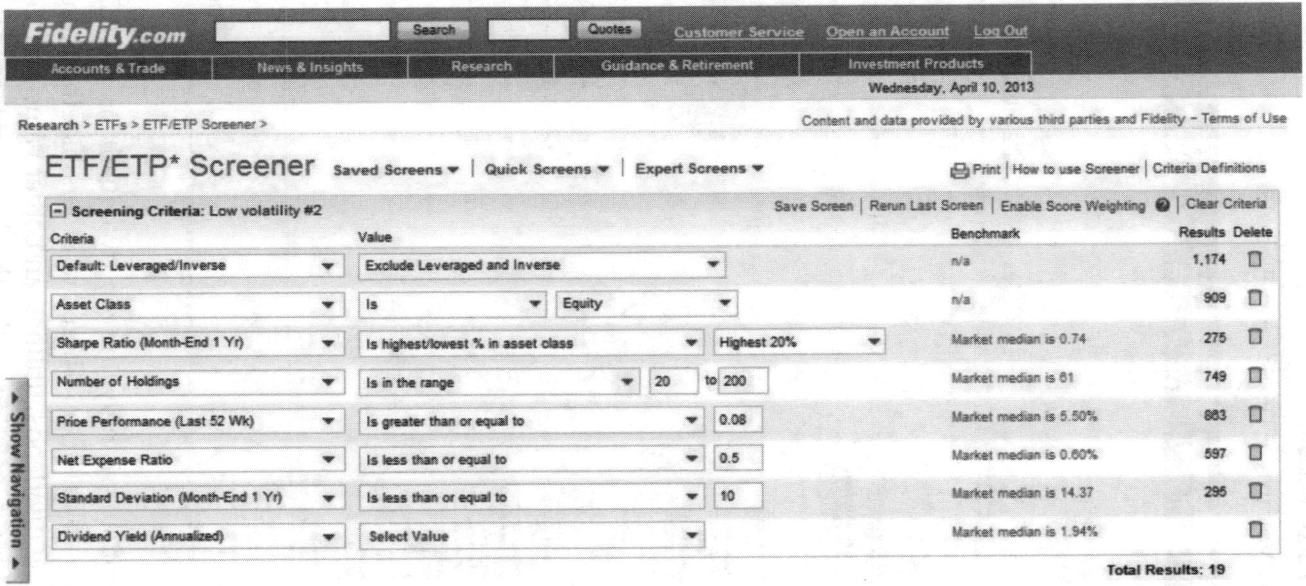

Criteria	Value			Benchmark	Results	Delete
Default: Leveraged/Inverse ▼	Exclude Leveraged and Inverse ▼			n/a	1,174	⬜
Asset Class ▼	Is ▼	Equity ▼		n/a	909	⬜
Sharpe Ratio (Month-End 1 Yr) ▼	Is highest/lowest % in asset class ▼	Highest 20% ▼		Market median is 0.74	275	⬜
Number of Holdings ▼	Is in the range ▼	20	to 200	Market median is 61	749	⬜
Price Performance (Last 52 Wk) ▼	Is greater than or equal to ▼	0.08		Market median is 5.50%	883	⬜
Net Expense Ratio ▼	Is less than or equal to ▼	0.5		Market median is 0.60%	597	⬜
Standard Deviation (Month-End 1 Yr) ▼	Is less than or equal to ▼	10		Market median is 14.37	295	⬜
Dividend Yield (Annualized) ▼	Select Value ▼			Market median is 1.94%		⬜

Total Results: 19

FIGURE 8.2

Low Volatility ETF Screen Results

Action	Score	ETF Name	Symbol	ETP Type	Default: Leveraged/Inverse	Asset Class	Sharpe Ratio (Month-End 1 Yr)	Number of Holdings	Price Performance (Last 52 Wk)	Net Expense Ratio	Standard Deviation (Month-End 1 Yr)	Dividend Yield (Annualized)
☐	87	SELECT SECTOR SPDR-CONSUMER STAPLES	XLP	ETF	No	Equity	2.14	43	+19.83%	0.18%	8.80	2.69%
☐	86	VANGUARD CONSUMER STAPLES ETF	VDC	ETF	No	Equity	2.08	109	+18.59%	0.14%	8.97	2.56%
☐	85	POWERSHARES S&P 500 LOW VOLATILITY PORTFOLIO	SPLV	ETF	No	Equity	2.28	101	+18.14%	0.25%	7.92	2.68%
☐	85	SCHWAB US DIVIDEND EQUITY ETF	SCHD	ETF	No	Equity	1.78	101	+16.21%	0.07%	9.28	2.73%
☐	84	POWERSHARES KBW PROPERTY & CASUALTY INSURANCE PORTFOLIO	KBWP	ETF	No	Equity	2.91	25	+29.35%	0.35%	9.67	2.50%
☐	83	SPDR S&P DIVIDEND ETF	SDY	ETF	No	Equity	2.11	85	+18.46%	0.35%	8.94	2.82%
☐	83	FIRST TRUST MORNINGSTAR DIVIDEND LEADERS	FDL	ETF	No	Equity	2.03	100	+18.91%	0.45%	9.60	3.51%
☐	83	ISHARES DOW JONES SELECT DIVIDEND	DVY	ETF	No	Equity	2.06	101	+15.04%	0.40%	7.95	3.42%
☐	82	ISHARES HIGH DIVIDEND EQUITY FUND	HDV	ETF	No	Equity	1.89	75	+16.89%	0.40%	9.16	3.18%
☐	81	GUGGENHEIM S&P EQUAL WEIGHT UTILITIES	RYU	ETF	No	Equity	2.01	40	+21.05%	0.50%	9.75	3.18%
☐	81	VANGUARD DIVIDEND APPRECIATION ETF	VIG	ETF	No	Equity	1.63	148	+14.61%	0.13%	8.74	2.16%
☐	80	ISHARES MSCI USA MINIMUM VOLATILITY INDEX FUND	USMV	ETF	No	Equity	2.05	126	+17.41%	0.15%	8.39	1.69%
☐	79	ISHARES S&P GLOBAL CONSUMER STAPLES	KXI	ETF	No	Equity	1.92	104	+18.35%	0.48%	9.50	2.43%
☐	78	FUNDAMENTAL PURE LARGE CORE PORTFOLIO	PXLC	ETF	No	Equity	1.70	68	+16.90%	0.39%	9.35	2.26%
☐	77	MARKET VECTORS RETAIL ETF	RTH	ETF	No	Equity	1.96	26	+19.75%	0.35%	9.07	1.71%
☐	77	GUGGENHEIM S&P EQUAL WEIGHT CONSUMER STAPLES	RHS	ETF	No	Equity	2.38	43	+23.41%	0.50%	9.64	2.02%
☐	76	POWERSHARES S&P 500 HIGH QUALITY PORTFOLIO	SPHQ	ETF	No	Equity	1.84	137	+15.82%	0.29%	8.20	1.76%
☐	75	ISHARES DOW JONES US CONSUMER GOODS SECTOR	IYK	ETF	No	Equity	1.88	120	+15.66%	0.47%	8.67	2.01%
☐	73	ISHARES DOW JONES US CONSUMER SERVICES SECTOR	IYC	ETF	No	Equity	2.10	182	+22.54%	0.47%	9.82	1.35%

Fidelity.com — Search — Quotes — Customer Service — Open an Account — Log Out

Accounts & Trade — News & Insights — Research — Guidance & Retirement — Investment Products

Wednesday, April 10, 2013

Total Results: 19

Total results meeting all criteria : 19 AS OF 11:57 am ET 04/10/13

Default View (criteria) — Edit View | Save View | Download

⊕ Don't see a security you expected?

Select an action... — OK

* How Scores Are Determined   ✅ Trade For Free

*The ETF/ETP Screener includes many types of Exchange-traded funds (ETFs) and Exchange-traded products (ETPs). It can include ETPs not registered under the Investment Company Act of 1940.

Not surprisingly, the top two qualifiers are ETFs in the consumer staples sector. There are others like these on the list: ETFs targeting dividends, utilities, and other value-oriented ideas.

More interesting is the third item returned on the list: the PowerShares S&P 500 Low Volatility Portfolio, symbol SPLV. This

ETF is the largest of the new breed of low volatility specialty funds that aim squarely at the low volatility investor's objectives: decent returns with relatively low risk. With a Sharpe ratio of 2.28, an annual return of 18.14 percent (compared to an 11.4 S&P 500 return over the same period, a standard deviation of 7.82 compared to a market average of 14.37, and an expense ratio of 0.25 percent) what's not to like? A closer look makes sense; these funds should be a core idea for low volatility investors.

THE LOW VOLATILITY ETF UNIVERSE

We've discussed low volatility funds with low volatility characteristics. Now we move to Low Volatility Funds: funds set up specifically with a low volatility objective and style. It's nice to have a fund that does exactly what you want to do; it makes for easy selection, especially for a foundation portfolio, so that you can spend your time adding other investments that require more analysis.

Low Volatility Funds select the lowest volatility components (usually measured by standard deviation) of broader market indexes like the S&P 500 or S&P Midcap 400 for the underlying index (in our example, the S&P 500 Low Volatility Index, published and maintained by Standard & Poor's). These indexes are often weighted in the fund inversely proportionally to volatility, so you're getting the highest concentration of the lowest of the low volatility components. These funds work: as of early 2013, the Sharpe ratio has been well above market averages for all Low Volatility Funds. The performance is real: both healthy returns and low volatility are evident from examining the Sharpe ratio components. Most have a decent dividend as well.

As of early 2013, there are 12 funds specifically tied to the low volatility strategy. As the fund market has recognized low volatility as something more customers want, the list, compiled from the ETF Database—an ETF portal at http://etfdb.com—is shown below:

- PowerShares S&P 500 Low Volatility Portfolio (SPLV)
- iShares MSCI USA Minimum Volatility Index Fund (USMV)

- iShares MSCI Emerging Markets Minimum Volatility Index Fund (EFMV)
- iShares MSCI All Country World Minimum Volatility Index Fund (ACWV)
- iShares MSCI EAFE Minimum Volatility Index Fund (EFAV)
- PowerShares S&P Emerging Markets Low Volatility Portfolio (EELV)
- PowerShares S&P International Developed Low Volatility (IDLV)
- PowerShares S&P 500 Downside Hedged Portfolio (PHDG)
- PowerShares S&P SmallCap Low Volatility Portfolio (XSLV)
- SPDR Russell 1000 Low Volatility ETF (LGLV)
- SPDR Russell 2000 Low Volatility ETF (SMLV)
- PowerShares S&P MidCap Low Volatility (XMLV)

SPLV: A Look Under the Hood

When evaluating an ETF (or anything, for that matter), statistics are helpful, but they don't tell the whole story. I always look under the hood, mainly at two things: first, what's actually in the portfolio, and second, how the underlying index is defined and constructed. The index definition explains strategy and a few important tactics, like how the component securities are weighted in the portfolio. The individual holdings show the result, and I like to compare it with my own sense of what should be in the portfolio. My basic question is obvious: "Would I want to own that portfolio?" If the answer is yes, the fund makes sense as an investment.

Figure 8.3 takes apart the SPLV fund, again from Fidelity's Portfolio Composition page:

What's not to like? In fact, eight of these Top 10 holdings are on my *100 Best Stocks to Buy 2014* (Adams Media, 2014) list. These are all strong, stable companies with few surprises, strong expectations, and a good track record for dividends and dividend growth. Check. For further confirmation, it's worth going the next step, to view all holdings.

FIGURE 8.3

The PowerShares S&P 500 Low Volatility Portfolio

Portfolio Composition: **SPLV**
POWERSHARES S&P 500 LOW VOLATILITY PORTFOLIO

31.5799 ⬆ 0.2599 (0.83%) AS OF 12:06:37PM ET 04/10/2013

Trade | Add to Watch List | Set Alert | Hypothetical Trade |

ETP's Prospectus Stated Objectives

The investment seeks investment results that generally correspond (before fees and expenses) to the price and yield of the S&P 500® Low Volatility Index (the "underlying index"). The fund generally will invest at least 90% of its total assets in common stocks that comprise the underlying index. Volatility is a statistical measurement of the magnitude of up and down asset price fluctuations over time. It generally invests in all of the securities comprising the underlying index in proportion to their weightings in the underlying index. The fund is non-diversified.

Holdings AS OF 04/10/2013

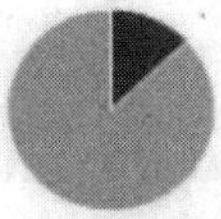

■ Top 10 Holdings	13.13%
■ Other Holdings	86.87%

Top 10 Holdings(Total Holdings: 101)

JNJ	Johnson & Johnson	1.45%
PEP	PepsiCo Inc	1.36%
GIS	General Mills Inc	1.33%
CLX	The Clorox Co	1.32%
HNZ	H.J. Heinz Co	1.32%
ED	Consolidated Edison Inc	1.30%
NEE	NextEra Energy Inc	1.28%
SCG	SCANA Corp	1.27%
CPB	Campbell Soup Co	1.26%
D	Dominion Resources Inc	1.24%

†Part or all of this cash position may represent cash-in-lieu of marketable securities and not actual cash. Click here for more information.
○ View all Holdings by Weight

A Look at the Underlying Index

The best way to learn the strategy of any ETF is to learn about its underlying index, and the best way to do that is to go straight to its source, the index provider. The best way to do *that* is simply to do a search on the full index name. You'll get to the mother site, in this case, the Standard & Poor's website (http://www.standard-andpoors.com). Here's what S&P has to say about their S&P 500 Low Volatility index:

> The S&P 500® Low Volatility Index measures the performance of the 100 least volatile stocks in the S&P 500. The index is designed to serve as a benchmark for low volatility or low variance strategies in the U.S. stock market. Constituents are weighted relative to the inverse of their corresponding volatility, with the least volatile stocks receiving the highest weights.

If you want the more complete mathematical story (for example, "volatility" is based on the standard deviation of the last 252 days' price changes) and weighting methods (methodology is jargon), there are links on this S&P page. From this we know what kind of stocks they choose, and how they're weighted in the index, giving confidence, along with actual performance, that the fund is aligned with our interests.

THE INVERSE UNIVERSE

One way to defeat volatility is to choose investments that don't change a lot and don't move a lot, while producing steady returns over a period of time. Another way is to counter, or hedge against, volatility by buying something that goes up when everything else is going down. As a stock or fund investor, don't you love it when your investments go up while others are tanking? That's the idea behind the inverse universe. You can buy highly specialized funds designed to go up while others are going down.

Such inverse funds are part of a larger family of leveraged and inverse funds, which employ an assortment of tactics including shorting underlying securities, buying downside derivatives (futures and options), assorted swaps, and other financial instruments designed to increase in value when an underlying index declines. Inverse funds go up when the underlying index goes down and vice versa; leveraged funds use derivatives to rise *or* fall by a factor, usually 2× or 3×, the actual index move. A 3× fund is designed to go up three times as much as a move in the underlying index. Of course, it goes *down* 3× as much when the market drops. Taking the concept to its final destination, a leveraged inverse fund is set up to go *up* by 3× the amount of a *downward* index move and will do just the opposite—down 3×—if the index moves up.

So, especially with a 3x-leveraged inverse index fund, you could get a lot of up in an otherwise down market with a relatively small investment. Low volatility investors, using these or other less-leveraged investments, can set aside a small portion of their portfolio, perhaps 3 to 10 percent, to counteract a downward market move, hence hedging their total portfolio risk. Back in Chapter 6 the idea was illustrated by the black triangle in Figure 6.3, showing the tiered portfolio with an inverse component.

Using an inverse investment acts like a counterweight on your portfolio, and using a leveraged inverse investment makes the counterweight heavier. Of course, it acts like a counterweight on the upside: if the markets and underlying indexes rise, you'll lose on a small segment of your portfolio. Note that, unlike options and futures discussed in the next chapter, you can hold on to these instruments forever; there is no time limit. These investments are typically short term and thus rotational or opportunistic in nature but can also be used to provide a long-term hedge or anchor in the foundation portfolio. It gets complicated pretty quickly, so it's best to show some examples to help absorb the concept.

As of early 2013, the use of inverse and leveraged products had grown rapidly as individual and especially professional investors began to use them widely. Fidelity shows 100 leveraged ETFs in its 1,391 ETF universe and 117 inverse ETFs; unfortunately, they don't break out leveraged inverse ETFs in their counts. These ETFs typically go long or short on the major market stock indexes: S&P 500, large cap, mid cap, etc., some with geographic focus and some that focus on individual sectors like financials or technology or even more precise slices, like cloud computing and solid-state drives. Some inverse and leveraged ETFs aim outside the stock market toward gold, silver, Treasury securities, gold mining stocks, and similar.

Sampling the Inverse Universe

Again, the best way to explain can be through illustration. The following two tables are adapted from a stock trading site called TraderMike.net, originally launched by a Stanford-educated professional trader and now run by Reink Media among a set of trading sites. The page at TraderMike, at http://www.tradermike.net/inverse-short-etfs-bearish-etf-funds/, shows inverse funds broken down by families. The following two tables show two of the more interesting and useful families:

TABLE 8.1

Inverse Market ETFs

ETF Name	Symbol	Benchmark Index
Short QQQ	PSQ	Nasdaq-100
Short Dow 30	DOG	DJIA
Short S&P 500	SH	S&P 500
Short Mid Cap 400	MYY	S&P Mid Cap 400
Short Small Cap 600	SBB	S&P Small Cap 600
Short Russell 2000	RWM	Russell 2000
UltraShort QQQ	QID	Nasdaq-100
UltraShort Dow 30	DXD	DJIA
UltraShort S&P 500	SDS	S&P 500
UltraShort Mid Cap 400	MZZ	S&P Mid Cap 400
UltraShort Small Cap 600	SDD	S&P Small Cap 600
UltraShort Russell 2000	TWM	Russell 2000
UltraPro Short QQQ	SQQQ	Nasdaq-100
UltraPro Short Dow 30	SDOW	DJIA
UltraPro Short S&P 500	SPXU	S&P 500
UltraPro Short Mid Cap 400	SMDD	S&P Mid Cap 400
UltraPro Short Russell 2000	SRTY	Russell 2000

Table 8.1 shows 17 inverse ETFs tied to major market indexes: the S&P 500, the Nasdaq 100, and so forth. If these indexes go up, the funds will go down by a corresponding amount. You can choose the S&P 500 as a broad hedge, or go narrower to hedge with the PSQ Nasdaq 100 short fund, if you believe that a market decline might be more narrowly confined to the more aggressive, growth-oriented Nasdaq. The UltraShort series applies 2x leverage; the UltraPro series applies 3x leverage, if you want to get there with a smaller investment and the risk of a larger penalty if you're wrong.

Now, suppose you believe that any future downturn or recession is most likely to hit the financial sector first and hardest, as it did in the Great Recession of 2008. If you really want to tailor your hedge this way, a company called Direxion markets a series of inverse 3x funds that address specific sectors or geographies, as shown in Table 8.2. Again, you can get a big bang for your buck to hedge your entire portfolio, or an aggressive long play in any of these sectors or geographies. As a footnote, some of these come with amusing ticker symbols: COWS for the agriculture sector, SICK for healthcare, and perhaps the best of all, YANG for Chinese markets.

Inverse Universe Pros and Cons

As with all investments, and particularly specialty investments like leveraged and inverse ETFs, one must carefully consider the upsides and the downsides. The upside of inverse and especially leveraged inverse funds is that they give you hedging protection with an increasingly broad set of indexes. A small investment tucked away in a corner of your portfolio can give a relatively large hedge, and can make your overall portfolio more stable. You get the comfort of at least one green arrow in a 300-point Dow drop that will help you sleep at least a bit at night.

The downside mainly centers on cost: These funds are relatively expensive, most being north of 1 percent and higher if fancy leveraging tools are deployed. They're a little like playing with fire—good if you know what you're doing and nothing terribly unforeseen happens, bad if, say, an index that underlies your 3x inverse hedge goes wildly higher. And even if you're more

TABLE 8.2

Direxion Inverse Sector ETFs

ETF Name	Symbol	Benchmark Index
Daily Large Cap Bear 3x	BGZ	Russell 1000
Daily Mid Cap Bear 3x	MWN	Russell Midcap Index
Daily Small Cap Bear 3x	RTY	Russell 2000
Daily Agribusiness Bear 3x	COWS	DAZ Global Ag Index
Daily Basic Materials Bear 3x	MATS	S&P Materials Select Sector Index
Daily Energy Bear 3x	ERY	Russell 1000 Energy
Daily Financial Bear 3x	FAZ	Russell 1000 Financial Services
Daily Technology Bear 3x	TYP	Russell 1000 Technology
Daily Health Care Bear 3x	SICK	S&P Health Care Select
Daily Real Estate Bear 3x	DRV	MSCI US REIT Index
Daily Semiconductor Bear 3x	SOXS	PHLX Semiconductor Sector Index
Daily China Bear 3x	YANG	BNY Mellon China Select
Daily Developed Markets Bear 3x	DPK	MSCI EAFE Index
Daily Emerging Markets Bear 3x	EDZ	MSCI Emerging Markets
Daily Latin America Bear 3x	LHB	S&P Latin America 40
Daily Russia Bear 3x	RUSS	DAX Global Russia+
Daily 7-10 Year Treasury Bear 3x	TYO	NYSE 7-10 Year Treasury Bond Index
Daily 20 year Plus Treasury Bear 3x	TMV	NYSE 20 Year Plus Treasury Bond Index

comfortable with a safer overall portfolio with diminished overall volatility, the volatility of these components, especially when leveraged, can be unsettling. Still, these tools should be considered by experienced and wise low volatility investors.

OTHER STUFF: FIXED INCOME

Now we move on from funds, which are a more or less universal tool to access an assortment of asset classes, to the other stuff. The first stop on the other stuff tour is fixed income investments: investments

that—at least in theory—are designed to retu
income stream with no, or relatively little, ch

Fixed income investments represent the u
model. By investing in bonds, or even more so,
fixed price investments, you're effectively parking yu
in port to earn the expected return while avoiding the hig.
of the rest of the investing world. Recent risk-free governmer.
bond yields in the 3 percent range confirm this, and most yields
for shorter-term instruments with more fixed prices, CDs being
the clearest example, have fallen below 1 percent: less than the
rate of inflation and leaving all aspects of economic growth on the
table for others. Safe, but you aren't likely to meet your investing goals with these investments. And if you venture toward the
mouth of the port to get a little more yield, you will encoun-
ter risks today that most bond investors could have ignored in
the past.

What are those risks? To stimulate the economy, the U.S. Fed
and most central banks have gone on a bond-buying binge to put
more cash into the economy, spur employment, and avoid a costly
and painful deflation cycle like that experienced in Japan. Unfortunately, that has driven bond prices artificially high, creating what
many think might be a bubble that pops or deflates when the central banks eventually stop this practice. That might not be the last
"storm" to hit the bond market, for the excess cash in the system
could also trigger a large inflationary cycle, which could further
erode the price of bonds and reduce the effective returns of other
investments.

So while fixed income investments do indeed reduce volatility (as shown in the chart in Chapter 1) and protect you from
many more obvious financial storms, they are far from risk free.
With lower reward and higher risks than in the past, they still
represent a ship-in-port investment but aren't as immune as
previously to economic storms, the overabundance of debt, and
the whims of public policy. In this section we'll focus mainly on
bonds, and the bond funds that make sense for most individual
investors.

ONDS AND BOND STRATEGIES

In this section, we'll examine some of the risks and commonsense strategies for deploying bonds in your portfolio. As an individual investor, it probably doesn't make sense to invest in individual bonds. It's a complex and murky market; individual bonds are hard to evaluate and transaction costs are high; thus it's more of a world for professionals. You probably won't use most of the more sophisticated quantitative techniques used by major bond players like pension funds to manage risk. Furthermore, with bonds, more diversification is good and overdiversification is less costly than it is with stocks, and you aren't really trying to beat market returns anyway. Thus, your bond ship in port is probably best set up as a bond fund, so we'll give a few pointers on bond funds, bond ETFs in particular.

The Risks of Bonds

Bonds are subject to many of the same external and internal risks as stocks. In most times they correlate negatively—when the stock market sells off, there's a flight to quality—a deliberate reduction of risk—executed by buying bonds, and vice versa. When investors feel more confident, they move back toward riskier investments. However, the Great Recession showed us that at times bonds can be positively correlated, too, and for that and reasons of other risks noted below, aren't always safe in port either.

Specifically, bond investors take on three major risks:

- *Credit risk* is illustrated by the simple question: "Will I get my money back?" Bonds are a promise to pay back an amount borrowed at a specific maturity date, and if a company (or country or municipality) can't meet its obligations, you lose. Investors look for quality (investment grade, AAA rated, etc.) and will try to reduce the time to maturity; less can go wrong in one year than in 30. And for individual investors, buying a fund with dozens, maybe hundreds, of individual bonds goes a long way to reduce credit risk.

- *Interest rate risk*: Bonds are fixed-income investments, and if you buy a bond you expect a certain return. If interest rates today are 3 percent, the price of the bond will reflect that. Now, if market interest rates for that time to maturity happen to rise to 6 percent, what happens to the price of your bond? It will, in theory, be cut in half, to match the return to today's higher market rate. Interest rates traditionally have moved according to economic cycles; today, with central bank intervention, they can change rapidly as a matter of central bank policy. Like credit risks, investors seek shelter from interest rate risk by shortening the time to maturity; less can happen, and the principal will be paid back sooner, so there's less price depreciation to worry about.

- *Inflation risk*: Bonds are bought today with today's dollars (or appropriate local currency) and paid back in tomorrow's dollars. If inflation rises during the holding period, those future dollars will be worth less, driving a decline in the value of the bond. Shorter times to maturity alleviate inflation risks, as do inflation-adjusted bonds like so-called TIPS—Treasury Inflation-Protected Securities—U.S. government bonds that adjust the payout to account for inflation. Like other bond risk factors, investors reduce time to maturity to lower inflation risk, and may also hedge it with gold or other common inflation hedges.

Managing risk means examining credit quality, especially if you're buying individual bonds, and time to maturity. A shorter time to maturity mitigates interest rate and inflation risks, because you're going to get paid back at full price sooner. So volatility—and returns—are reduced. The trick to bond investing is to find the Goldilocks point between time to maturity and return: too short time to maturity and returns will be minuscule, especially these days; too long, and you're rolling the dice on inflation and interest rates. Most ship-in-port bond investors these days are opting for intermediate maturities.

BONDING WITH QUANTS

Professional bond investors, and a select few individuals with enough wealth to manage and the inclination to do it solo, deploy a few quantitative techniques mainly to manage bond risk. Yes, the quants have been here, too, and are well entrenched on the staffs of large investment houses and pension funds that manage large bond portfolios. Are you surprised?

Here are three popular concepts, the first of which especially merits further research if you're a big investor in individual bonds.

- *Laddering* is a strategy for individual bond buyers to reduce volatility and avoid having to redeploy too much of the portfolio at the wrong time. Essentially, you spread the maturities across a number of future years to reduce risk and average out the returns.
- *Duration*—modified duration most specifically—is a rather complex mathematical concept that gets you, at the end of the day, to how much a bond portfolio value will change per a single percent change in the interest rate. A duration of 7.8 means a bond portfolio will decline 7.8 percent for every 1 percent risk in interest rates. Recall that the longer till maturity, the more interest-rate risk you endure, so the longer the average maturity, the more sensitive bond prices are to changes in interest rates. Bond portfolios with low durations have, on average, shorter maturities. Duration is a fairly direct risk measure available as a screenable statistic for most bond funds. Lower duration means lower volatility and risk.
- *Immunization* is a technique not unlike its medical counterpart, where bond portfolio managers inject bonds of differing maturities to optimize risk and returns.

If you really want to become a bond portfolio manager—for your own portfolio or someone else's—you should read up on these concepts. Like most other quant stuff, you can put these concepts into play conceptually without grinding up a lot of computing time.

Types of Bonds

Like stocks, bonds aren't just bonds: there are different types you can buy, along with different maturities, risk profiles, etc. Here are a few of the majors, with a brief description of pros and cons:

- *Government bonds* are issued by the treasuries of major governments. U.S. government bonds come in different sizes and maturities and are generally equivalent to the risk-free investment as repayment is assumed to be automatic—credit risk is zero. But as noted earlier, and as you might expect, returns are low. Large amounts of corporate cash, pension assets, etc., are parked in the port of government bonds.

- *Corporate bonds* are issued mostly by large corporations, and as such bring credit risk into the picture—and, as a result, a chance for better returns. Yields directly reflect credit quality and time to maturity. Investors should look at quality ratings from bond rating agencies (investment grade, AAA-rated, etc), and a look at the company as you would a stock isn't a bad idea either.

- *Municipal bonds* come in many flavors and are issued by state and local governments and various public agencies. They bring a little credit risk into the picture, as these government agencies cannot simply print money to pay their future obligations, and there have been a few bankruptcies. These instruments also carry tax advantages. Yields will typically fall in between government and corporate bonds.

- *High-yield bonds* are, as the name implies, corporate (and some municipal) bonds that pay more than average returns but carry more than average credit risks. You might see yields as much as 50 percent higher than normal corporate issues. It's very important to diversify credit risk away here; high-yield bond funds are the only practical way to play.

- *Convertible bonds* are a special niche in the market, where a bond is convertible into shares of a company's stock at a stated price, usually much higher than today's. As a consequence, they retain the safety of a bond with some appreciation potential, but current returns in the form of interest are

usually diminished and replaced with appreciation potential. These bonds can make sense for some more aggressive
investors still seeking some port safety but are hard to analyze, buy, and sell. Again, funds probably make sense here.

- *TIPS*, or Treasury Inflation-Protected Securities, are special
  government bonds designed to track inflation and pay back
  an increased amount to compensate for it. They are the ulti-
  mate port investment, reducing volatility to near zero and
  hedging against inflation to boot, but return almost nothing today. For me, TIPS (and CDs, for that matter), are not
  just ships in port, they're in dry dock. As such, they could
  be used for a small portion of truly safe foundation capital,
  knowing they will reduce your overall average returns in
  most markets.

- *Floating-rate notes*: To get around interest-rate risks, some
  issuers have started issuing bonds and notes that allow the
  interest rate to float, sort of like an adjustable-rate mortgage. This mitigates the interest-rate risk, but you'll sacrifice some income, especially if rates don't rise. Too, they are
  typically tied to short-term rates and rate indexes, so if short
  rates stay low and longer-term rates rise, you may come out
  behind. If you're worried about inflation or higher interest
  rates, these notes may be a safe low volatility haven, and
  they typically pay better than TIPS. New funds, like the
  Van Eck Investment Grade Floating Rate ETF (FLTR), are
  starting to address this niche; these are worth a look.

BOND FUNDS

Most individual low volatility investors, especially those deploying the tiered approach from Chapter 6, seek to allocate time to
what's most likely to achieve better-than-market returns; otherwise, simple index investments work best. As such, the goal is
to leave much of the foundation portfolio to manage itself. Since
bonds are mainly foundation investments, and funds allow an
investor to take a more hands-off approach, bond funds are the
obvious way to approach bonds.

Bond ETFs are probably the best way to manage the bond part of your portfolio. They're simpler, easier to understand, and easier to use, and since yields are low, expense control is even more important. Why? A bond fund may return only 3 or 4 percent; if you're taking 0.50 or 0.60 percent out as the expense ratio, you're giving up as much as 20 percent of the return for the service.

Good screeners allow you to shop the type of bond, credit quality, maturity objectives, and geography, with the ability to select on return, volatility, size, number of holdings, etc. For most bond ETFs, expenses typically run between 0.20 percent and 0.60 percent. ETF yields range between 2 and 4 percent for investment grade and 4 and 6 percent for high-yield corporate bond funds. These funds typically have 50 to 400 holdings—plenty of diversification. Remember, overdiversification is not as harmful here because you're not trying to beat anything. These funds have very low standard deviations and hence very high Sharpe ratios, as high as 3.

In the ETF space, the sweet spot might be Vanguard Intermediate-Term Corporate Bond ETF (VCIT), with an annualized dividend of 3.3 percent, 47 holdings, investment grade, expenses of 0.12 percent, and a Sharpe ratio of 2.97. Its long-term brother, Vanguard Long-Term Corporate Bond ETF (VCLT), gets a more substantial 4.4 percent yield, but with higher volatility, the Sharpe ratio drops to a still respectable 1.4. A fund with more holdings may be more diverse, but that will drive the expense ratio higher.

The Fidelity screener works well for bonds and, most important, screening statistics are available to individuals without accounts.

ARE YOU A PREFERRED INVESTOR?

Preferred stocks are shares of equity issued by corporations that act more or less as a hybrid of a stock and bond. Preferred shares are paid a fixed dividend and do not share in the earnings and dividend growth of a company. Typically, they are issued by banks and other financial institutions eager to show more equity and less debt on their balance sheets.

As equities, preferred stocks have no fixed maturity date or payback to investors. As such, they yield better than long-term bonds but carry considerable interest-rate risk. There are some convertible preferred issues as well. Preferred stocks go in and out of favor, and are currently in favor as investors seek higher yields. But when interest rates rise, look out. Like most fixed income investments, funds are probably the way to play. The PowerShares Preferred Portfolio ETF (PGX), yielding over 6 percent at press time, might be a good port in which to park some foundation money.

WANT TO *REALLY* REDUCE VOLATILITY? PAY OFF THE MORTGAGE

Got some extra cash to park for a decent return and virtually no volatility or downside risk? Simply put—if you're a home-owner—consider paying off or paying down your mortgage.

You'll get a fixed income equal to the amount you would have paid on the mortgage, maybe 5 to 7 percent if it's an older mortgage. And it can't lose value like a bond; there is no infla-tion, interest rate, or credit risk. The only real risk is to your own liquidity—this cash is now tied up in the mortgage and can't be reclaimed without refinancing—but a home-equity line of credit or something simpler can deal with that. Are you incur-ring home-price risk? No more so, really, than you already were with the mortgage.

Professional advisors sometimes advise against paying off a mortgage. They bring up the diminished liquidity, but that's not an issue if you have liquidity or cheap credit elsewhere. Are they perhaps concerned that you won't have as much invest-ment capital (for them) to play with?

Paying off a mortgage should be considered as an ultralow volatility foundation investment choice.

OTHER STUFF: REAL ESTATE

Time was, not too long ago, when real estate, especially residential real estate, was considered the ultralow volatility investment. "They ain't making any more of it" was the popular mantra; you simply bought and waited for appreciation; depreciation was out of the question.

We all know what happened to that.

Now, to be sure, even with the bubble and subsequent crash, real estate hasn't fared too badly from a volatility standpoint compared to other long-term investments, as was shown in Chapter 1. However, when mixed with leverage, the common practice for most individual investors, the volatility picks up quite a bit.

In my view, one's own home should be a residence first and an investment second. People should buy what they can afford, what they can afford to maintain and keep up, and not get too carried away with leverage. Follow those rules and volatility shouldn't be too much of a concern.

More interesting here is the consideration of real estate as an investment. Most would consider the purchase of rental properties, with relatively steady rents and a gradual mortgage payoff representing returns even if prices aren't growing. The volatility, of course, comes not only from prices but also the absence of renters and the presence of unexpected repair and maintenance costs. This sort of volatility suits some investors and chases others away. Overall, diversifying into real estate makes sense, but the volatility will depend a lot on the specific property involved and your own ability to maintain it and keep it rented. Most important is to avoid too much leverage and to commit too much of your asset base to this form of investment.

The Reality of REITs

REITs, or Real Estate Investment Trusts, should be considered by any investor constructing a low volatility portfolio. Although there are some technical differences, REITs are analogous to funds; they buy specific properties to assemble into a portfolio, typically collecting income from those properties and distributing it to investors. REITs offer the fund advantages of professional management and diversification, and have offered decent returns with moderate market volatility over the years. A recent Fidelity stock screen on Common Stock REITs yielded 235 results with an average three-year beta of 1.17 and recent dividend yields in the 5 to 10 percent range. Unlike bonds, these dividend yields can grow.

You can choose among different types of REITs. General REITs invest in all kinds of properties, but there are residential REITs, hospitality REITs specializing in hotels and hotel franchises, healthcare REITs specializing in healthcare facilities, and geographic REITs specializing in international and other geographies. Most REITs don't use leverage, so you don't run that risk, but leveraged REITs do exist, which will boost both returns and risk. REIT funds, like the Vanguard REIT ETF (VNG), buy baskets of REITs, giving an additional volatility buffer for a modest additional expense.

With the 2008 real estate crash lessons mostly learned and a relatively stable real estate and especially rental market, REITs and REIT funds make sense as low volatility foundation investments. As other stuff investments go, they move the ship a few miles farther out of port toward reaching your investment goals.

OTHER STUFF: COMMODITIES

Commodities are popular low-correlated or sometimes negative-correlated investments to accompany a more traditional stock-bond-real estate portfolio. The traditional wisdom is that commodities support economic growth, but in a different way than stocks—the more growth, the more demand for commodities—and a lot of that growth, as the story goes in recent years, is from China. Additionally, commodities act as a hedge against inflation; the more dollars there are to chase the same amount of goods and services, including commodities, the higher commodity prices go.

Third—and an important principal to commodity investors—commodities act as a cleaner, purer supply-and-demand fundamentals investment. That is, you don't have to invest in a management team, you don't have to be right about consumer preferences, channel strength, etc.; you take these internal risks out of play when you buy commodities. You aren't vulnerable to managers who fail to understand the business or change in the business or, worse, aren't looking out for shareholder interests.

All that said, you do retain external risks of the economy and economic policy, and you do retain the personal risks of emotion and less-than-rational trading in the markets. Commodity markets and trading are a more specialized activity, largely done through derivatives (to avoid truckloads of soybeans being dumped in your driveway) and specialized brokers operating under less stringent rules, as many traders trading through MF Global, a trading company that ran aground in late 2011, discovered.

Commodities also take on another problem directly related to their supply-demand behavior: demand begets supply—that is, as demand grows, prices rise, and farmers plant more corn, miners mine more gold and silver, households sell jewelry, and so forth—thus causing a rise in supply. What might appear to be a favorable supply-demand balance can change quickly. As such, and for other reasons, like droughts, mine troubles, and policy, commodities can be quite volatile. Commodities like precious metals and energy can be negatively correlated at times. Most have low (not negative) market correlations, but they tend to have higher correlations than most people think, and can be just as vulnerable as equity investments in tough economic times. They probably should be used sparingly in a low volatility portfolio, mainly as a hedge against long-tail economic events and inflation.

As with bonds, funds and especially ETFs can be a good way to inject some commodity exposure into a portfolio. ETFs cover narrow and wide bands of the commodity space, from gold, silver, or oil specifically, or precious metals and energy or agricultural commodities or softs as a group. Funds that invest in physical assets, or ETNs tied directly to a commodity price, are usually better than funds that invest in futures, as the next box explains.

CAN YOU CONTANGO?

Actually, you probably don't *want* to contango if you're a commodity fund investor.

The first commodity ETFs specialized in buying commodity futures, the common way for individual investors to play commodities. That was fine, except many, like the U.S. Oil Fund (USO), regularly lost money, even when the underlying commodity went up in price. Why? Because of what market pros call the *contango effect*.

These ETFs bought futures contracts, whose price, by definition as a derivative, was driven by volatility and the time to expiration (see the Black-Scholes model explanation in Chapter 5 if this isn't clear). Each time a contract was purchased there was some premium in the price for time-to-expiration possibilities. As the contracts moved toward expiration, that premium decayed normally. When the contract expired, the fund may have recorded a gain, a loss, or stayed the same, but had to enter into, or roll over into, another contract, paying the premium once again. These ongoing payments of premiums ate into the gains and even, in some cases, produced losses on gently rising underlying prices.

To avoid contango, simply invest in physical asset holders or high-quality ETNs—or special futures funds designed to avoid contango.

As of early 2013, there are 128 commodity ETFs available on the Fidelity ETF screener, including 23 leveraged and/or inverse funds. Of the 128 ETFs, 78 are of the ETN type; they don't invest in futures or physical assets. (It should be noted that because of obvious physical characteristics, most physical asset funds are in the precious metal segment.) Of the 128 funds, 27 are in the Agriculture sector, 32 are in Energy, 18 are in Industrial Metals (aluminum, copper, tin, zinc, lead, etc.), 30 are in Precious Metals, and the rest are considered "Multi" commodity investments. The expense ratio averages 0.60 percent, not insignificant, and can run a lot higher, although many higher-volume, less-specialized funds do better.

You can screen on expenses and common volatility measures, like beta and standard deviation. Beta, in this case, is correlated against standard commodity indexes, not the S&P 500, and you'll see a wide variation of beta figures. Searches across the commodity fund space will show a high variation of beta from one fund to another. Standard deviations are similar to those found for stocks but, again, with a high variation from one fund to another.

Solid portfolio hedges against long-tail economic disasters might include the SPDR Gold Fund (GLD), which holds physical gold and is priced at roughly one-tenth the actual spot price of the metal. The ETFS Physical Precious Metal Basket Shares (GLTR) are also worth a look. Energy plays are harder because it is more difficult to avoid contango; some funds do it through specialized hedging strategies, like the PowerShares DB Energy Fund (DBE), but expenses for all energy funds are higher than the commodity average of 0.60 percent. Shop carefully. Agriculture commodities have the same problems, but the E-Tracs UBS Bloomberg CMCI Food ETN (FUD), a broad play on all food ingredients, is worth a look.

Adding a sprinkling of these funds to your asset base may help you sleep at night, as well as help reduce overall portfolio volatility, especially in highly volatile stock markets. But a little goes a long way, and most do not provide much insulation against volatility over the long term. Shop carefully.

CURRENCIES

When you think of buying and selling international currencies, what immediately comes to mind is rapid, fast-paced, 24-hour trading—speculation—in currencies. While this image prevails, and isn't altogether inaccurate, it turns out that currency fluctuations are relatively much lower than equity and most other markets. A one-cent change in the dollar against the euro is headline news, though it is less than 1 percent in reality. If you look at any currency chart, especially one showing percent changes, it will show relatively mild volatility.

Why do currencies appeal to some low volatility investors? Because, first and obviously, they don't move much. As with commodities, no surprise earnings reports or competitive action will knock a currency out of bed. Second, if you follow (and understand) policy, you can see pretty much where a currency is headed over the long term; a currency accompanied by low interest rates, aggressively stimulative economic policy, trade deficits, and government budget deficits will decline in value.

In recent years, the United States and, now, Japan, follow this model, and many U.S. investors choose to hedge against current inflationary policies by buying currencies, especially in countries with solid economic fundamentals (like Norway or Switzerland) or with strong commodity export bases (like Australia or Canada). Both are viewed as strong hedges in case of longer-term dollar malaise, which could result from current policies of flooding the economy with cash, and could be aggravated by, say, a bond market crash or some other dollar crash trigger.

Again, for low volatility investors, funds are the right way to play this space. There are 36 currency funds in the Fidelity ETF space, all giving some form of protection from decline in the value of a dollar. The PowerShares DB US Dollar Bearish Fund (UDN) is a general play; the WisdomTree Commodity Currency Fund (CCX) is another play, but be warned that expenses in the 0.40- to 1.00-percent range can eat up modest potential gains pretty quickly.

I will also step outside my normal methods at this point to mention a colleague, Axel Merk, who runs a series of traditional mutual funds targeted toward currencies and writes an exceptional newsletter explaining the impacts of policy change on currencies and international economics. His company is Merk Investments, well worth a look (and newsletter signup) at http://www.merkinvestments.com. If you believe in currencies and really want to leave the driving to someone else, this is the place to go.

KEY CONCEPTS

▶ ETFs are probably best for low volatility investors; they are less expensive, more transparent, diverse, and easy to screen.

▶ Specific ETFs that use a low volatility strategy are now available.

▶ With any fund, it's important to look under the hood to see what the fund owns.

▶ The "inverse universe" gives you an easy way to hedge your portfolio against volatility.

▶ Bonds carry more risk today than most think, and three kinds of risk ongoing. Consider bond funds or even paying down a mortgage to give bond or bond-like exposure.

▶ Commodities can be a good hedge against poor business performance. Specialized commodity ETFs and ETNs are probably the way to go.

▶ Currencies can work as a low volatility inflation hedge.

CHAPTER 9

Playing the Other Side of the Table: Using Options to Reduce Volatility

Options are derivatives. Now, when most investors—especially low volatility investors—come across the word *derivatives*, the small hairs on the back of their necks immediately tense up and stand at attention. Low volatility? Derivatives? Can't use those two words in the same sentence, can we? Yikes!

Gamblers, among others, know that there are two sides to the table. (Oh my, now we're bringing *gambling* into the discussion?) I hear you cry—but have no fear, because gamblers know that they take one side of the table and the dealer, or house, takes the other. Most games are set up so that the money is made by the dealer off the risks taken by the gambler, while the gambler hopes to get lucky once in a while. The dealer (and the house) make most of the money off the risks the gambler is taking. In the leading strategy we will introduce in this chapter, known as selling covered calls, you'll learn to play the house side of the table. In the two other strategies, you'll learn ways to *transfer* your risk to someone else, as if you're working with an insurance agent.

This isn't a book about derivatives. If it were, we probably wouldn't be including low volatility investing in the title. Instead, it is about reducing volatility in your portfolio. It turns out that if you take the right side of certain option plays, you can *reduce* risk or *transfer* your risk to someone else. You can bend the risk/reward curve in your favor, to protect yourself against long-tail events, turn potential volatility into current cash, and limit your overall downside risk.

Now, back to the word derivative for just a moment. A *derivative* is, according to Wikipedia, a "financial instrument which derives its value from the value of underlying entities such as an asset, index, or interest rate." Derivatives are used most often to gain leverage or to hedge an investment; the price of a derivative does not move one-for-one with the price of the underlying asset. The world of derivatives is very complex; some derivatives trade on exchanges, while others, like swaps, are created by hand to service the needs of individual traders. We will focus on the most common and transparent exchange-traded variety of derivatives: equity (stock) and index options.

This chapter is about how to use derivatives to both boost income and hedge a portfolio, two objectives consistent with the premise of low volatility investing. We will explore three strategies:

- Buying *put* options to *transfer* downside risk
- Selling *covered call* options to earn current cash and *reduce* downside risk
- Buying *call options* on riskier stocks to *reduce* downside risk

Before examining those three low volatility strategies, we'll first do another field guide—not a textbook—on put and call options, what they are, and how they work. Then, consistent with other parts of this book, we'll explore the three different strategies above for using options to reduce volatility, with brief discussions of the mechanics and an example.

KNOWING YOUR OPTIONS: EQUITY, INDEX, AND OTHER

In the past 20 years, markets for listed or exchange-traded options have flourished. Options can be bought and sold for thousands of companies, large and small, and on specialized investments, like ETFs or even stock indexes themselves. The Chicago Board Options Exchange (CBOE) is the largest trading venue, but there are others.

The CBOE and its accompanying training and educational materials (http://www.cboe.com) are some of the best places to become familiar with options trading and trading strategies.

PUTS AND CALLS: WHAT THEY ARE AND HOW THEY WORK

Equity options come in two basic types: puts and calls. A *call* option is a contract to buy 100 shares of an underlying stock at a specific price *on or before* a specific date. The price is known as the *strike price*, the date is known as the *expiration*. So, if you buy one XYZ June 30 call, you are buying a contract allowing you to buy 100 shares of XYZ at $30 each anytime before the June expiration. What do you pay for that call option contract? Similar to insurance, you pay an amount known as a *premium*, determined by several factors expanded on below.

A *put* option works in the other direction: an XYZ June 30 put contract gives you the right to *sell* 100 shares of XYZ at $30 on or before the expiration date. When you buy a put, you're buying protection against a downside move in the underlying asset.

What Are Equity Options Worth?

In the above XYZ June 30 call example, it is easy to see that the option has value at expiration if the stock closes above $30, and is worthless if the option closes below that level. Likewise, the XYZ June 30 put has value if the stock closes below $30. But what is the value of that option before the expiration? In April or May? That's where much of the interest in options arises.

As we first saw in Chapter 5 in the discussion of the Black-Scholes option pricing model, the value of an option is determined by three factors: (1) the difference between the current stock price and the strike price, (2) the time to expiration, and (3) the volatility of the underlying investment. Obviously, if the current price of a security is above the strike price, the call option will have value—and *more* value the larger the difference—while the put option has no theoretical value.

But this value, sometimes known as *intrinsic* value, is just one factor. The longer the time to maturity, the more events can occur that will change the fortunes of the underlying investment, and the more chance the stock price has to exceed the strike price. Thus, an option expiring nine months from now has more possibilities than one expiring next week, and will be priced accordingly. Finally, the volatility, or variability, of the underlying stock influences the value of the option. A stock that regularly moves between 20 and 40 has more potential to produce winners for buyers of a 30 call than one that only moves between 28 and 32. Thus, the premium will be higher.

These factors play together in mathematically complex ways to drive the price of options. The Black-Scholes model calculates option values and, while useful, the behavior of prices is best understood by visual experience gained by examining the option chain over time.

Option Chains

An *option chain* is simply the list of available options on a security. For XYZ stock, there may be put and call options trading at 15, 20, 25, 30, 35, 40, and 45. Whether or not an option is available depends on the interest of market makers and the market in general; there simply isn't enough interest in a June 60 call for a stock trading in a 25 to 30 range for market makers to set one up. But as the price approaches 60, that option may appear, and it will appear if it becomes the next strike, that is, if the stock closes above 55.

To see what options are available for a stock, simply enter the stock ticker symbol in a financial portal or a broker site and look for an option chain or similar button, sometimes under an option tab.

Buying and Selling Options

Options are bought and sold through most online brokers. Today's markets are highly liquid, and you can easily see what you'll get if you sell or pay if you buy an option. Most trade in penny increments like stocks. Like stocks, brokers charge modest commissions for trading options contracts (1 contract = 100 shares in most cases); typical commissions run just slightly higher than stocks.

Most of the larger stocks have options that trade in monthly and quarterly expiration increments, and certain very active stocks now trade in weekly expirations. There are also longer-term options known as LEAPS, or Long-Term Equity AnticiPation Security contracts, which have expiration increments up to three years out, usually expiring in January of that year, as in a January 2015 call. Obviously, LEAPS will have a high premium for time value.

Most brokerage websites and, again, the CBOE website offer solid facts and instructional materials covering options, option trading, and option strategies.

WHAT DO I MEAN BY BENDING THE RISK/REWARD CURVE?

Can you fundamentally change the risk/reward profile of an investment? Not really. You can't really change the external, internal, and personal risks of an investment or the world around it, other than by reducing exposure or avoiding the investment altogether. Just like buying car insurance, if you drive, you can reduce the probability of an accident by driving safely, but you can't eliminate accidents altogether. However, you can change the financial outcome of that accident by buying insurance. Changing the financial outcomes in your favor is giving up something, usually money, to get something else: less volatility. That's what I mean by bending the risk/reward curve. Here's how options can help you do that:

- Buying puts is most like buying insurance: you'll take a small loss (paying a premium) to protect against a larger one. It's the most direct way to *transfer* your downside risk.

- Selling covered calls gives up large potential gains in favor of current income. You also get enhanced protection on the downside.

- Buying call options gives up a little cash now to achieve a large possible gain but avoids the risk of a major fall in the price of the underlying asset.

The rest of this chapter explores these three scenarios.

Buying Puts: An Investment Insurance Policy

Puts are the right to sell a given number of shares at a price by an expiration date. Buying a put is analogous to buying casualty insurance as you might for your house or car, but in this case it's for an investment or for your entire portfolio. You're *transferring* some or all of your risk to another party.

Here's how it works. If you buy 100 shares of stock XYZ at $29.50, you might consider buying a June 29 put: the right to sell at $29 by the third week of June. That option gains intrinsic worth when XYZ drops below $29, and so far as your portfolio is concerned, gives you a downside floor for that stock. If the stock drops *toward* $29, the put value will rise, if it drops *below* $29, it is *in the money* and will rise equally with the fall of the stock. Thus, at $29, less the premium you paid, you're 100 percent protected from further downside in the stock. If, in this case, you paid a $1.50 premium for the put, your downside floor is $27.50.

Figure 9.1 illustrates:

FIGURE 9.1

Put Buying Scenario

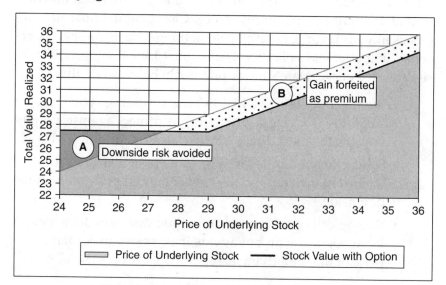

If you buy the put, you're sacrificing the amount of the premium ($1.50 in this case) from your potential gain; that's represented by area B on the chart. But you're getting the downside protection shown as triangle A. If the stock drops to $27.50 or lower, the total value of your investment will remain $27.50. The chart illustrates the bending of the reward curve, from the steady rise to the right representing the stock performance with no options, to the knee curve, shown as a heavy black line, with options involved.

Put buyers are looking for peace of mind. The best time to buy puts is when everything feels good and the markets (or the stocks under consideration) are calm or, better yet, going up. During volatile markets, when most people think about buying puts, the premiums go up because everyone wants to buy puts. The downside of put buying is that premiums paid are real cash and will diminish your returns in a steady or rising market. And, like your car insurance, put options expire and you have to write the check all over again.

Many low volatility investors buy a few puts here and there just for some protection and peace of mind, usually far out of the money to avoid large cash outlays. Some buy puts covering the broader market —on stock indexes or on ETFs mirroring the stock indexes—such as the SPDR S&P 500 Trust (SPY). Recently, a nine-month put covering a 10-percent drop in the SPY ETF (from 155 down to 140) cost $3.80 per put—$380 per contract—and that price will vary according to the market volatility experienced at the moment. In guarding against a 20- percent drop, that $3.80 invested would rise to approximately $15 ($1,500) at expiration if the 20-percent drop occurred.

Some put buyers will take large positions far out of the money (perhaps, 20- percent below the current price) knowing that even a small move downward will drive the put price higher, especially if the down move happens well before expiration. A similar 20-percent down move (strike price $125) sold recently for $1.80. Their goal is to sell when the put moves from, say, $1.80 to $3.60, a 100-percent gain, which could be realized with a far smaller downward move early on in the cycle. They're not only protected, they actually make money well before the put reaches an in-the-money state.

ISN'T SELLING SHORT THE SAME THING?

If you're a more experienced investor, you've heard of short selling: that is, borrowing shares to sell into the market, hoping to repurchase them profitably at a lower price later. Perhaps you've even done it.

Short selling, like buying puts, is a way to bet on downward moves in the market or in individual stocks. It works, and you can hedge a portfolio to the downside by selling short. However, the risk of loss is unlimited, as the markets, or the stocks shorted, can go up forever. In addition, you pay interest to the broker to borrow the stock, and you pay the owner any dividends he or she would have received from the company or fund being shorted.

As a consequence, you really need to know what you're doing. Short selling works, but it's not for the sleep-at-night investor. You can accomplish the same thing with puts, although you do pay a modest amount for the convenience. And for the extra sleep.

Over time, you might realize, especially in volatile markets, that, like most other forms of insurance, such portfolio insurance is expensive to buy. Most investors keep the cost down by buying deep out of the money puts tied to market indexes for that just-in-case scenario, but it also works if you're in a stock that might exhibit some future volatility. All that said, buying puts can give you peace of mind, and it's a worthwhile tool to have in your low volatility bag of tricks.

THE PROBLEM WITH CHASING LONG TAILS

You may recall from the last chapter that the inverse universe of inversely correlated funds gives similar downside protection, mainly for baskets of equities. In some ways it is better protection because it lasts longer: forever, really. The problem is that it takes a larger capital commitment. The chief advantage to the put-buying approach is that you can get a lot of protection for a relatively small premium paid; the disadvantage is that you're dealing with an expiration date; if what you're trying to protect against doesn't happen, you lose and have to pay again. Just like car insurance.

Investors can go nuts chasing these long tails. They know they're right; the markets are overdone, perhaps even in a bubble. But they lose; over and over again. The old adage "The market can stay irrational longer than you can stay solvent" enjoys no finer hour.

If you want to avoid this cycle of paying up for insurance over and over again, you might try the inverse universe approach instead. It's all about choices, and a combination of the two strategies might serve you best at the end of the day.

Selling Covered Calls: Turning Volatility into Cash

Earlier on I explained the purchase of call contracts, that is, contracting to buy 100 shares of XYZ at $30 by the third Friday of June. That trade wins if the price closes above $30 plus the premium paid for the option and brokerage commission by that date.

But what if you *sell* that call option? What if you *collect* a $1.50 premium for allowing someone to buy 100 shares of XYZ at $30 by June *from you*? Picture yourself as the green-visored dealer or insurance agent on the other side of the table and you get the idea. Collecting money by selling options becomes a major play for the low volatility investor, generating both short-term income and downside protection.

Here's how it works: if you buy or own 100 shares of XYZ, you can sell a covered call option (covered by your ownership of the underlying security), usually for a strike price slightly above your purchase price. Why slightly above? It's to get the most time and volatility premium, and to lock in a sale price, if the stock rises, above your purchase price. So you make money on the premium and on a small amount of price appreciation. As an example, if you buy or own 100 XYZ at $29.50 and sell, or *write*, a June 30 call at

$1.50, you'll collect $1.50 for the option plus the 50-cent gain from $29.50 to $30 if the stock appreciates to $30 or higher. You can do this for virtually any stock in your portfolio; you don't have to go out and buy the underlying stock to do this.

What are you actually doing? You are giving up, or *transferring*, the potential of a larger future gain—say, if the stock rises to $34 or $35—for a more certain $1.50 collected at the time the option is sold. You're giving up what *might* happen in favor of a certain current income: a proverbial bird in hand. At the same time, you still retain most—but not all—of the ordinary investment risk that the stock price might decline. Why not all? Because if the stock you bought drops to $28, you still break even, as you sold a call for $1.50 on shares bought or valued at $29.50. If the stock drops further, you lose, but again, the losses are offset by the premium collected plus transaction costs.

Picturing It

Figure 9.2 shows the above transaction graphically:

FIGURE 9.2

Covered Call-Writing Scenario

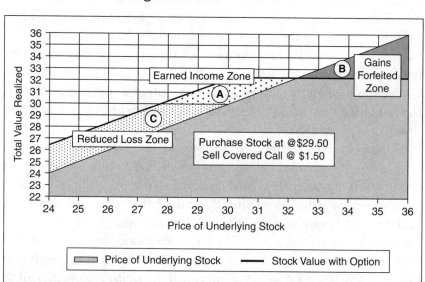

You buy or own 100 shares of XYZ at $29.50 and sell a June 30 call contract for $1.50. The slope of the straight up-and-to-the-right line shows the possible price outcomes with no options involved; you may realize any value along the sloping line.

By selling the option, you transfer a *possibility* for larger gains (B) to the option buyer, receiving the premium—current income—as compensation. The total value of this investment at different price points is represented by the heavy stock value with option line. This is the bent risk/reward curve.

If the stock price goes below $28, you'll lose, but the losses will be reduced by the option premium collected (C). The parallelogram (A) represents the sweet spot of this transaction; that is, you pocket the income, forgo no larger gains, and incur no net depreciation of your capital. Most likely you turn around and repeat the transaction after expiration, collecting another premium for the next option period. If all goes right, sustained short-term income can be generated from your investments.

Writing Covered Calls in Practice

Writing covered calls is a strategy to improve returns by generating short-term income and to play defense by reducing losses. While most people think derivatives and options are risky and not for them, writing covered calls effectively reduces your risk by transferring it to someone else. However, gains forfeited can be significant, and if you take away the upside on all of your investments, particularly with options written for long expiration time frames, long-term performance can be affected, particularly since downside exposure is retained.

Writing covered calls on a limited portion of your portfolio is usually best. That way you preserve upside gains on much of the portfolio. Some stocks may be acquired just to write covered calls. This works especially well on more volatile, lower-priced stocks that command relatively high option premiums. Here especially, you're turning volatility to your advantage: in this case, cash.

Among the best uses of covered calls is to *write*, or sell, them when underlying stocks already in the portfolio reach the high end of recognizable trading ranges. Selling calls on a portion—perhaps half—of the position captures some income while preserving some of the growth opportunity. In sum, covered calls can be used to harvest income and reduce downside risk, and to take some risk off the table from appreciated investments. This explanation doesn't cover all nuances of this strategy, but it gives an idea of how this powerful tool is used, and with practice you'll get good at it.

BUYING CALLS: A WAY TO REDUCE DOWNSIDE RISK

When you sell call options, there is a buyer, and that call buyer takes on risk by betting on the price appreciation of the stock (triangle B in the diagram above). As a call buyer, he or she buys an out-of-the-money call, and unless the stock rises past the stock price, they lose everything. But you also gain *leverage*—buy that XYZ June 30 call for $1.50, and if the stock moves to $35 (a 17-percent gain) you realize a value of $5, a more than 200-percent gain! So you get a larger possible reward, but you also do something else: you limit your downside risk. What's the most you can lose? The $1.50: the price of the option.

So buying calls, in this sense, is a risk-reducing play. When you buy a call, the premium paid is the maximum amount risked. So, if you buy the XYZ June 30 calls at $1.50, the $1.50 is the maximum amount you can lose, whereas if you buy the stock outright, you can lose much, or even all, of the share value, $29.50 in the example. However, since the option has value only when the stock rises above 30, the *probability* of losing everything up to $1.50 is higher when you buy the option.

Many active investors buy calls when stocks get oversold or hit the bottom end of trading ranges, or when they are unsure about a particular investment. If it sounds like a good idea but they want less exposure to the downside, they can buy a call option. In that sense, buying the call option reduces the volatility simply by taking some of it away (as in prices dropping to $27, $26, $25, and so forth. Many also buy calls to get an active but limited downside, exposure) to a sector, a low- or negatively correlated hedge, like gold through the SPDR Gold Trust (GLD), or the broader market itself through something like the SPDR S&P 500 Trust (SPY).

Some active investors buy in-the-money calls as a simple alternative to buying shares. There are two reasons for this. First, if the stock drops or goes flat because of time value and the value of possibilities, these calls tend to decline in value more slowly than the underlying stock, providing some near-term downside protection. Secondly, some investors take an option position to avoid laying out the entire share price of the stock. Keep in mind that the main risk of options comes from the time element: when buying a stock, there is no time limit to achieve a gain—you own it forever—while with an option, the stock must perform in the given time. So while you risk less capital, you do pay a risk premium and you do incur the risk of time.

USING INDEX AND SECTOR OPTIONS

Index, sector, and ETF options extend the concept of equity options into market sectors and collective baskets of stocks. Thus, it becomes possible to buy or write calls on the S&P 500 as a whole, or virtually any other component of the market. As with equity options, low volatility investors can use these options to hedge against other investments and to generate short-term cash. There are options traded on major stock market indexes or averages, and options are also traded on many ETFs, thus giving active investors several ways to use options on major segments of the market.

ETF options allow investors to use them to hedge, generate cash, or gain long-term exposure to a market or market segment. As ETFs represent diversified portfolios, price movements are relatively modest compared to individual stocks, so premiums are relatively low. Still, covered call options can be used to generate some income against ETF holdings in a foundation or rotational portfolio and hedge against a downturn. You can protect from long-tail risks by buying ETF puts, or hedge with an inversely correlated investment like gold (the SPDR Gold ETF is a good vehicle).

ETF options are also a good way to play a vastly oversold market or sector. If the markets take a major spill, one can buy a call option on a SPDR S&P 500 ETF or the PowerShares QQQ Trust ETF (which covers the Nasdaq 100, known popularly as *"cubes"*) ETF. If the index rebounds, there is good upside potential; if it doesn't, or if it declines further, you are only out the premium paid. Keep in mind that, as with all options, the greater the volatility, the higher the premium you'll pay.

As you dig further into options and gain experience, there are lots of other strategies that can be used, mostly to be deployed as combinations of different types of options to reduce and transfer risk. Spreads, straddles, strangles, and others all play with timing, price, and trading ranges of underlying stocks to push the risk/ reward curve around and produce income and/or gains and/or loss protection in the right circumstances. What's been covered so far is probably enough; those more specialized strategies are more for traders and aren't core techniques of the low volatility investor. Likewise, futures contracts and options on futures contracts may also enter the advanced lexicon, but it makes the most sense to stick with equity and ETF options to start out.

GETTING STARTED AS AN OPTION INVESTOR

The concept and use of equity options strengthen with time and practice. Investors new to the game should observe these instruments and their behavior over time, and begin with modest investments. Over time, each investor develops his or her own comfort zone for such issues as whether to trade in-the-money or out-of-the-money options, whether to sell covered calls or buy puts, and what time horizons to use. Investors learn price behavior over time, and to look for what makes sense in the context of their entire portfolios, without committing too much cash or locking in losses or giving away too much potential gain. Active option investors become familiar with certain stocks and their options, and many play short-term equity options on them each month. Others use longer-term options as stock surrogates or to hedge against major downside market activity. The cliché "to each his own" applies well to the strategic use of options.

VIX: A CANARY IN THE COAL MINE OF OPTION OPPORTUNITY

"VIX," or Volatility IndeX, was designed by and is published by the Chicago Board Options Exchange (CBOE). But unlike other indexes, there's no underlying market or basket of stocks. Rather, as covered in Chapter 5, it represents implied market volatility calculated as a single number from actual prices paid for S&P 500 equity options.

VIX serves as a guide to overall market volatility, and thus the price of options. The VIX index ranged from about 11 to about 28 during the 52-week period ending March 31, 2013. The all-time high of almost 90 occurred in October 2008.

A VIX below 15 implies low volatility, signaling a relatively less expensive period to *buy* options because time premiums— either puts or calls—will be lower. A VIX greater than 20 implies high volatility or uncertainty in the markets. High volatility signals relatively high-option premiums, a relatively good time to write or *sell* options. (A high VIX can also signal a good time to *buy* put options as downside protection, but know that your premiums will be higher.) The *trend* in VIX also provides useful signals. Many investors consider a steadily rising VIX as a sign of a market trend reversal, and a good time to sell covered calls or buy puts.

You can trade futures or options on VIX directly, but betting directly on volatility can be a high-volatility game. You can also trade an assortment of ETF products designed to track VIX, like the iPath S&P 500 VIX Short-Term Futures ETN (VXX). But, for most low volatility investors, the best use of VIX is to gauge whether it's a good time to buy or sell options. It's an indicator of opportunity as well as the cost of—and the need for—protection.

KEY CONCEPTS

▶ Options are user-friendly, market-traded derivatives that give low volatility investors opportunities to reduce or transfer risk.

▶ Options can be bought or sold (written) on equities, ETFs, or indexes, giving you ways to profit and/or hedge risk for individual stocks, sectors, or the entire market.

▶ *Call* options are contracts to buy a security at a set *strike price* at or before the *expiration date; put* options are contracts to *sell* the underlying security.

▶ The *premium* is what you pay (or collect) for an option, and it works like an insurance premium.

▶ By *buying puts,* you transfer the downside risk of a security or portfolio to someone else, and *pay* the put premium to do so.

▶ *Selling covered calls* allows you to transfer the opportunity for future gains to someone else, *collecting* the premium as profit and as an offset to your downside risk.

▶ *Buying calls* allows you to participate in a stock or ETF while limiting your downside risk. You pay the premium to limit your risk and to gain leverage.

CHAPTER 10

Getting into the Habit: Becoming a Low Volatility Investor

We've covered the principles and laid the groundwork. The final task ahead is to put the principles together into a low volatility investing style that you can use, one that fits your preferences, your needs, your investment choices, and, most of all, your comfort zone.

Here's how we'll do that in this final chapter. First, we'll tie together the thought processes into building a portfolio that works, a real example. Second, we'll take a broader look out onto the playing field of habits and practices I believe necessary to become an effective low volatility investor, arriving at a set of Seven Habits of Highly Successful Low Volatility Investors you can make your own.

CREATING YOUR LOW VOLATILITY PORTFOLIO

At the end of the day, as a low volatility investor you want an investment portfolio that meets your financial objectives, which for most of us I'll call "retirement plus": a suitable cushion and number for retirement, plus something extra to meet financial goals, needs, and wants along the way. But you also want that portfolio to accomplish those goals quietly, with a minimum of upsets, a minimum of nerves, a minimum of complex mathematics, and, most likely, a reasonable amount of effort on your part, because you're busy doing other things in life.

In Chapter 6 I laid out a tiered portfolio building model, or an asset allocation model, if you choose, that makes sense with these two objectives in mind. It is consistent with the idea of reducing the time you spend analyzing investments. It is also consistent with the idea of saving the cost (and lost opportunity) of having others do the legwork for you. Over time, as we saw in Chapter 3, those few percentage points, even fractions of a percentage point, deducted from your account in fees—or worse, underperformance—can cost a lot over the long run.

That model divided the portfolio into three primary tiers: the foundation portfolio; the largest and most stable base, a rotational portfolio, giving exposure to current trends and favored sectors of the market; and an opportunistic portfolio, set up to capture short-term opportunities to generate short-term cash. Refer to Figure 6.2 to recall the basic model. For our portfolio example, we'll use a relatively conservative construct, with an 80-percent foundation base, as shown in Figure 10.1:

FIGURE 10.1

Sample Tiered Portfolio Base

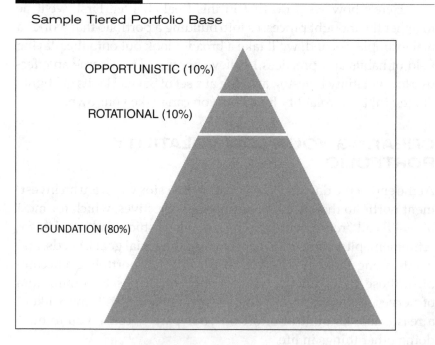

OPPORTUNISTIC (10%)

ROTATIONAL (10%)

FOUNDATION (80%)

Recall that the foundation portfolio is set up to meet or slightly beat expected market returns, often with stable and somewhat defensive investments. Dividend-paying stocks with rising dividends and growing prospects while at the same time exhibiting low downside risk and volatility are a pretty good fit. These investments can be stocks or funds, and can be augmented by fixed-income securities, real estate, or other investments that meet this general profile. The purpose of the rotational and opportunistic portfolios is to achieve better-than-market returns, perhaps with more volatility, but these portfolios are small enough to contain risk and to avoid consuming too much of your investing time and bandwidth.

A LOW VOLATILITY PORTFOLIO CONSTRUCT

To illustrate how all the low volatility concepts presented so far come together, I'll walk you through a sample low volatility portfolio. Keep in mind that this is one way, one construct, out of millions of possible constructs and mixes of investments. It is intended as a model only, not a formula or recipe for a low volatility portfolio. It is like learning how to play chess by watching others do it: no two games, including your next one, will be played the exact same way.

How your portfolio is put together is entirely up to you, not only because the portfolio needs to suit your tastes, intuitions, and the facts at the time, but also because many of the investments (and the mix of investments) may not even be available, or priced right, at the time. An obvious example occurs if you're investing through a company 401(k) retirement plan: you have only a limited set of investments available, but you can fit this retirement account and its available investments—usually funds—into your greater portfolio construct. The portfolio construct that follows gives a general idea of how to set it up, but specific investments are many and varied, and there are literally thousands you can choose from that meet these same goals.

Here's my model portfolio:

The Foundation: 80 Percent

This foundation portfolio is designed to be relatively low maintenance and to concentrate on steady state, low volatility stocks and
funds that produce current income while maintaining some capac-
ity for growth. I divided it into four sub segments, as described
following the table.

Portfolio Fraction	Portfolio Component	Contents and Criteria	Sample Investments
30%	Classic low volatility stocks	• 3–5 Quality stocks • Yield > 3% • Growing dividends • Beta < 0.80	• Kimberly-Clark • Procter & Gamble • Waste Management • DuPont • Abbott Labs
30%	Low volatility funds	• 2–3 Funds or ETFs • Yield > 2% • Beta < 0.80 • Low-volatility strategy • Fixed-income funds	• PowerShares Low Volatility Portfolio (SPLV) • iShares Dow Jones Dividend (DVY) • First Trust Morningstar Dividend Leaders (FDL) • PowerShares Preferred (PGX)
10%	Real estate income	• Yield > 4% • REITs or REIT funds	• Vanguard REIT ETF (VNQ) • iShares FTSE NAREIT Residential Plus (REZ)
10%	Inflation hedge	• Gold • Commodity fund • Currency fund	• SPDR Gold ETF (GLD) • ETFS Physical Precious Metal Basket Shares (GLTR) • Merk Currency Funds (Merk Investments)

The four sub segments:

1. *Classic low volatility stocks* are blue chip issues set up to take
    advantage of economic growth, to get a decent yield and
    raises in that yield while maintaining a fair amount of safety.
    They have a low beta and a solid track record for dividends
    and dividend growth, and are strong players in their indus-
    tries. These—and others—can be found on my *100 Best Stocks
    to Buy* lists (Adams Media, published annually).

2. *Low volatility funds* are added to gain additional diversification and a more scientific modeled or quantitative
   approach offered by the new low volatility style ETFs.
   I listed the SPLV fund, but there are 11 others available
   in that category, and you can also use an ordinary index
   or large-cap fund here, too. Especially at first, you can
   move some of the classic low volatility stocks portfolio
   here if you want to leave the driving to others. This
   segment can also be used for fixed income or other types
   of income funds if you so choose.

3. *Real estate income*: to get some exposure to this traditionally stable, income-producing sector, and exposure to
   other types of real estate besides residential, (i.e. your
   own home). This segment could be a larger allocation if
   you don't own a home; perhaps smaller if your home is
   a big chunk of your entire net worth. If you own rental
   property you may also want to dial back this segment.
   Specialized healthcare, commercial, or hospitality REITs
   can work here, too.

4. *Inflation hedge* is a just-in-case segment tied to preserving
   or even growing value if inflation kicks in and the dollar
   or your local currency depreciates. These investments are
   typically low correlated, sometimes negatively correlated.
   For instance, if commodity prices rise, input costs for the
   steady-Eddie low volatility stocks will rise, creating headwinds for those investments, and commodities will help
   offset this concern. Gold can work here, too.

The Rotational Portfolio: 10 Percent

Here, we're taking a broad view of trends in the economy—up or
down—and trying to get in front of those trends. The rotational
portfolio and the components suggested here are entirely optional,
but they can give you a chance to play certain in-favor sectors
of the market, particularly when it's tough to discern individual
stocks or you don't know enough about individual companies or

investments. Here you may also stash away some low or inversely correlated investments from your inverse universe, investments designed as parachutes—investments that gain in periods of turbulence and high volatility. Having a rotational portfolio isn't mandatory; it's a matter of choice if these sorts of investments work for you.

Portfolio Fraction	Portfolio Component	Contents and Criteria	Sample Investments
5%	Sector Investments	• 1–3 in-favor sector ETFs, e.g., energy, healthcare, infrastructure. agriculture, biotech	• Market Vectors Agribusiness ETF (MOO) • iShares Dow Jones Healthcare Providers (IVF) • First Trust North American Energy Infrastructure Fund (EMLP) • SPDR S&P Biotech ETF (XBI)
5%	Inverse or low correlated	• 1–2 inverse or inverse leveraged funds	• ProShares Short S&P500 (SH) • Proshares UltraShort 2x S&P500 (SDS) • Direxion Daily Financial Bear 3x (FAZ)

The two sub segments:

1. *Sector investments* can be whatever you think is where the puck is going in the marketplace and economy. Healthcare and energy are always popular; less commonly on the radar are infrastructure, biotech, or even something as specialized and new as social media.

2. *Inverse or low correlated* is part of the inverse universe described in Chapter 8 and is specialized, powerful, and somewhat expensive investment vehicles but handy to have when the road gets rough. You can invert the broad market with or without leverage. You can also get more

specific; I showed the Direxion Daily Financial Bear 3x ETF as an example of a tool to use if you think the next crisis might start in the financial sector, if financial companies are particularly vulnerable to rising interest rates, or any of a number of other scenarios.

The Opportunistic Portfolio: 10 Percent

Opportunistic investments are, well, opportunities, and those opportunities can lie almost anywhere. This is your play money deployed more aggressively to seek higher returns and short-term cash. These more aggressive, more-watched investments are put into play to achieve bigger returns, thus acting as a kicker and pulling along the return of the entire portfolio. This should be money you don't fret too much about losing; it shouldn't be your grocery money.

Portfolio Fraction	Portfolio Component	Contents and Criteria	Sample Investments
5%	Hot stuff	• 1–3 ETFs (or stocks) in the hottest or most aggressive sectors or stocks, like emerging markets, cloud computing, etc • SPDR S&P BRIC 40 ETF (BIK) • High beta, greater than 1	• SPDR S&P Emerging Asia Pacific Fund (GMF) • PowerShares Dynamic Networking Portfolio (PXQ) • First Trust ISE Cloud Computing Index Fund (SKYY) • CREE stock, VMWare stock, etc.
5%	Strategy and strategy funds	• 1–3 ETFs investing in special strategies or turnaround situations • Covered call plays	• Individual stock(s) set up for buy/write covered-call strategy • PowerShares S&P500 BuyWrite Portfolio (PBP) • First Trust Value Line 100 (#1 Timeliness) ETF (FVL)

The two sub segments:

1. *Hot stuff* is whatever is making headlines today with prom-
   ising growth prospects. You can invest in individual stocks
   or funds covering emerging markets or a particular country or set of countries, or a hot topic, like cloud computing,
   networking, domestic oil drilling, nanotechnology, etc., or
   in individual stocks like our Cree, Inc., maker of LED lighting and components.

2. *Strategy and strategy funds* are where you deploy some
   capital toward special strategies designed to produce
   enhanced returns. Selling covered calls is an example. You
   can, of course, buy individual stocks to do this, but there
   are also funds (yes, there are funds for almost everything!).
   I've listed the PowerShares BuyWrite Portfolio ETF (PBP)
   as an example. Another strategy idea is to consider stocks
   rated 1 for timeliness by Value Line—and guess what—
   there's an ETF that does this, too: the PowerShares Value
   Line 100 ETF (PVL).

OKAY, SO THERE'S AN ETF FOR EVERYTHING I WANNA DO—HOW DO I FIND IT?

With more than 1,300 ETFs out there, how do you find the one
aligned to the strategy you're looking for? As with most things,
the Internet makes it pretty easy.

Screeners can help, but there are two faster ways to helicop-
ter in on the choices. First, you can do a simple search-engine
search on a strategy, like "Low Volatility ETF," "Dividend ETF,"
or "Australian Currency ETF." It works. You can also check out
the ETF Database at http://etfdb.com. The ETF Database types
page gives a complete list sliced and diced in just about every
way you can think of, with the number of funds that qualify. Want
an inverse bond ETF? An ETF specializing in social media? Rare
earth and strategic metals? You'll find those entries on this list.

Finally, in case you're wondering, Figure 10.2 shows how this portfolio construct looks as a figure:

FIGURE 10.2

Sample Tiered Portfolio

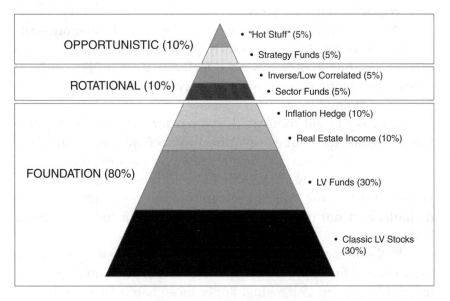

OPPORTUNISTIC (10%)
- "Hot Stuff" (5%)
- Strategy Funds (5%)

ROTATIONAL (10%)
- Inverse/Low Correlated (5%)
- Sector Funds (5%)

FOUNDATION (80%)
- Inflation Hedge (10%)
- Real Estate Income (10%)
- LV Funds (30%)
- Classic LV Stocks (30%)

Remember, this is just one way to build your low volatility portfolio. Start with a clean slate (or with the investments you currently have) and build it up. This probably works best for portfolios exceeding $50,000 or so; otherwise your segments may be spread too thin, transaction costs will be too high, and you won't get enough return to justify the time spent fine-tuning these segments. For smaller portfolios, it probably makes the most sense to retain the Classic LV Stocks and LV Funds tiers in the foundation portfolio and not divide the rotational and opportunistic tiers; just invest in what makes sense at the time. It's easier to manage four sub segments.

And remember, too: This is not an investment recommendation, only a recommended thought process.

TURNING PRINCIPLES INTO HABITS

Investors have obvious goals: to produce wealth and to preserve capital. Anything an investor does should address both goals, preferably simultaneously. As an investor, you're motivated to succeed and, over time, you build a set of strategies and tactics to help you achieve those goals.

When it comes to achieving investing goals, former one-mile record holder Jim Ryun gives us a quote intended for the world of running, but that enjoys no finer hour than in the world of investing: "Motivation is what gets you started. Habit is what keeps you going."

It's easy to get motivated. It's harder to learn the ropes—the skills and techniques—required to become a good investor. But what may be hardest of all, once you gain experience and enjoy some investing success, is to turn those skills into habits. Habits that become built in, second nature, repeatable and predictable, and not only lead to good results but help you avoid bad ones.

Without consistent habits, low volatility investors will make mistakes and find themselves off in the weeds. Good investing habits are like a good golf swing: apply those habits to every investment choice and you won't succeed every time, but your chances for success will brighten considerably.

SO JUST WHAT IS A HABIT?

A habit, according to the online Free Dictionary by Farlex is:

- A recurrent, often unconscious pattern of behavior that is acquired through frequent repetition and
- An established disposition of mind or character.

As an investor, you need to not only learn to do it well but also to do it with some consistency, and do it without struggling to remember what you did last time. As a low volatility investor, you're not likely to be as active trading in the markets as some other investors, and you may not watch as closely. But that said, any investor—active, inactive, aggressive, or low volatility—has a duty to keep up with his or her investments. For the low volatility investor and others, it's important to develop certain habits, routines, or thought processes for:

- choosing investments,
- watching and managing investments, and
- selling or replacing investments.

Analogous to the golfer with a well-learned and repeatable golf swing, or a chef with certain ways of measuring, adding, and blending ingredients, with the right habits, you'll increase the chances for success.

With that, I bring you:

THE SEVEN HABITS OF HIGHLY SUCCESSFUL LOW VOLATILITY INVESTORS

Habit #1: Get and Stay Informed

Earlier in this book I shared a Katherine Neville quote, "What can be measured can be understood; what can be understood can be altered." Here I expand that idea to encompass all sorts of information about the external environment and internal workings of your investments.

Unless you outsource your investing to others, you can't do this without knowing at least something about the economy, the business environment, and the marketplace environment in which your investments exist. Low volatility investors should pay attention—not a constant, 24/7 vigil, but pay attention to financial news, other news that may affect your existing portfolio, future investments, and overall market sentiment.

You should have a set of favorite investing resources available, if not at your fingertips, at least somewhere nearby for review easily and often. I believe all investors should have:

- A favored investing portal to track the price of their investments, movements of the broader markets, economic news, and news directly involving their investments. Portals like Google Finance and Yahoo!Finance work and contain useful company information, stock price history, yields, charts, beta measures, and other good low volatility investing information. Increasingly, most online brokerage sites provide the same and more. It's worth a peek through these portfolios daily, if you want; if you're really set up for low volatility, maybe once a week or so.

- Favored business news sources. Portals are good, but they don't always give the depth or quality that I think gives a good sense of what's going on. I still like to read newspapers, and the *Wall Street Journal* (WSJ) continues to be an excellent information source. As I shared in Chapter 7, I read the Marketplace section before the Money & Investing section; it tells more about businesses and less about stocks. The *New York Times* and the *Economist* are also good reads and, of course, the online versions of all of these work OK, too. I try to give at least a half hour a day to the *WSJ* and an hour a week to the *Economist*.

- Investment analysis resources. Here I find Value Line simply the best for stocks, especially the high profile foundation stocks I depicted earlier in this chapter. It isn't cheap, but it often can be found in local libraries. I find Morningstar (www.morningstar.com) to be good for funds and ETFs, as well as most brokerage sites. I think Fidelity is particularly good for ETFs and does a good job with stocks, too. For commodities I don't really have any favorites; for currencies, I like Merk Investments, as mentioned earlier.

Like many things, it isn't just about having these resources, it's about *using* them. Good low volatility or any other kind of investors develop their own set of favored resources and learn to use them regularly.

TO GET HELP OR NOT TO GET HELP

I get asked this question a lot: "I'm not comfortable about doing this all myself, and I'm not even sure I have the time. What if I brought in a financial planner or advisor?"

Good question, especially if your investing goals really fit the low volatility model. And this is as good a place as any to answer it.

As with any service, you must, at the end of the day, decide if you're getting what you paid for—a return on your investment, as it were. Hiring a professional can give you access to their analysis and information sources, and can save you a lot of time. Their job is to keep their finger on the pulse, so you might not have to do as much research or watch things as closely. Some advisors may have special portfolio-building tools at their disposal that can more scientifically evaluate the potential volatility of your portfolio.

I've been trained as an advisor but have never actually done it for money, nor do I intend to. But I know what they do and have interacted with a lot of them. Most advisors err on the side of caution. They don't want to upset clients, or get into something they can't get out of and can't explain. Good advisors are careful and thorough and serve your needs well and get access to investments you might not have access to or even think of.

The trouble is, while you may get the cautious, sleep-at-night approach you seek, you will also be challenged to beat the market, and depending on the fee structure (often 1 percent of assets annually for a fee-only" advisor) and/or of the investments they choose, you may be giving up a percentage point or two to market returns right out of the gate. The secret, of course, is to find an advisor who does things you're comfortable with and outperforms the market—and who can show you conclusively, with actual data, that he or she actually does outperform. If not, you're probably better off buying a low-cost index or low volatility fund.

A good advisor can really help free up time and help you sleep at night (if not, find another advisor.) Advisors can allow you to manage some of your investments, while leaving the driving to someone else for the remainder. That approach may come automatically with company-sponsored retirement plans, or may be something you elect to do.

There are no right answers here: it is about what a particular advisor can do for you, and whether or not that makes you feel better about achieving your low volatility investing goals.

Habit #2: Be Cognizant of Change

Businesses change, economies change, markets change, and change causes volatility, especially when it isn't expected. Being cognizant of change means not ignoring it, but it doesn't mean overreacting to it; it means keeping your finger on the pulse and making sound judgments about what the change really means.

Business change is natural. Customer preferences change, competitors change, input costs change, labor costs change; the list is endless. Over time, the pace of change has accelerated. Railroads and consumer film photography enjoyed a 100-year cycle, and radio was the thing for 30 years before television took over. Now, with the rapid pace of technology, new technologies and the businesses built around them may last only a few years; even the once unassailable Microsoft is feeling the pinch of technology migration away from PCs. Somewhat surprisingly, Eastman Kodak succumbed to technology change, while railroads, hardly known for innovation over the years, have emerged into a second century of business excellence by adapting to technology and marketplace change.

Where does this leave the low volatility investor? Low volatility investors naturally side with the businesses and industries that have legs. These businesses keep up and prosper as business cycles come and go and technologies evolve. The trick is to figure out whether change is real and permanent or short term and something that can be managed, adapted to, or solved. Will Microsoft (and Intel and HP and Dell and others) adapt to the tablet revolution? Will Apple continue to dominate it? Those are the key questions for investors in those industries. Low volatility investors must stay up with change and assess the impact these change in industries, businesses, technologies, and sentiment will have on their investments. Even a low volatility stock like Campbell's Soup has gone through a lot of change lately.

It's all about seeing the bigger picture; about seeing what's really changing. A soft quarter or even a soft year doesn't necessarily mean the business has changed, even though a stock may become more volatile in the short term. For Campbell's Soup, it's a migration away from canned products and toward healthier foods that they need to grapple with. As a low volatility investor, try to assess the undercurrent, the climate that produced the weather, not the heavy weather itself.

Habit #3: Always Look Under the Hood

When you invest, by definition, you are deploying your own hard-earned capital into an asset with the expectation of receiving a return on that investment. If you buy a stock, you're investing in a business run by others. In return for providing that capital, you expect those others to do a good enough job, and that the business is a good enough business to produce a decent return.

As such, why would you buy an asset, especially a business, without knowing much about it? The truth is that it is easy to buy shares, funds, commodity futures, even real estate. It's an easy transaction requiring you to know little if anything about the asset. But that's where you can really go wrong.

The value investing mantra "Buy a stock like you're buying the entire business" applies here. Investing will typically seem less risky and less volatile if there are no surprises. If you do your homework, the asset that you buy may still be volatile, but it will be a volatility that you understand in advance, and understand the reasons for in advance. That can make a huge difference.

As Buffett says, "Risk comes from not knowing what you're doing." As such, the habit here is to do your homework and always look under the hood at a company, its fundamentals and marketplace position and, if a fund, what investments are in the fund; if real estate, it's the location and income potential of that real estate. Understand the risks external and internal to the investment, then buy the asset as if you were buying the whole thing and needed to know how to run or manage it. Such a careful, rational approach reduces unforeseen volatility. Don't just rely on diversification to manage risk.

Habit #4: Stay in Your Comfort Zone

This habit seems fairly self-explanatory, yet it's surprising how many investors get caught up in the moment or let their greed, or peer pressure, or even an eager professional advisor overrun their fears, and push the button on an investment that doesn't make sense.

The following points help clarify:

- *Do only what allows you to sleep at night.* If you can't focus on work, fun, or family, and have a glazed look on your face most of the time or are cranky or have to rush to your computer every Sunday night to see how the Asian markets are opening for Monday, you're probably in too far. You should consider changing your approach or getting help.

- *Invest what you can afford to lose.* Again, it sounds pretty basic, but many forget this, and take risks with funds that may cause enormous regret (divorces, blown college savings, etc.) if they're lost. If you invest the bulk of your assets in relatively stable foundation assets and let your hair down on a small percentage, you'll reduce the impact of any downside risk, really, turning volatility in your favor because it can work to the upside, too.

- *Avoid temptation.* Particularly when the markets are rising, it's easy to be drawn into the psychology of missing out on something, keeping up with your friends, etc. It's easy to imagine how this ends. Also, investors are always looking for that great idea, that can't-miss company or technology that tempts us all. I've lost on companies that made videoconferencing technologies (25 years before Cisco made it mainstream) and a company that recycled old tires to be burned as energy. Both were good ideas at the time –but not good businesses.

Know what you're investing in, and do an honest, pros-and-cons appraisal of whether it really makes sense.

Habit #5: Don't Overreact or Underreact

This habit logically follows the first four, particularly Habit #2, Be Cognizant of Change. Investors, particularly those sensitive to downside moves and losing in general, tend to follow the flocks out the door at the first sign of trouble. Others, of course, are doing the same, so it becomes a rout, fear feeds on fear, and you end up getting wiped out, only to have cooler heads prevail and move the investment higher the next day. Bet you've seen that one too many times, especially when earnings are announced, etc.

The habit is really to be clear-eyed, to do what makes the most sense. Don't follow crowds. Don't panic. But don't ignore change or look the other way, either; if something really has changed, you need to do something about it and not allow it to circle the drain into oblivion.

Which brings us to another question I'm often asked: "When should I sell?" Most investing books—including mine—are aimed at figuring out what to buy and when to buy it. Sound familiar? But, yes, buying is only half the equation. When's the best time to sell?

I have one simple mantra: sell when there's something better to buy. You may have an investment that's done horribly, but does it make sense to sell it? Especially if the price is already down and less than what you paid for it? The answer is yes, but only if there's something better to buy. That's the analysis: "Is there a better place for my capital?" There probably is, if the fundamentals of the asset have changed. But if the market is tanking, maybe the investment you have is still right. That's really a buy decision: would you buy the same investment today, given today's facts and market?

Note that cash may be the something better to buy. Now it gets a little trickier but stays on the side of rationality: if you would be better off in cash than the investment in question, then sell it and convert it into cash.

Habit #6: Think in Terms of Risk and Reward

Especially if you're the risk-averse type, constantly seeking shelter or calmer waters, there's a tendency to think more about the risk of something than the reward. That's OK as far as it goes; on the surface you'll feel more comfortable. But the problem is—and you saw this coming—you'll end up with the proverbial money in a mattress (or CD, which is almost the same thing) and your earnings, or returns, will suffer.

Don't forget about the reward part. We're not talking about greed here, only reasonable returns, 1 or 2 percent ahead of the market. That 1 or 2 percent margin can make a huge difference.

As such, you shouldn't cave in to fear or simply hide your head in the sand from the markets. You'll be safe, but you may also be sorry some day. Keep a balanced view between risk and reward and you're more likely to come out ahead while still feeling comfortable.

Habit #7: Don't Be Afraid to Make Mistakes

Again, don't hide your head in the sand. Not every decision will be perfect; in fact, you will lose occasionally. It's a fact of life. The important thing is not to overcommit to any one asset, and not get angry or take your emotions out on the market, either by withdrawing or, worse, throwing good money after bad because you *knew* you were right. Remember the saying: markets can stay irrational longer than you can stay solvent.

Learn to stay rational even in the face of adversity and headwinds. Assess your mistakes, don't ignore them. Furthermore, there's something to learn from every mistake, so learn it! And keep on investing.

REMEMBER: THERE'S NO FORMULA

What works for you, and allows you to sleep at night, is ultimately your set of personal low volatility principles. This book has been designed to help you figure out what those are.

KEY CONCEPTS

▶ A tiered portfolio tuned to your preferences and situation is the best way to allocate assets in a low volatility construct.

▶ Sixty percent of your portfolio in high-quality, low volatility, dividend-paying stocks and Low Volatility funds is a good place to start.

▶ It's okay to get outside help managing a low volatility portfolio; just make sure you're getting a return on your investment. If you still can't sleep at night and still underperform the markets, it isn't the right kind of help.

▶ The Seven Habits of Highly Successful Low Volatility Investing:
  ○ Get and Stay Informed.
  ○ Be Cognizant of Change.
  ○ Always Look Under the Hood.
  ○ Stay in Your Comfort Zone.
  ○ Don't Overreact or Underreact.
  ○ Think in Terms of Risk *and* Reward.
  ○ Don't Be Afraid to Make Mistakes.

INDEX

ABOUT THE AUTHOR

Peter Sander is an author, researcher, and consultant in the fields of personal finance, business, and location reference. He has written 39 books, including *The 100 Best Stocks to Buy 2014, Value Investing for Dummies, The 25 Habits of Highly Successful Investors, What Would Steve Jobs Do?,* and *101 Things Everyone Should Know About Economics.* He is also the author of numerous articles and columns on investment strategies. He has an MBA from Indiana University and has completed Certified Financial Planner (CFP®) education and examination requirements.